PRINCIPLES AND PRACTICES OF STUDENT HEALTH

VOLUME ONE

# FOUNDATIONS

# PRINCIPLES AND PRACTICES OF STUDENT HEALTH

## THREE VOLUMES

Volume One: **FOUNDATIONS**
Editor: Helen M. Wallace, MD, MPH

Volume Two: **SCHOOL HEALTH**
Editors: Guy S. Parcel, PhD
Judith B. Igoe, MS, RN, FAAN

Volume Three: **COLLEGE HEALTH**
Editor: Kevin Patrick, MD, MS

PRINCIPLES AND PRACTICES OF STUDENT HEALTH

## Volume One

# FOUNDATIONS

EDITORS

**Helen M. Wallace, MD, MPH** • Foundations
Professor, Maternal and Child Health
Graduate School of Public Health
San Diego State University
San Diego, California

**Kevin Patrick, MD, MS** • College Health
Director, University of California, San Diego, and
San Diego State University General Preventive Medicine Residency
Director, Student Health Services
San Diego State University
San Diego, California

**Guy S. Parcel, PhD** • School Health
Professor and Director
Center for Health Promotion
Research and Development
The University of Texas Health Science Center at Houston
Houston, Texas

**Judith B. Igoe, MS, RN, FAAN** • School Health
Associate Professor and Director
School Health Programs
University of Colorado Health Sciences Center
Schools of Nursing and Medicine
Denver, Colorado

with forewords by

Ernest L. Boyer, PhD
Julius B. Richmond, MD
Vince L. Hutchins, MD, MPH

THIRD PARTY PUBLISHING COMPANY
OAKLAND, CALIFORNIA, U.S.A.

# ACKNOWLEDGMENTS

The Editors want to express their gratitude to the many experts who have been willing to share their knowledge and expertise, and who have taken the time to write the individual chapters for these three volumes. We also want to acknowledge the significant contribution of Charlotte Shindledecker Seidman, RN, FNP, MHS, MPH, who did the text editing and indexing of all three volumes. Paul Mico, our publisher, gave us important ideas about content in planning the book, especially from his discipline of health education. Chris Morris assisted with many of the graphics used in the book, as did Patrick Kammermeyer. Finally, we would like to thank Dan Nowak, Vice President of Student Affairs, San Diego State University, and the staff of the SDSU Student Health Center for providing some of the support necessary for the production of this book. The publisher joins in the acknowledgment of Charlotte Seidman's contribution. In addition to the able assistance she provided to the Editors and chapter authors on the technical preparation of their manuscripts, she was especially helpful with her advice regarding in-house style and on the overall presentation of this Work.

## PRINCIPLES AND PRACTICES OF STUDENT HEALTH

Three Volumes:

One:    Foundations
Two:    School Health
Three:  College Health

Copyright © 1992 by Third Party Publishing Company

Library of Congress Catalog Card Number: 91-67600

International Standard Book Numbers:
For the complete work: **0-89914-034-3**
For Volume One: **0-89914-035-1**
For Volume Two: **0-89914-036-X**
For Volume Three: **0-89914-037-8**

Manufactured in the United States of America
Third Party Publishing Company
A division of Third Party Associates, Inc.
P.O. Box 13306, Montclair Station
Oakland, California 94661-0306, U.S.A.
Telephone: 510/339-2323
Fax: 510/339-6729

Publisher, and Design: Paul R. Mico
Electronic Composition: Patrick Kammermeyer

# CONTENTS

VOLUME ONE: **FOUNDATIONS**

# PREFACE

The history of health care for students, from preschool through college, has been wrought with too few resources, insufficient infrastructure to support service delivery, ambiguous roles for health personnel, and confusion surrounding the relationship of the student health program to the school system or university and to other community health systems. Nevertheless, the deteriorating health status of children and youth coupled with the need to take advantage of the school and college settings as ideal environments for developing health life-styles warrants the development of new, and the support and improvement of existing, student health systems. Given the complexity and urgency of the needs that must be met, it is today's challenge to overcome the fragmented approach and institutional inertia that have characterized the past, and design a comprehensive, integrated student health care system guided by an overall philosophy of disease prevention and health promotion.

Health care was first widely provided in schools and colleges in the early 1900s. It was almost always associated with the simple goal of screening for communicable disease. Since then, school health programs have evolved from the provision of basic preventive health care and health education to an expanded focus on the provision of primary health care services and health promotion to students with special health needs. The latter is aimed at the "new morbidities," i.e., early adolescent pregnancy, emotional disorders, sexually transmitted diseases, and other life-style-associated phenomena that require psychosocial and behavioral interventions and new types of services.

It must be emphasized that an increasing number of primary, secondary, and post-secondary students today need basic primary health care due largely to their un- or under-insured status. The 1984 National Health Interview Survey found that at least 4.5 million (14%) students ages 10 to 18 are in these categories, and that those from poor and/or minority households are least likely to have health insurance. Current estimates are that as many as 30 percent of college students lack any form of health insurance and that another

ix

15 percent may be seriously under-insured. For a variety of reasons, this problem has become worse in the early 1990s.

Growing numbers of acute and chronically ill and impaired children and youth are in school and college today as a result of the Education for All Handicapped Children's Act of 1975 (PL 94-142), and the more recent PL 99-457. These individuals require complex nursing and health care and the best place to do so is often at school or in college. Among the common treatments these students require are bladder catheterization; endotracheal suctioning, ileostomy, and ureterostomy care; nasogastric tube feedings; and physical, occupational, and communication therapy.

The traditional primary and secondary school health program that has grown out of this history consists of the three core components of health services, health education, and health protection (measures intended to promote a physically, socially, and psychologically healthy environment). Yet, in spite of this evolution to a varied and sophisticated level of care, these school health programs are commonly a series of unrelated activities and projects for which there exist no unifying mission, goals, or objectives. School nurses orchestrate case management services for medically fragile students independent of health teachers who plan health education curricula, while environmental inspection for health hazards is arranged and implemented by someone else in the school organizational structure. The bottom line is that these school health efforts are fragmented at a time when a consolidated and effective system of health care is needed more than ever to ensure the well-being of students, faculty, and staff.

A similar circumstance has occurred with the evolution of college and university health services. What began as simple dispensaries on a few campuses to deal with the communicable disease problems of students attending college away from home has evolved into a panoply of models of delivery of services ranging from simple triage and referral performed by nurses to full-scale primary and secondary health care centers staffed with a range of health professionals. However, as with primary and secondary education, little in the way of unifying mission, goals, or objectives for these services has developed in the higher education arena. A reactive, "medical model" approach is common, even in the face of overwhelming evidence that the key causes of morbidity and mortality among college students are associated with behavior and life-style and are either partially or completely preventable. It is the rare institution of higher education that explicitly integrates a high level of commitment for the health and well-being of their students, and their graduates, into all levels of institutional policies and procedures.

The logical resolution of these issues is for health planners and providers to redesign student health care systems to meet today's needs. However, planners and providers of student health services have held what sociologists refer to as a "boundary dweller" position: they are members of two organizations – the school or college and the community health care system. Usually, boundary dwellers succumb to a natural inclination to assume the role most frequently in use in, or most acceptable to, their organization. The school nurse may be more comfortable playing the role of teacher than of health care provider and thus may avoid important clinical activities. The college health physician may be best suited to simply "be a doctor" and avoid questioning the impact of institutional alcohol-use policies on patient management. Yet neither of these approaches is satisfactory given what we know about the integrated nature of the causes – and the solutions – of the challenges facing our children and youth.

With this series of volumes, we have chosen to address student health issues for students at all levels of education – primary, secondary, and post-secondary. To our knowledge, this has not been attempted before. It is our conviction, however, that there is much more in common between the "worlds" of school health and college health than has heretofore been acknowledged. Each field responds to health needs in educational contexts. Each has as its central beneficiary a developing human being confronted with the many challenges of growth and identity formation. Each field addresses that most complex period of life known as adolescence. And, in the interest of both a higher order of integration of our activities and a stronger, more unified approach to making our case to others, each field can benefit from a greater level of understanding of the other.

Much remains to be done to design the student health care systems that we need. Key to achieving this is acceptance of the concept that student health care involves many different disciplines commonly associated with multiple institutional and community resources, agencies, and programs. Once accepted, this notion then begs the issue of the need for enhanced communication between and among these resources. This communication is essential if we are to attain the economies of scale, both human and financial, that are paramount to the attainment of the level and complexity of services needed. Of equal importance is a unifying mission of student health care. We posit that the overriding mission of such activities is to promote health, prevent disease, and to provide for environments capable of developing the full potential of each student. It is only in this way that we can insure that the student health care needs of today and tomorrow will be met.

Helen M. Wallace, MD, MPH
Kevin Patrick, MD, MS
Guy S. Parcel, PhD
Judith B. Igoe, MS, RN, FAAN

# FOREWORD

Ernest L. Boyer, PhD

School and college health professionals have always dispensed more than aspirin, bandaids, and the proverbial "tender loving care." Student health offices have provided not only first aid, but also the first line in health care for many of America's children and young people. It is often the school nurse who discovers that a child has faulty vision or impaired hearing, or who brings a child's need for dental treatment to the notice of the family. In college, the health center is often the first place to which students turn when stricken with disease, addiction, or serious depression and self-doubt.

The publication of *Principles and Practices of Student Health* could not be more timely, because today, more than ever, the primary health care needs of many students will be diagnosed at school, or not at all. The numbers of poor children are rising, thrusting upon school nurses special responsibilities for attending to basic health needs. And adding to the burden is the ever larger role that schools and colleges have assumed in trying to head off or cope with alcohol and drug abuse, sexually transmitted diseases, AIDS, unplanned pregnancies, and the many other perils young Americans face today.

The situation is critical, especially in schools. In a 1990 Carnegie Foundation survey, over two-thirds of the nation's primary and secondary teachers reported that poor health was a problem among students in their school. Teen pregnancy and parenting were cited as a serious or somewhat serious problem by nearly 80 percent of secondary school teachers; while 24 percent said alcohol was a serious problem, and 60 percent said it was a somewhat serious problem for young people in their school.

Wherever one looks, the numbers are numbing, especially given the typically poor resources allocated for student health. For many school professionals, the job is not unlike the approach taken by overworked doctors and nurses on the front lines during times of war. Often, they are so overextended that they must make their own triage decisions and allocate their precious time in ways that leave unattended some student health needs that sorely need to be addressed. Clearly, school health professionals need the best training and guidance they can get in making these decisions, and in organizing their efforts, so as to be efficient while remaining reassuring and humane.

This large territory is well-mapped in these three volumes on Student Health. Here is where nurses, doctors, and others responsible for student health can go for the latest information on how to recognize and evaluate the signs and symptoms of abuse, disease, addiction, and distress. Here is where student health professionals can go for information on the developmental transitions that affect children's health and well-being; on the many subtle connections between health and learning; and for models for organizing school health services, which are informed by a broader vision of what constitutes student health. In this vision, diagnosis, referral, and treatment are essential, but they are only the first steps.

As the authors of *Principles and Practices of Student Health* make clear, wellness is a goal that must be pursued in many ways. If we are to adequately serve the health needs of our children and young people, school and college health professionals must seek – and receive – better support for their task. This means that adequate financial support must be provided for student health services, of course. But it also means that a healthy environment must be created throughout the school or campus, and, indeed, in their surrounding neighborhoods, as well.

Today, there is a growing acceptance of the idea that something constructive about school health can and should be done. In schools and campuses around the country, urgent discussions are taking place on how to mobilize everyone – students, teachers, parents, and staff – for the task. School health professionals are playing a vital role in these discussions, and understanding that the whole community is implicated in the wellness of children and young people is an essential fact that health professionals can help people from varied walks of life to see. Good nutrition, physical fitness, social confidence, emotional stability, and general knowledge about health are essential conditions for wellness. They are conditions that all adults working or living with children have the responsibility to strengthen, foster, or create.

Making schools and colleges and their neighborhoods safer and healthier environments should be a top priority both for health and for education policy today. Throughout the country, innovative ways are being found to fund school health offices, to upgrade the professional status of school health professionals, to extend school health services, and to link them more closely to local community needs. The challenge is to build on these new and promising models that see the connections between health and learning, schools and neighborhoods, and students' academic and non-academic life. School and college health professionals are uniquely situated to help the larger community to understand student health problems, and to envision the breadth of appropriate response.

# FOREWORD

## Julius B. Richmond, MD

These volumes on student health are a welcome addition to the library o
those interested in improving the health of children and adolescents. It i
surprising, since we require all children to attend school, that so little attentio
has been directed specifically to the health of students. Now, at last, we hav
a comprehensive sourcebook for those in the various health professions whe
work with children in their student years.

These volumes go beyond the usual considerations of the practice of healtl
professionals, for they present the context in which students are growing an
developing. Today's problems are in part the consequence of historical progres
in improving the health of children. The revolution in biology of the pas
several decades has resulted in a dramatic decline in morbidity and mortalit
from the acute infectious and gastrointestinal diseases of childhood. Decline
in infant mortality rates, although not as great as we would like to see, hav
resulted in the saving of the lives of many low birthweight infants who ar
vulnerable to developmental disabilities. These changes have transforme
pediatric practices and services in recent years.

A consequence of these changes has been a considerable shift from th
acute disorders to developmental disabilities and long-term illnesses, whicl
have major implications for the health of students. The student's primary tas
is learning, and these are health issues with profound implications for educa
tion. Society has recognized this linkage of health and education through th
passage of the Education for All Handicapped Children's Act (PL 94-142), t
which has been added PL 99-457 to include children in preschool years. Thu
all health professionals caring for children and adolescents must be prepare
to deal with learning disorders and the impacts of chronic illnesses on learning
processes. While the implementation of this legislation is somewhat uneven ir
communities across the country, there is no question but that it has stimulate
improved programs for students and better training and research, whicl
ultimately leads to higher quality programs.

The transformation of student health services has also resulted from other changes in the context of practice. We have witnessed much greater ethnic diversity among the children in our schools. The number of children living in poverty and its intensity has increased; immunization rates in low-income populations have decreased; drug abuse has become a pervasive concern; teenage pregnancy rates are difficult to reduce; and acquired immunodeficiency syndrome (AIDS) has become a major risk, as have other sexually transmitted diseases. These ethnic, social, and economic issues and their political implications are important for every health worker. These volumes provide a state-of-the-art book to help in dealing with these difficult issues; they are also of help in comprehending the health problems for those young people who drop out of school.

The new complexity is resulting in efforts to reorganize services for students. Thus, while the establishment of school-based clinics is not a novel concept, there is considerable movement to expand such programs, probably due in part to the considerable fragmentation of services that has developed over the past several decades. The expansion of Medicaid and other services to low-income populations is a welcome effort that can help those involved in student health to finance the improvement and expansion of their efforts. As we move toward expanded state – and perhaps, ultimately, national – universal health insurance programs, we should make every effort to incorporate adequate provision for better student health programs.

It is interesting to observe the recent improvements in high school and college-age health programs. There is a growing sophistication concerning the opportunities in these programs to foster improved personal health practices that will carry over into adult life. It is also appropriate to note that in the preschool years, programs such as Head Start have comprehensive health services and it is important that students in the school years be assured of continuity of these services.

Student health programs provide unique opportunities to teach health promotion and disease prevention. Since the 1979 Surgeon General's Report, *Healthy People*, and its recent update, *Health Goals for the Year 2000*, our knowledge base for fostering health-enhancing behaviors has improved. In the many settings in which health professionals work with students they can serve as educators as well as service providers.

Thus, it is clear that those who provide student health services face many complex challenges and opportunities. Their activities should result in improved services, training, and research that will lead to better health for children and adolescents. These volumes should go a long way toward establishing an interdisciplinary profession of student health services as it clarifies these issues.

# FOREWORD

Vince L. Hutchins, MD, MPH

With the publication of *Principles and Practices of Student Health,* a longitudinal view is presented of health and health delivery issues concerning school-age children, adolescents, and young people from the perspective of school health.

Health services, health education, and a healthful school environment are generally accepted as the three principal components of comprehensive school health. Despite rather common agreement on these three components of a comprehensive school health program, wide differences exist among the 16,000 school districts in the U.S. Some provide innovative programs of health services and education, including provision of primary care in the school setting, while others make little or no provision for even basic health services for enrolled children. Budget constraints frequently mean a reduction or elimination of some or all health services to school-age children.

Concern is increasing about the health of the millions of school-age children and youth in our society. The focus of this concern has broadened from physical health to other conditions – behavioral disturbances, learning disabilities, substance abuse, mental health disorders, injuries (both intentional and non-intentional), sexually transmitted diseases, child abuse, adolescent adjustment, suicides, and homicides – as well as the age-old health problems such as infectious disease, malnutrition, and vision and hearing defects.

At any one time, approximately 99 percent of 6-to-15-year olds and about 90 percent of 16 and 17 year olds are enrolled in school. Once children are in school, many of their health and developmental problems are identified because a considerable number of these problems relate to their school performance. Many of these children are also seen by health care providers in the private or public sector.

As a result, health information on these children exists in a variety of settings – private sector, public agencies, and the schools. These data could be used more effectively to develop a rational base for delineating policy, planning, allocating resources, and evaluation if there were common recognition and communication.

It is important to understand that school health programs function within a system of health care, including the physician in private practice as well as the community health agencies. School health practice must be integrally related to this network for resolution of the school population's health-related problems.

With their newly evolving role in systems building, the State Title V Maternal and Child Health (MCH) program should be in the vanguard of promoting this network and communication within it. The State MCH program should be identifying the health needs of this population and taking action to plan, promote, and coordinate health services responsive to their needs. All of this should be accomplished through a public process.

The family, however defined, must continue to have a central role in all aspects of child health. The health services and programs should be implemented in ways that work with and for the family, involving and capitalizing on their strengths and supplementing and supporting their roles as necessary.

The health of school-age children should become a community-wide concern and not be viewed as the sole domain of any single part of the system. Services appropriate to a child and a family's needs, as noted, may need to come from the health care delivery system, the educational system, or the community and social services system. Thus, each must be considered in planning for services. Informed leadership, mutually identified goals and objectives, and coordinated action become critical for a successful community-based program, the end result of which will be healthy school-age children and youth.

# Contributing Authors, All Three Volumes

**Diana Abramo,** Doctoral Candidate, New York University; P. O. Box 1801 Old Chelsea Station, New York NY 10011

**Martha Adams, BSN, FNP, MSN,** Assistant Professor, University of North Dakota College of Nursing; Co-ordinator, Child Health Program, Grand Forks ND 58202-8195

**Richard M. Adams, MD,** Director, School Health Services, Dallas Independent School District, Dallas TX 75204

**Zili Amsel, ScD,** Acting Director, Division of Epidemiology and Prevention Research, National Institute on Drug Abuse, Rockville MD 20857

**Elizabeth Bacon, MS,** Director, Disabled Student Services, San Diego State University, San Diego CA 92182

**Suzanne M. Bianchi, PhD,** U.S. Bureau of the Census, Housing and Household Economic Statistics Division, Washington DC 20233

**Anne Bourgeois, MS, RD,** Obesity Specialist, NHLBI Information Center, P.O. Box 30105, Bethesda MD 20824-0105

**Pamela A. Cooper Bowen, MD, MPH,** Director, Princeton University Health Services, Princeton NJ 08544-1004

**W. David Burns,** Director, Student Health Services; Assistant Vice President for Student Life Policy and Services, Rutgers University, New Brunswick NJ 08903

**Ernest L. Boyer, PhD,** President, The Carnegie Foundation for the Advancement of Teaching, 5 Ivy Lane, Princeton NJ 08540

**Willard Cates, Jr, MD, MPH,** Director, Division of Training, CDC Epidemiology Program Office, CDC, Atlanta GA 30333

**Donald F. B. Char, MD,** Director, Student Health Services; Professor of Pediatrics, University of Hawaii at Manoa, East West Road, Honolulu HI 96822

William A. Christmas, MD, FACP, Director, Student Health Center Clinical Associate Professor of Medicine, College of Medicine, University of Vermont, Burlington VT 05401

Dominic Cittadino, DDS, Director and Staff Dentist, Student Emergency Dental Service, Southern Illinois University at Carbondale, Carbondale IL 62901

MarJeanne Collins, MD, Director, Student Health Service; Associate Professor of Medicine, Associate Professor of Pediatrics, Hospital of the University of Pennsylvania, Philadelphia PA 19104-4283

James P. Comer, MD, MPH, Professor, Child Psychiatry; Director, Yale Child Study Center, Yale University School of Medicine, New Haven CT 06510

Carol N. D'Onofrio, DrPH, Associate Professor of Public Health, University of California at Berkeley, Berkeley CA 94720

Murray M. DeArmond, MD, Director, Student Health Services, University of Arizona, Tucson AZ 85721

Connie A. Diggs, RN, NP, MPA, Director, Student Health Center, California State University, Los Angeles, Los Angeles CA 90032-8411

John M. Dorman, MD, Director of Public Relations and Outreach, Cowell Student Health Center; Clinical Associate Professor of Pediatrics, Stanford University, Stanford CA 94305

Johanna Dwyer, DSc, Professor of Medicine in Community Health, Tufts University School of Medicine, Boston MA 02111

Linda H. Edwards, MSN, DrPH, School Health Co-ordinator, Illinois Department of Public Health, Springfield IL 62761

James H. Evans, MS, Assistant Professor of Behavioral Sciences; Director, Chemical Dependency Counselor Training Program, San Diego City College, San Diego CA 92101-4787

Nell Faucette, EdD, Associate Professor of Physical Education, University of South Florida, Tampa FL 33620

Gail C. Frank, DrPH, MPH, RD, Nutritional Epidemiologist, Professor of Nutrition, California State University, Long Beach, Long Beach CA 90840-0501

Karen A. Gordon, MPH, EdD, Director, Health Education, Princeton University Health Services, Princeton NJ 08540

Ted W. Grace, MD, MPH, Director, Clinical Services, San Diego State University Student Health Services, San Diego CA 92182

Joel Grinolds, MD, MPH, Staff Physician, Liaison to Disabled Student Services, San Diego State University Student Health Services, San Diego CA 92182

Debra W. Haffner, MPH, Executive Director, Sex Information and Education Council of the U.S. (SIECUS), West 42nd Street, New York City NY 10036

Steven L. Harris, MD, MS, Clinical Assistant Professor of Family and Emergency Medicine, USC; Chief of Medical Staff, California State University, Los Angeles, Los Angeles CA 90032-8411

Nils Hasselmo, PhD, President, University of Minnesota, Minneapolis MN 55455

Karen Hein, MD, Professor of Pediatrics, Associate Professor of Epidemiology and Social Work, Albert Einstein College of Medicine, New York NY 10467

Wylie C. Hembree, MD, Director, Student Health Services, Health Sciences Campus; Associate Professor of Clinical Medicine and OB/GYN, Columbia University, New York NY 10032

Alan R. Hinman, MD, MPH, Director, National Center for Prevention Services, CDC, Atlanta GA 30333

Vince L. Hutchins, MD, MPH, consultant, Carnegie Corporation, New York City.

Judith B. Igoe, MS, RN, FAAN, Associate Professor and Director, School Health Programs, University of Colorado Health Sciences Center, Denver CO 80262

Elaine M. Johnson, PhD, Director, Office for Substance Abuse Prevention; Associate Administrator for Prevention, Alcohol, Drug Abuse, and Mental Health Administration (ADAMHA) of the USDHHS, Rockville MD 20857

Diane H. Jones, MSW, PhD, Medical Sociologist, Center for Chronic Disease Prevention and Health Promotion, Centers for Disease Control, Atlanta GA 30333

Richard P. Keeling, MD, Director, Department of Student Health; Associate Professor of Internal Medicine, University of Virginia, Charlottesville VA 22902

Steven H. Kelder, BS, MPH, Doctoral Student, Division of Epidemiology, School of Public Health, University of Minnesota, Minneapolis MN 55455

**Douglas Kirby, PhD,** ETR Associates, P.O. Box 1830, Santa Cruz CA 95061-1830

**Joel C. Kleinman, PhD,** (deceased), former Director of Analysis, National Center for Health Statistics, Hyattsville MD 20782

**David P. Kraft, MD,** Executive Director, University Health Services University of Massachusetts at Amherst, Amherst MA 01003

**Richard D. Krugman, MD,** Director, C. Henry Kempe National Center for the Prevention and Treatment of Child Abuse and Neglect; Professor of Pediatrics and Acting Dean of the University of Colorado School of Medicine, Denver CO 80262

**Felice D. Kurtzman, MPH, RD,** Assistant Professor, Department of Biological Chemistry, School of Medicine, UCLA, Los Angeles CA 90024-1703

**Myra Lappin, MD, MPH,** Director, Student Health Service, San Francisco State University, San Francisco CA 94132-4200

**Carl G. Leukefeld, DSW,** Director, Drug and Alcohol Abuse Research Center, University of Kentucky, Lexington KY 40506

**Frances Marcus Lewis, RN, PhD,** Evaluator, Cancer Information System, Fred Hutchinson Cancer Research Center, Seattle; Professor, Department of Community Health Care Systems, University of Washington Seattle WA 98195

**Chris Y. Lovato, PhD,** Assistant Professor, Graduate School of Public Health, San Diego State University, San Diego CA 92182

**Ralph Manchester, MD, FACP,** Chief, Medical Care Section, University Health Service; Associate Professor, Department of Medicine, University of Rochester, Rochester NY 14642

**Mary L. Michal, MD,** Associate Professor, Department of Pediatrics; Director, Developmental/ Behavioral Pediatrics, East Tennessee State University, Johnson City TN 37614-0002

**Brenda S. Mitchell, PhD,** Director, Behavioral Science and Health Promotion, Institute for Aerobics Research, Preston Road, Dallas TX 75230

**Patricia A. Motz, EdD, RNC,** Director, Health Services, Denver Public Schools, Denver CO 80203

**Philip R. Nader, MD,** Professor of Pediatrics; Chief, Division of General Pediatrics; and Director, Community Pediatrics, University of California at San Diego, San Diego CA 92103

**National Health/Education Consortium, c/o Rae Grad,** National Commission to Prevent Infant Mortality, Switzer Building, Washington DC 20201

**Anne Marie Novinger, RN, MA,** Specialist, Health Services, Glendale Community College, Glendale CA 91208

**Patrick W. O'Carroll, MD, MPH,** Chief, Intentional Injuries Section, Epidemiology Branch, Division of Injury Control, National Center for Environmental Health and Injury Control, CDC, Atlanta GA 30333

**Janice Ozias, RN, PhD,** Supervisor of Nursing Services, Austin Independent School District, Austin TX 78757-2147

**Guy S. Parcel, PhD,** Professor and Director, Center for Health Promotion Research and Development, The University of Texas Health Science Center, Houston TX 77225

**Carole Passarelli, RN, PNP, MS,** Editor, Journal of School Nursing; Associate Professor, Pediatric Nursing Program, Child Division, Yale University School of Nursing, New Haven CT 06536-0740

**Kevin Patrick, MD, MS,** Director, UCSD-SDSU General Preventive Medicine Residency Program, University of California at San Diego; Director, Student Health Services, San Diego State University, San Diego CA 92182-0567

**Mary Ann Pentz, PhD,** Associate Professor, Department of Preventive Medicine, University of Southern California; Institute for Health Promotion and Disease Prevention Research, North Lake Avenue, Pasadena CA 91101

**Cheryl L. Perry, PhD,** Associate Professor of Epidemiology; Chair, Community Health Education, Division of Epidemiology, University of Minnesota School of Public Health, Minneapolis MN 55455

**R. Morgan Pigg Jr., HSD, MPH, FASHA,** Editor, Journal of School Health; Professor and Chair, Department of Health Science Education, University of Florida, Gainesville FL 32611-2034

**Deborah Prothrow-Stith, MD,** Assistant Dean for Government and Community Programs, Harvard University School of Public Health; Lecturer, Health Policy and Management Department, Harvard University, Boston MA 02115

**Julius B. Richmond, MD,** John D. and Catherine T. MacArthur Professor of Health Policy, Emeritus, Harvard University School of Public Health, Boston MA 02115

**Frederick P. Rivara, MD, MPH,** Director, Harborview Injury Prevention and Research Center, Seattle; Professor of Pediatrics, University of Washington, Seattle WA 98104

**George M. Robb,** Associate Vice President for External Relations, University of Minnesota, Minneapolis MN 55455

**Carolyn C. Rogers, MA,** Demographer, Economic Research Service (USDA), Washington DC 20005

**James F. Sallis, PhD,** Associate Professor of Psychology, San Diego State University, San Diego CA 92182

**Linda E. Saltzman, PhD,** Behavioral Scientist, Intentional Injuries Section, Epidemiology Branch, Division of Injury Control, National Center for Environmental Health and Injury Control, CDC, Atlanta GA 30333

**Allan J. Schwartz, MA, MS, PhD,** Associate Professor of Psychiatry and of Psychology; Chief, Mental Health Section, University Health Service, University of Rochester, Rochester NY 14642

**John R. Seffrin, PhD,** Professor, Health Education; Chair, Department of Applied Health Science, Indiana University, Bloomington IN 4740

**Toby Simon, MEd,** Associate Dean, Student Life, Brown University, Providence RI 02912

**Bruce G. Simons-Morton, EdD, MPH,** Research Scientist, The Prevention Research Branch, Division of Epidemiology, Statistics, and Prevention Research, National Institute of Child Health and Human Development, Rockville, MD 20892

**Beverlie Conant Sloane, MPH, PhD,** Director, Health Education, Dartmouth College; Assistant Professor, Department of Community and Family Medicine, Dartmouth Medical School, Hanover NH 03755

**Jack C. Smith, MS,** Chief, Statistics and Computer Resources Branch, Division of Reproductive Health, Center for Chronic Disease Prevention and Health Promotion, CDC, Atlanta GA 30333

**Howard R. Spivak, MD,** Associate in Pediatrics, New England Medical Center Hospital, Boston; Associate Professor of Pediatrics, Tufts University School of Medicine, Boston MA 02111

**Richard Strauss, MD,** Associate Professor of Preventive Medicine and Internal Medicine; Team Physician, Athletic Department; Director, Sports Medicine Clinic, Student Health Services, The Ohio State University, Columbus OH 43210-1240

Paula Swinford, MS, CHES, Director of Health Education, Student Health and Counseling Services, University of Southern California, Los Angeles CA 90089-0311

Alex Thomas, PhD, Associate Professor, Educational Psychology Department, Miami University, Oxford OH 45056

Kenneth C. Troutman, DDS, MPH, Professor of Clinical Dentistry; Director, Pediatric Dentistry Post-doctoral Program, Columbia University School of Dental and Oral Surgery, New York NY 10032

Deborah Klein Walker, EdD, Assistant Commissioner for the Bureau of Parent, Child, and Adolescent Health, Massachusetts Department of Health, Boston MA 02111

Helen M. Wallace, MD, MPH, Professor of Maternal Child Health, Graduate School of Public Health, San Diego State University, San Diego CA 92182

Leighton C. Whitaker, PhD, Director, Psychological Services for Swarthmore College; Swarthmore PA 19081

J. Robert Wirag, HSD, Director, Student Health Center, University of Texas at Austin, Austin TX 78713

Joel Yager, MD, Professor, Department of Psychiatry and Biobehavioral Science, School of Medicine, UCLA; Director of Residency Education; Senior Consultant, Adult Eating Disorders Program, UCLA, Los Angeles CA 90024-1703

Laurie S. Zabin, MD, Associate Professor, Department of Population Dynamics, The Johns Hopkins University School of Hygiene and Public Health; Associate Professor, Department of Obstetrics and Gynecology, JHU School of Medicine, Baltimore MD 21205

Christine Heustis Zimmer, BSN, MA, Administrator, University Wellness Programs, Sindecuse Health Center, Western Michigan University, Kalamazoo MI 49008

Joseph E. Zins, PhD, Professor, Department of Early Childhood and Special Education, University of Cincinnati, Cincinnati OH 45221

VOLUME ONE

# FOUNDATIONS

# Health Status Indicators
# for School-Age Children
JOEL C. KLEINMAN, PhD

The nation's health has increased dramatically over this century and child health has shown the greatest improvement. Concomitantly there has been a major change in the important indicators of child health. During the first half of this century, infectious disease was the primary threat to child health. With the advent of immunizations, antibiotics, and other effective medical interventions, mortality and morbidity from infectious diseases declined sharply. As we enter the last decade of this century, child health problems have become more strongly associated with social problems. Improving child health has increasingly come to focus on issues like family structure and support, access to health and social services, injuries, violence, and substance abuse. Underlying these issues is the high rate of poverty among United States children: In 1987, one-fifth of all children under 18 (44 percent of black and 39 percent of Hispanic children) lived in families below the poverty level.[1] Children now have the highest poverty rate of any age group in the U.S.

In this chapter, we will discuss a number of health status indicators for monitoring trends and variations in child health. These indicators are not meant to be exhaustive but rather to illustrate the potential for using health data to assess major problems in child health and to understand the limitations in using such data for tracking progress in child health. A more detailed discussion of child health indicators is presented in reference 2. It is important to recognize that the age groups traditionally used to present child health statistics do not always correspond to appropriate developmental stages of childhood and adolescence or even school placement (e.g., the 10-14 age group used in vital statistics spans students in elementary, and junior and senior high schools).

# MORTALITY

Death rates for children have dropped precipitously during the first half of the century.[3] Between 1900 and 1950, death rates for each of the age groups 5-9, 10-14, 15-19, and 20-24 years decreased by 70 percent to 80 percent. For the younger age groups (5-14 years), death rates since 1950 continued a large and steady decline through 1985. For adolescents and young adults, however, there was essentially no change between 1950 and 1970, but a resumption of the decline between 1970 and 1985. Since 1985 the death rates for children 5-14 have remained essentially constant while those for 15-24 year olds have increased.

In 1979, the U.S. Public Health Service released its 1990 Objectives for the Nation.[4] One of the 1990 goals was to reduce the death rate for children 1-14 years of age from the 1977 level of 42.3 deaths per 100,000 to 34. That goal was achieved with a 1988 death rate of 33.2 per 100,000. The goal for adolescents and young adults (age 15-24) was to reduce the rate from 114.8 observed in 1977 to 92 by 1990. After initial progress through 1985 to a rate of 95.9, there was a sudden increase in the death rate to 102.3 in 1986, followed by a decline in 1987 to 99.4, but another increase in 1988 to 102.1. These adverse trends in the overall rates reflected the patterns of three of the leading killers in this age group: motor vehicle injuries (MVIs), homicide, and suicide.

The Health Objectives for the Year 2000[5] call for further reductions in the death rate for children 1-14 to 28 deaths per 100,000 and resumption of the decline among the 15-24 age group to a rate of 85 per 100,000.

In recent years, external causes of death (i.e., injuries, homicide, and suicide) account for half the deaths in the 5-14 year age groups and more than three-quarters of the deaths among 15-24 year olds. However, the leading causes of death vary by age, race, and sex. The Year 2000 Objectives include specific targets for reduction in childhood death rates from MVIs, drowning, and residential fires; and reduction in adolescent death rates from MVIs, homicide, and suicide.

Motor vehicle injuries are the leading cause of death among 5-9 year olds. Nearly three-fifths of the deaths from MVIs were pedestrian-related (i.e., the child was killed as a result of being struck by a motor vehicle) and black children were almost twice as likely to die from a pedestrian-related MVI. Fires and drownings were also among the leading causes of death, with death rates from fires for black children four times higher than for white children and death rates from drowning twice as high for black children.

For children 10-14, MVIs were also the leading cause of death for three of the four race-sex groups; among black females the death rate from cancer was slightly higher. Furthermore, among black males 10-14 years old, drowning was a close second. Death rates among black children in this age group were substantially higher than among white children for homicide (triple), drowning (quadruple), and fires (triple).

The teenage years 15-19 represent the only age group for which there is essentially no difference in all-causes death rates between blacks and whites. However, the patterns of mortality were substantially different. MVIs were the leading cause for white teenagers while homicide was the leading cause for black teenagers. Death rates from MVIs were nearly three times as high for whites as for blacks while homicide was five times as likely among blacks as whites. Suicide is the second leading cause for whites and the fourth leading cause for blacks with the rate for whites double that for blacks. Deaths from drowning and fires were twice as high among black teenagers. The death rate for teenage boys was more than twice the rate for teenage girls with the sex ratio particularly high for suicide (4), homicide (4 for blacks), and drowning (9). Deaths from MVIs have declined substantially between 1970 and 1985 but have been stable from 1985 to 1988. The homicide rate among black male teenagers has increased sharply in the past few years, from 39.3 in 1984 to 77.4 in 1988, the highest level ever recorded.

Data on mortality are generally available only for whites and blacks. However, 1988 death rates for Hispanics, Asians, and American Indians were presented in broad age groups in a recent report.[6] For children 1-14, the death rate from all causes was highest for blacks (49 per 100,000) and American Indians (44) and similar for whites (30), Hispanics (30), and Asians (24). Injuries were the leading cause of death in all these ethnic groups. For those 15-24 years of age, American Indians had the highest death rate (162 per 100,000) followed by blacks (145), Hispanics (113), and whites (95). Asians had the lowest rate, 57 per 100,000. The differentials by cause were even greater. American Indians had the highest death rate from injuries (89 per 100,000), while Asians (29) and Blacks (37) had the lowest. Blacks had the highest homicide rate (59 per 100,000) followed by Hispanics (28) and American Indians (22). Whites (8) and Asians (7) had the lowest homicide rates. American Indians had the highest suicide rate (26 per 100,000) while blacks (8), Asians (6), and Hispanics (10) had the lowest. Whites were intermediate with 14 suicides per 100,000.

The chief advantage of mortality data is the fact that they are available over a long period of time (since the turn of the century) for small geographic areas (cities and counties from national vital statistics and zip codes or census tracts from state and local vital statistics). Although mortality data represent important health indicators, they account for only a small portion of the health risks faced by children and adolescents. In order to identify other important health problems we need to consider indicators that go beyond mortality.

## MORBIDITY

Unlike mortality data, morbidity data are derived from a variety of data systems and are generally based on sample surveys so that it is difficult to obtain data for states or smaller geographic areas. The major health surveys are those carried out by the National Center for Health Statistics (NCHS). The oldest is the National Health Interview Survey (NHIS), a sample survey of the non-institutionalized population of the U.S. in which data are collected through personal household interviews. The NHIS has been carried out annually since 1957. Information is collected on personal and demographic characteristics, illnesses, injuries, impairments, chronic conditions, and utilization of health resources. Special topics are covered in supplements to the basic survey. In 1981 and 1988 a Child Health Supplement was included that obtained additional information on child development, psychological problems, school functioning, and day care.

Although NHIS provides a wealth of population-based data on health characteristics, certain limitations must be kept in mind when using these data to assess child health. Most important is that the respondent (usually the child's mother) can report only those health problems of which she is aware. Undiagnosed conditions (e.g., allergies, mild asthma) will not be reported and so subgroups with greater access to health care will often appear to have greater incidence of such conditions. Furthermore, the structure of the questionnaire makes it likely that conditions that receive medical attention will be ascertained at a greater rate than those that do not. One example of this bias is that in 1988 the reported number of acute conditions per 100 of those under 18 years of age was 303 for whites and 186 for blacks.[7] Similarly, the number of bed days associated with acute conditions per 100 children in 1988 was higher for whites than blacks (404 vs 340). It is highly unlikely that black children actually have lower rates of acute conditions than white children given their poorer socioeconomic status (as well as their higher death rates). The more reasonable explanation is that awareness and the ability to afford medical consultation explains this disparity. On the other hand, however, reports of respondent-assessed health status do show large differentials in the expected direction. For example, in 1988, 2.4 percent of white children compared to 5.0 percent of black children were reported as having fair or poor health.[7] Data from NHIS therefore need to be interpreted very carefully.

Recognizing the limitations of NHIS, the NCHS also maintains the National Health and Nutrition Examination Surveys (NHANES), which are designed to assess the health and nutritional status of a representative sample of the U. S. non-institutionalized population through direct physical examinations as well as interviews. Because of their cost and complexity, the NHANES are carried out only periodically. Five surveys have been completed (1960-62, 1963-65, 1966-70, 1971-75, 1976-80) and a sixth (NHANES III) is being conducted in 1988-94. In addition, the Hispanic HANES, which focused on Mexican-Americans, Cuban-Americans, and Puerto Ricans residing in the New York area, was conducted in 1982-84. Because these surveys are based on standardized physical examinations and laboratory tests, they provide an unbiased assessment of health status for the NHANES subjects. Thus, NHANES data are often the basis for national standards for such measurements as height, weight, and hematocrit.

Growth retardation or growth stunting is generally defined as height-for-age below the fifth percentile of children in the U. S. population. Operationally, this is defined as the fifth percentile based on the participants in the Second National Health and Nutrition Examination Survey (NHANES II) conducted in 1976-1980.[8] Many studies have shown that low-income children, particularly from minority ethnic groups, have a higher prevalence of growth retardation.[9] The most readily accessible source for monitoring this indicator on a regular basis is the Pediatric Nutrition Surveillance System (PedNSS) maintained by the Centers for Disease Control (CDC). Unfortunately, however, this system is based on those children who are already enrolled in the WIC (Supplemental Food Program for Women, Infants, and Children) program and so high-risk children who do not participate cannot be monitored using this data system. The nutrition division of state and local health departments may also have data sources available on this issue.

Children with elevated blood lead levels are at increased risk for medical and behavioral problems. CDC has recommended that children with blood lead levels of 25 mg/dl or more be referred for further evaluation and treatment.[2] Data from NHANES II have documented much higher prevalence of elevated blood lead levels among black compared to white children and low-income compared to high-income children.[10]

"Iron deficiency is the most common single-nutrient deficiency in the United States and also the most common cause of anemia."[9] The measurement of the prevalence of anemia is complex and based on multiple biochemical indicators. The major population groups at risk are infants, adolescents, and women of childbearing age. Within these groups, the prevalence of iron deficiency is much greater among the poor, blacks, and Hispanics.[9] State and local data are usually based on simplified criteria of low hematocrit or hemoglobin levels derived from high-risk populations in public programs (e.g., the WIC program; the Early and Periodic Screening, Diagnosis, and Treatment [EPSDT] Program).

## SUBSTANCE ABUSE

The use of cigarettes, alcohol, and other drugs poses serious threats to the health of children and adolescents. The main source of data on substance abuse is the National Household Survey on Drug Abuse, carried out by the National Institute on Drug Abuse (NIDA). The survey covers the population 12 years of age and over living in households in the coterminous United States, asking about the use of selected substances during the month prior to interview. Data from these surveys show a decline in use of cigarettes from 25 percent of 12-17 year olds in 1974 to 12 percent in 1988.[6] Smoking among 18-25 year olds declined from 49 percent to 35 percent. Use of marijuana has also declined in recent years: after reaching a peak in 1979 (17 percent of 12-17 year olds and 35 percent of 18-25 year olds) the prevalence has been more than halved (6 percent of 12-17 year olds and 15 percent of 18-25 year olds in 1988).

Alcohol use followed a similar pattern, although the decline has not been as great. Among 12-17 year olds, 37 percent reported alcohol use in 1979 compared to 25 percent in 1988. For 18-25 year olds the decline was from 76 percent to 65 percent.[6]

The trends in cocaine use are more difficult to assess. The household survey shows a decline in cocaine use from 9.3 percent among 18-25 year olds in 1979 to 4.5 percent in 1988 (the proportion among 12-17 year olds was slightly over 1 percent in both years). However, data on drug abuse occurrences that have resulted in a medical crisis have been collected by the Drug Abuse Warning Network (DAWN). DAWN is based on a nonrandom sample of emergency rooms in 21 metropolitan areas. Data from DAWN show large annual increases (30-95 percent) in the number of cocaine-related emergency room episodes from 1985 to 1988 for 12-17 and 18-24 year olds. The number of episodes in 1989, however, did show a small decrease (10 percent) in both age groups.[6]

Another often-cited source of data on substance abuse is the Survey of High School Seniors carried out by the University of Michigan. Results from this survey can differ from the NIDA surveys because the most serious substance abuse problems occur among adolescents who drop out of school before becoming seniors.

## HEALTH SERVICES UTILIZATION

Access to health services is a critical component of health status. However, attention to cost containment and health promotion have led to decreased emphasis on access in recent years. Nevertheless, utilization of health services, particularly primary care, can help to avert more costly interventions and improve health status.

Data on health services utilization can be obtained from several sources. The NHIS includes information on utilization as reported by the respondent based on two-week recall for physician contacts and 12-month recall for hospital episodes. Differences in utilization by race and socioeconomic status are higher among children than any other age group. In 1985-87, black children under 18 had 2.8 visits per year compared to 4.5 visits for white children, despite the higher prevalence of fair or poor health among black children (4.8 percent vs 2.1 percent). Furthermore, among children in fair or poor health, blacks had 6.5 visits compared to 15.5 for whites.[11]

Differentials in hospital utilization are much smaller. Based on the 1985-87 NHIS data, the average annual number of hospital discharges per 100 children under 18 was 4.9 for whites and 5.4 for blacks. This excess among blacks was accounted for by their health status: the discharge rate for those in fair or poor health was 29.9 for whites and 28.1 for blacks while the rate for those in good or excellent health was 4.4 for whites and 4.2 for blacks.[11] It is of interest that although the overall hospital discharge rate in the U.S. is higher than in many industrialized nations, the discharge rate for children is relatively low. This discrepancy has been attributed to both positive and negative factors: the substitution of ambulatory for inpatient care and the lower rate of hospital utilization among poor children without health insurance.[12]

Data on hospital utilization are also available from the National Hospital Discharge Survey (NHDS). The NHDS is a continuous nationwide sample survey of short-stay hospitals in the U.S. that has been conducted since 1965. Within each hospital in the survey, a sample of discharges is selected and data are abstracted regarding the patient's age, sex, race, expected source of payment, discharge diagnoses, and procedures. Unfortunately, the race information is sometimes incomplete, leading to the possibility of biased racial comparisons. The information on expected source of payment could be useful in identifying barriers but it has only recently been added to the survey and has not yet been analyzed in detail, especially for children. Further research in these areas could make the NHDS an important source of data in the future.

One crucial aspect of ambulatory care utilization for children is the receipt of the recommended schedule of immunizations against preventable childhood diseases (diphtheria, tetanus, pertussis, measles, mumps, rubella, and polio). Data on immunization status for 1985 and earlier were collected through the United States Immunization Survey (USIS) conducted by the Census Bureau for CDC. This survey has been discontinued, but beginning in 1991 the NHIS will include periodically a battery of questions on childhood immunization. Data from the 1985 USIS show that nonwhite children were considerably less likely to be vaccinated than white children.[13]

## CONCLUSIONS

Although child health continues to improve, there remain large differentials among population subgroups, with ethnic minorities and the poor at particular risk. Further exacerbating these disparities is the increase in unmarried motherhood and divorce so that in 1988, 24 percent of all children under 18 (and 54 percent of black children) lived in single-parent households.[14] Health programs need to take a broader perspective than the treatment of disease, and focus on prevention of injuries, violence, and substance abuse, within the context of providing social support to children at high risk.

Acknowledgment

The editors and publisher thank Lois Fingerhut, a statistician with the National Center for Health Statistics, and Jennifer Madans, from Dr. Kleinman's office, for their help in the revision of this chapter and completion of the references.

## REFERENCES

1. U.S. Bureau of the Census: Current Population Reports P-60, No. 168. Money income and poverty statistics in the U.S., 1989. Washington, DC, U.S. Government Printing Office, 1990

2. Miller CA, Fine A, Adams-Taylor S: Monitoring Children's Health: Key Indicators. Washington, DC, American Public Health Association, 1989

3. Fingerhut LA, Kleinman JC: Trends and current status in childhood mortality, U.S., 1900-1985. National Center for Health Statistics. Vital and Health Statistics 3 (26). Washington, DC, U.S. Government Printing Office, 1989

4. Office of the Assistant Secretary for Health: Healthy People, the Surgeon General's Report on Health Promotion and Disease Prevention. Washington, DC, 1979

5. U.S. Department of Health and Human Services: Healthy People 2000: National Health Promotion and Disease Prevention Objectives. PHS. Washington, DC, U.S. Government Printing Office, 1990

6. National Center for Health Statistics: Health, United States, 1990. Hyattsville, MD, Public Health Service, 1991

7. Adams PF, Hardy AM: Current Estimates from the National Health Interview Survey: U.S., 1988. NCHS. Vital and Health Statistics 10 (173). Washington, DC, U.S. Government Printing Office, 1989

8. U.S. Department of Health and Human Services and U.S. Department of Agriculture: Nutrition Monitoring in the United States - A Report from the Joint Nutrition Monitoring Evaluation Committee. PHS. Washington, DC, U.S. Government Printing Office, 1986

9. Life Sciences Research Office: Nutrition Monitoring in the United States - an Update Report on Nutrition Monitoring. Federation of American Societies for Experimental Biology. Washington, DC, U.S. Government Printing Office, 1989

10. Annest JL, Mahaffey K: Blood lead levels for persons 6 months - 74 years, U.S., 1976-1980. NCHS. Vital and Health Statistics 11 (233). Washington, DC, U.S. Government Printing Office, 1984

11. Ries P: Health of black and white Americans, 1985-1987. NCHS. Vital and Health Statistics 10 (171) Washington, DC, U.S. Government Printing Office, 1984

12. Kozak LJ, McCarthy E: Hospital use by children in the U.S. and Canada. NCHS. Vital and Health Statistics 5 (1). Washington, DC, U.S. Government Printing Office, 1984

13. National Center for Health Statistics: Health, United States, 1989. Hyattsville, MD, Public Health Service, 1990

14. U.S. Bureau of the Census: Marital Status and Living Arrangements: March 1988. Current Population Reports P-20 (433). Washington, DC, U.S. Government Printing Office, 1989

# 2

# The Socioeconomic Status
# of America's Children and Youth

Carolyn C. Rogers, MA and Suzanne M. Bianchi, PhD

Significant changes have occurred in the structure of American families in the past two to three decades. More children today can expect to live in a single-parent family at some point in their lives due to both high rates of divorce and increased out-of-wedlock childbearing. As mothers of young children are more apt to work outside the home, many children are being cared for by other relatives or non-family members. American society has not fully adapted to the new realities of family life experienced by children, raising concern about the effects of family circumstances on the economic, social, and psychological well-being and academic development of children today.

The well-being of children is a multifaceted phenomenon. This chapter appraises the current situation of children, beginning with the size and composition of the child population. Next we examine recent trends in measures of children's well-being, including indicators of economic well-being, physical health, academic achievement, social behavior and attitudes, and emotional well-being.

## SIZE AND COMPOSITION

As of July 1989, there were approximately 64 million people under the age of 18 living in the United States (Table 1, next page). The overall size of the child population has fluctuated markedly during the past three decades, reflecting the high fertility of the postwar baby boom, the subsequent low fertility of the 1970s, and the increased fertility of the late 1980s. The number of children under 5 years old increased by 14 percent between 1980 and 1989, and is projected to crest in the 1990s and then decline by 2000. The elementary school-age population began to increase in the late 1980s and is expected to rise slowly into the next century. In contrast, the high school-age population declined by 16 percent between 1980 and 1989, but is expected to start increasing again in the 1990s.[1]

Although the number of children is increasing, those under age 18 now constitute a smaller fraction of the U.S. population than in the recent past (26 percent in 1989 compared with 36 percent in 1960). The youth-dependency ratio – the number of people under 18 years of age per 100 aged 18 to 64 years – decreased from a high of 66 per 100 in 1965 to 42 per 100 in 1988. A lower youth-dependency ratio is usually viewed as

### Table 1

### Number of Children by Age, Race, and Spanish Origin
### (numbers in millions)

|  | 1960 | 1970 | 1980 | 1989 |
|---|---|---|---|---|
| Total, aged 0-17 | 64.2 | 69.6 | 63.7 | 64.1 |
| Ages |  |  |  |  |
| 0-5 | 24.3 | 21.0 | 19.6 | 22.4 |
| 6-11 | 21.7 | 24.6 | 20.8 | 21.6 |
| 12-17 | 18.2 | 24.1 | 23.3 | 20.1 |
| Race and ethnic origin, 0-17 |  |  |  |  |
| White | 55.5 | 59.1 | 52.5 | 51.4 |
| Nonwhite* | 8.7 | 10.6 | 11.2 | 12.0 |
| Black | n.a. | 9.5 | 9.5 | 10.0 |
| Spanish origin | n.a. | n.a. | n.a. | 7.2 |
| Children as percentage of total |  |  |  |  |
| U.S. population | 36 | 34 | 28 | 26 |

Sources: "Preliminary Estimates of the Population of the United States by Age, Sex, and Race: 1970 to 1981," Current Population Reports. Series P-25, no. 917, Table 1; "Estimates of the Population of the United States by Age, Sex, and Race: 1980 to 1985," Current Population Reports, Series P-25, no. 985, Table 1; "U.S. Population Estimates, by Age, Sex, Race, and Hispanic Origin: 1989," Current Population Reports, Series P-25, no.1057, Table 2; 1970 census volume, "Characteristics of the Population, U.S. Summary," Table 52; 1960 census volume, "Characteristics of the Population, U.S. Summary," Table 155. n.a. – not available
* "Nonwhite" includes blacks, Indians, Japanese, Chinese, and all other races except white. Blacks constitute the great majority of nonwhites. People of Spanish origin can be of any race.

positive for society because it means that there are more adults available to support, supervise, and socialize young people. The child population in the year 2000 will contain a larger share of minority youth due to higher black and Hispanic fertility rates and substantial immigration of Hispanic and Caribbean blacks to the U.S.

# TRENDS IN MEASURES OF WELL-BEING

## FAMILY LIVING ARRANGEMENTS

In 1988, 46 million children – 73 percent of children under age 18 – were living in two-parent families, compared with 88 percent in 1960 (Table 2, next page). More than 13 million children in 1988 were living with their mothers only – 21 percent, compared with only 8 percent in 1960. These changes in family living arrangements are the result primarily of high rates of marital disruption and divorce and increased childbearing and rearing by unmarried women.[2,3] Based on current trends, 50 percent to perhaps 60 percent of children born today are projected to spend some part of their childhood in single-parent families.[4]

Racial differences in the family living arrangements of children have grown during the past three decades. The proportion of white children living with two parents declined by 12 percentage points (from 91 percent to 79 percent) between 1960 and 1988, but it declined even more for blacks – 28 percentage points, from 67 percent to 39 percent. Black children are more likely to spend some part of their childhood in a mother-only family than are white children. In 1988, the majority of black children (51 percent) lived with their mother only, compared with 16 percent of white children (Table 2, next page). Children in mother-only families often face multiple burdens, such as lower average income and higher unemployment. Never-married mothers are likely to have the additional disadvantages of younger age and less education. Furthermore, many of these children lack contact with or support from their absent fathers and must rely on government assistance for support.

## MATERNAL EMPLOYMENT AND CHILD CARE

Another profound change in children's lives is the increased probability of having a mother who works for pay outside the home. As of 1988, 62 percent of all children under age 18 had mothers who were in the labor force, compared with 39 percent in 1970.[5] Fifty-three percent of children under age 6, and 66 percent of those ages 6 to 17, had mothers who were

## Table 2

### Living Arrangements of Children Under 18 Years, by Race and Hispanic Origin: 1960, 1970, 1980 and 1988

| Living arrangement | 1960 | 1970 | 1980 | 1988 | Percent Change 1960-1988 |
|---|---|---|---|---|---|
| | | (numbers in thousands) | | | |
| **All Races** | | | | | |
| Children under 18 years | 63,727 | 69,162 | 63,427 | 63,179 | -8.6 |
| Percent living with: | | | | | |
| Two parents | 87.7 | 85.2 | 76.7 | 72.7 | -17.8 |
| One parents | 9.1 | 11.9 | 19.7 | 24.3 | 163.0 |
| Mother only | 8.0 | 10.8 | 18.0 | 21.4 | 164.9 |
| Father only | 1.1 | 1.1 | 1.7 | 2.9 | 149.7 |
| Other relatives | 2.5 | 2.2 | 3.1 | 2.3 | -7.4 |
| Nonrelatives only | 0.7 | 0.7 | 0.6 | 0.7 | 1.2 |
| **White** | | | | | |
| Children under 18 years | 55,077 | 58,790 | 52,242 | 51,030 | -7.3 |
| Percent living with: | | | | | |
| Two parents | 90.9 | 89.5 | 82.7 | 78.9 | -19.6 |
| One parent | 7.1 | 8.7 | 15.1 | 18.9 | 144.8 |
| Mother only | 6.1 | 7.8 | 13.5 | 16.0 | 141.3 |
| Father only | 1.0 | 0.9 | 1.6 | 2.9 | 165.7 |
| Other relatives | 1.4 | 1.2 | 1.7 | 1.6 | 5.7 |
| Nonrelatives only | 0.5 | 0.6 | 0.5 | 0.6 | 4.5 |
| **Black** | | | | | |
| Children under 18 years | 8,650 | 9,422 | 9,375 | 9,699 | 12.1 |
| Percent living with: | | | | | |
| Two parents | 67.0 | 58.5 | 42.2 | 38.6 | -35.5 |
| One parent | 21.9 | 31.8 | 45.8 | 54.1 | 176.6 |
| Mother only | 19.9 | 29.5 | 43.9 | 51.1 | 187.8 |
| Father only | 2.0 | 2.3 | 1.9 | 3.0 | 66.5 |
| Other relatives | 9.6 | 8.7 | 10.7 | 6.4 | -25.0 |
| Nonrelatives only | 1.5 | 1.0 | 1.3 | 1.0 | -28.8 |
| **Hispanic** | | | | | |
| Children under 18 years | (NA) | 4,006 | 5,459 | 6,786 | (NA) |
| Percent living with: | | | | | |
| Two parents | (NA) | 77.7 | 75.4 | 66.3 | (NA) |
| One parent | (NA) | (NA) | 21.1 | 30.2 | (NA) |
| Mother only | (NA) | (NA) | 19.6 | 27.2 | (NA) |
| Father only | (NA) | (NA) | 1.5 | 3.0 | (NA) |
| Other relatives | (NA) | (NA) | 3.4 | 2.7 | (NA) |
| Nonrelatives only | (NA) | (NA) | 0.1 | 0.9 | (NA) |

Note: Excludes persons under 18 years old who were maintaining households or families. Persons of Hispanic origin may be of any race.
Source: U.S. Bureau of the Census: "Marital Status and Living Arrangements: March 1988," Current Population Reports, Series P-20, No. 433 Table A-4.

in the labor force in 1988.[6,7,8] The impact of maternal employment on children depends on the family's socioeconomic status, age of the child, and whether the mother works full- or part-time. Working mothers add to the family's income, particularly important for low-income families. Employed mothers also have fewer children than unemployed mothers, and fewer siblings imply that more economic resources are available per child. Children with fewer siblings also tend to have higher academic achievement than those with more siblings.[9,10] Thus, to the extent that maternal employment increases family income and leads to smaller families, children will benefit both academically and financially.

As maternal employment has risen, the need for substitute care for the children of working mothers has increased and the location of this care has shifted outside of the child's home. In 1987, the most common child-care setting for children under 5 years with employed mothers was in another person's home – 36 percent – compared with 30 percent cared for in their own home and 24 percent in child-care centers or nursery or preschool programs during all or most of the time their mothers were at work.[11] Among full-time working mothers in 1987, 39 percent of their children were cared for in another home, 28 percent in group care or nursery-preschool care, and 24 percent in the child's home.[10] Although care of young children has increasingly moved outside of the child's home, often into group situations, family members continue to have a major role in the provision of care.

About three-quarters of children 5 to 14 years old are in school for most of the time their mothers are at work, and hence, school serves as a primary child-care arrangement.[12] For an important subgroup of these children, before- or after-school care is also needed to cover all the hours their parents are at work. In 1987, 22 percent of school-age children requiring a secondary arrangement in addition to school cared for themselves while their parents were at work.[11] The most accurate guess of the number of these "latch-key kids" – 2.1 million children 5 to 13 years old – is based on data collected in a 1984 Census Bureau survey.[13]

## ECONOMIC WELL-BEING

Children have consistently had a higher probability of being poor than adults, as seen in official poverty statistics available back to 1959. In the 1960s, poverty among children under age 18 declined substantially; the number in poverty dropped from 18 million in 1959 to 10 million in 1969, and the official poverty rate fell from 27 percent to 14 percent (Table 3, next page). As economic growth slowed in the 1970s, the number of children in poverty leveled off at approximately 10 million, with a poverty rate of nearly 16 percent. After 1978, the number of children in poverty increased, and peaked at almost 14 million in 1983, coinciding with the severe economic recession of the early 1980s. Poverty rates have declined since then, but as of 1988, 12.6 million children (20 percent) live below the poverty level, one-quarter more than the number of children in poverty throughout the 1970s.

Children in mother-only families have an almost one-in-two chance of being poor, compared with a less than one-in-ten chance for children living with two parents (Table 4, next page). In 1988, about 3.3 million mother-only families with children – or 45 percent – were in poverty. Children in mother-only families suffer economically because their mothers usually have low earnings, their fathers often do not contribute to their support, and their public assistance benefits have not kept up with inflation during the 1980s.

### Table 3
### Number and Percent Below Poverty Among Children and
### Working-Age Adults, by Race for Selected Years: 1959 to 1988
### (numbers in thousands)

|  | Persons Under Age 18 | | Persons Age 18-64 | |
|  | Number | Percent | Number | Percent |
|---|---|---|---|---|
| All Races |  |  |  |  |
| 1959 | 17,552 | 27.3 | 16,457 | 17.0 |
| 1969 | 9,691 | 14.0 | 9,669 | 8.7 |
| 1979 | 10,377 | 16.4 | 12,043 | 8.9 |
| 1983 | 13,911 | 22.3 | 17,767 | 12.4 |
| 1988 | 12,584 | 19.7 | 15,812 | 10.5 |
| White |  |  |  |  |
| 1979 | 6,193 | 11.8 | 8,110 | 6.9 |
| 1983 | 8,862 | 17.5 | 12,347 | 10.0 |
| 1988 | 7,483 | 14.6 | 10,867 | 8.3 |
| Black |  |  |  |  |
| 1979 | 3,833 | 41.2 | 3,478 | 23.8 |
| 1983 | 4,398 | 46.7 | 4,694 | 29.2 |
| 1988 | 4,364 | 44.2 | 4,278 | 24.4 |
| Hispanic |  |  |  |  |
| 1979 | 1,535 | 28.0 | 1,232 | 16.8 |
| 1983 | 2,312 | 38.1 | 2,148 | 22.5 |
| 1988 | 2,653 | 37.9 | 2,501 | 20.7 |

Source: U. S. Bureau of the Census: Money Income and Poverty Status in the United States: 1988, Current Population Reports Series P-60, No.166, Table 19

The character of poverty is affected by the availability of Aid to Families with Dependent Children (AFDC) and non-cash benefits. Of approximately 11 million AFDC recipients in fiscal year 1988, 67 percent were children, representing 11 percent of the total child population and 65 percent of children in poverty.[14] Although the average value of cash benefits from state welfare programs for poor families with dependent children has declined, the economic security of families with children (particularly mother-only families) has been bolstered by non-cash benefit programs introduced in the late 1960s and 1970s – programs such as food stamps, subsidized housing, and Medicaid.[15] Non-cash benefit programs continue to provide benefits to substantial numbers of needy families with children.

The growing number of two-parent families in poverty has also contributed to the higher poverty among children during the 1980s. Poverty in these families is due largely to the stagnation in the real wages of fathers.[16] Most of these "working poor" do not qualify for any public assistance except food stamps, and many are not covered by health insurance. The income from working mothers, smaller families, and delayed

Table 4
Poverty Status of Families with Children Under Age 18 by
Family Type For Selected Years, 1959 to 1988
(numbers in thousands)

| Mother-only Families, No Husband Present | Total Families | Families Below Poverty Number | Percent |
|---|---|---|---|
| 1959 | 2,544 | 1,525 | 59.9 |
| 1969 | 3,384 | 1,519 | 44.9 |
| 1979 | 6,035 | 2,392 | 39.6 |
| 1983 | 6,622 | 3,122 | 47.1 |
| 1988 | 7,361 | 3,294 | 44.7 |
| Married Couple Families | | | |
| 1959* | 24,448 | 3,818 | 15.6 |
| 1969* | 26,443 | 1,707 | 6.5 |
| 1979 | 25,615 | 1,573 | 6.1 |
| 1983 | 25,216 | 2,557 | 10.1 |
| 1988 | 25,598 | 1,847 | 7.2 |

*Data for 1959 and 1969 include a small number of male-headed, single-parent families.
Source: U.S. Bureau of the Census: Money Income and Poverty Status in the United States: 1988, Current Population Reports Series P-60, No 166, Table 20

childbearing are factors that have helped ameliorate the poverty conditions experienced by these families.

Racial differences in childhood poverty are substantial; black children and Hispanic children are especially apt to be poor. The racial gap in childhood poverty has decreased since 1959, but racial differences persist because a growing proportion of black children live in mother-only families and such families are more apt to be poor.[17] In 1988, 56 percent of black mother-only families with children were poor and over one-half of black children lived in mother-only families. The poverty rate in white mother-only families was also quite high (38 percent) but only 16 percent of white children lived in such families.[18] Even among two-parent families, the likelihood of black families living in poverty (almost 13 percent in 1988) was twice that of white families (6 percent).[18]

Children's economic well-being is reflected not only in poverty trends but in the average level and distribution of income among families with children. Average family income (in real terms) for families with children fell in the first half of the 1980s, but rebounded in the latter part of the decade. By 1987, the median income for families with children under age 18 was $29,892, down slightly from the 1979 level of $30,005 (adjusted to 1987 dollars).[19] Real income for children in two-parent families increased by 5 percent between 1979 and 1987, whereas the family income for children in mother-only families decreased by 16 percent.[19] In 1987, mother-only families received an average annual income of $9,838, only 28 percent of the $35,423 average for children in two-parent families.[19] Hence, the growth in mother-only families has been accompanied by a growing inequality in the economic circumstances of children.

Even with economic disparities by race and family type, today's smaller family size means that more income is available to each child at any given family income level. The dramatic increase in employed mothers has enhanced the money income available to children, at least in two-parent families. Moreover, the higher educational attainment of parents today is advantageous for children because more educated parents are, on average, better able to provide an adequate family income. They are also typically better equipped to assist children with homework and enhance the home learning environment.[20]

## PHYSICAL HEALTH

The overall physical health of U.S. children is better today than in 1960, although the rate of improvement for some health indicators has declined in recent years. The infant mortality rate – the proportion of babies who die within the first year of life – was 9.7 in 1989 (9.7 infant deaths per 1,000 live births), less than half of what it was in 1960 (26.0).[21] Although infant mortality rates have improved for both blacks and whites, a racial gap persists. In 1987, the black infant death rate was 17.9 (down from 44.3 in 1960), compared with a rate of 8.6 for whites (down from 22.9 in 1960).[21] Death rates for preschool and school-age children have also declined substantially. Although mortality rates provide only a partial picture of children's health status, these dramatic declines attest to real improvements in the physical health of young people.

One way to help ensure a healthy infant is for the expectant mother to obtain prenatal care early in the pregnancy. Yet for one out of every 20 babies born in the U.S., the mother has not obtained prenatal care or has obtained care late in the pregnancy. Young teenagers, school dropouts, unmarried women, and black women are at greater risk of not obtaining timely prenatal care. Pregnant women who do not obtain timely prenatal care are also more likely to produce babies of low birth weight and babies who die during the first year of life.[22]

Many communicable diseases once common to childhood, such as diphtheria, polio, and measles, have been eradicated or greatly reduced in frequency.[23,24,25] By the time U.S. children enter school, virtually all of them have been immunized against measles, mumps, rubella, diphtheria, and polio.[26] While children still have bouts of acute illness or minor injuries from time to time, most grow up physically healthy. Eight out of ten children are described by their parents as being in "very good" or "excellent" health, and all but about 3 percent are rated in at least "good" health.[27]

With progress made in conquering many of the traditional diseases of childhood, public health experts and the media have shifted their attention to other child health problems, such as the prevention of accidental injury and child abuse/neglect by parents and other caretakers. Accidental injury is the leading cause of death to children after the first few months of life. Drowning, burns, choking and other forms of suffocation, falls, and poisoning are other common causes of injury and death in childhood. Motor vehicle accidents represent a large fraction of serious injuries and childhood deaths, especially among older children. Nearly 10 million emergency room visits and at least one night in the hospital for 1 in every 130 children occur annually.[28] Many forms of unintentional injury to children and youth have been combated with success; for example, improvements in child motor vehicle safety are due in part to the beneficial effects of government regulations.[14] The number of child abuse cases –

childhood injuries and deaths resulting from attacks by parents, relatives, acquaintances, or strangers (or self-inflicted, such as teenage suicide) – is less than the number due to unintentional causes, but such incidents of intentional injury/death tend to generate more public attention and concern.

A number of child health indicators – mortality rates, health ratings, and some measures of illness and injury – show substantial disparities in the health status of children from different segments of American society. Black and Hispanic children, especially those in central cities or rural areas, are less healthy, on average, than non-minority children.[14] The health status of poor children and children whose parents are less well educated is below average. Socioeconomic and ethnic disparities are also seen in children's use of physician and dental services, with children from poor and minority families receiving less-frequent care than those from middle-class, non-minority families,[29] despite the fact that children from poor families are more likely to need medical or dental care. Furthermore, only about two-thirds of children from families below the poverty line are covered by some form of health insurance, compared with nearly 90 percent of children in families with incomes at least twice the poverty line.[30] Health insurance coverage also varies by family type, with more than 85 percent covered in two-parent families, and less than 70 percent in mother-only families.[14]

## School Enrollment and Academic Achievement

American children start school earlier and stay in school longer than in the past. Nursery or preschool attendance has increased markedly in the past two decades; in 1988, 38 percent of 3- and 4-year-old children were enrolled in nursery schools, pre-kindergarten or kindergarten programs, or child care centers with an "educational curriculum," up from 11 percent in 1965.[31] Attending nursery school is more common among children in the suburbs of metropolitan areas (generally more affluent) than in central cities or non-metropolitan areas.[32] With compulsory school attendance for children ages 7 to 15 years, enrollment has been virtually universal for this age group since 1960.[33]

More teenagers remain enrolled in school, and high school graduation rates are higher today than in the past. In 1960, 85 percent of white 16-to-17-year olds and 76 percent of their black counterparts were enrolled in school. By the late 1980s, 93 percent of students this age, regardless of race, were still enrolled in school.[33] About 85 percent of white 20 to 24 year olds in 1986 had graduated from high school, a rate virtually unchanged since the mid-1970s.[33] Among blacks, the rate of high school graduation has increased in recent years; by 1986, 81 percent of 20-to-24-year-old blacks were high school graduates. Although the dropout rate has been reduced substantially in recent years,[31] disproportionate numbers of high school dropouts are still found in families with low socioeconomic status and non-Asian minority backgrounds.[34] Dropout rates for minority students are also considerably higher in the inner cities of the largest metropolitan areas than in other parts of the country.[14]

Academic competence is just as important as higher enrollment and graduation rates, and there is widespread concern over what children are learning in school today. The National Assessment of Educational Progress (NAEP) measured academic achievement in reading, mathematics, and science for a national sample of school-age children 9, 13, and 17 years old at selected intervals in the 1970s and 1980s. The NAEP has not found a deterioration in fundamental reading, writing, and arithmetic skills; overall student performance in these basic areas either remained constant or improved slightly in the past two decades. Evidence has been found, however, of a decline in verbal and mathematical achievement involving complex reasoning.[35,36,37] Recent cohorts of students have not performed well on exercises measuring their understanding of mathematical concepts, their ability to apply computational skills to the solution of practical problems, or exercises measuring inferential comprehension.[35]

Deterioration in student knowledge and proficiency in more advanced topics and skill areas during the late 1960s and 1970s has been evidenced in a number of large-scale testing programs. The average test scores of college-bound high school seniors on the Scholastic Aptitude Test (SAT) dropped appreciably between 1963 and 1980.[35,38,39,40] The Educational Testing Service has concluded that the continuing decline in scores after 1971, however, was not due to changes in the composition of high school seniors taking the test. The downward trend in SAT scores seems to have ended, with a small improvement in average verbal scores between 1981 and 1985 and in mathematics scores between 1981 and 1987.[39,40,41] Even with improved SAT scores in the 1980s, average scores remain considerably below those of 25 years ago.

Large-scale testing programs also indicate that academic achievement among black and Hispanic students has improved notably over the past 25 years. Ethnic minorities and other groups whose achievement levels have traditionally been below average – namely, students in the South, those in disadvantaged urban communities or rural areas, and students whose parents have less than a high school education – have shown gains in reading, writing, and mathematical skills.[39,40,42] Over the past decade, the average scores achieved by black and Hispanic students on standardized college admission tests – either the SAT or the American College Testing (ACT) examination – have also increased. Despite the gains made by black and Hispanic students, their average levels of reading, writing, and mathematics remain well below the performance level of children in the nation as a whole.

In sum, two divergent trends in academic achievement are evident. On the one hand, the academic achievement of today's best students appears to be significantly lower than that of the best students of the early 1960s. On the other hand, the achievement of minority students and those from lower class family backgrounds has improved since the early 1960s, although at a slower pace in the most recent decade and remaining at a level well below that of middle-class non-minority students.

## SOCIAL BEHAVIOR AND ATTITUDES

Profound changes have occurred in the social behavior and attitudes of teenagers over the past three decades. Theft and violence, use of illicit drugs, and early sexual activity outside of marriage all became much more prevalent during the late 1960s and early 1970s, leveling off or diminishing somewhat in the late 1970s and early 1980s. Today, most forms of deviant behavior remain more common than in the early 1960s.

The teenage arrest rate from the National Crime Survey (NCS) was 102 arrests per 1,000 young people ages 13 to 17 years in 1985. Thirty-two percent of these arrests were for property crimes: arson, auto theft, burglary, and larceny. Four percent of the arrests were for violent crimes: aggravated assault, murder, rape, robbery, and non-negligent manslaughter. The remainder of the arrests were for vandalism, liquor-law or drug-abuse violations, disorderly conduct, and simple assault.[43,44,45] Today's teenagers play a smaller part in overall crime than a decade ago due to recent stabilization in the teenage arrest rate and to a smaller proportion of teens in the population.

Despite these trends, the number of juveniles in custody has increased slightly in the past few years, due in part to tougher public policies about keeping offenders of all ages incarcerated for the duration of their sentences.[46] Black teens are overrepresented in violent crimes (such as robbery) that are likely to lead to arrest and prosecution.[47] Minority youth in general are overrepresented among juveniles arrested or held in correctional facilities; approximately half of the juveniles in custody are from ethnic minorities.[43,46]

The use of marijuana and other illicit drugs – cocaine, amphetamines, and other stimulants; LSD and other hallucinogens; inhalants; barbiturates; and heroin – by teenagers became more prevalent during the 1960s and 1970s. Public attention has focused on the increased use of illicit drugs among young people due to concern about negative health and motivational effects and to the possibility that regular use might lead to addiction. Teenage drug use may also be a risk factor in serious injury from automobile accidents, fights, or other unfavorable incidents as well as early sexual intercourse and pregnancy. Marijuana has been the most popular drug used, with 56 percent of all young adults ages 18 to 25 years in 1988 reporting having ever tried marijuana.[48,49,50] Use of nearly all drugs has declined from peak levels reached in the late 1970s or early 1980s, with the exception of cocaine, which continued to increase into the mid-1980s.[49,50]

Alcohol is by far the most common intoxicant used by adolescents, and no other illicit drug (not even marijuana at its peak) comes close to the level of teenage alcohol use.[49,50] As of 1988, 90 percent of 18 to 25 year olds had ever used alcohol and 65 percent were current users (compared with 15 percent who currently used marijuana). Because teenage drinking is so widespread, it is likely that the negative personal and societal effects of teen alcohol abuse far exceed the effects attributable to teenage drug abuse.

Teenage sexual activity outside of marriage has increased and occurs at earlier ages. While leveling off in recent years, teen sexual activity still remains more common than in the past, with 53 percent of female teenagers in 1988 reporting that they had ever had intercourse.[51] Because many teens do not use contraceptives when they initiate sexual activity, this has resulted in a large number of adolescent pregnancies.[52] Among female teenagers 15 to 19 years old in the mid-1980s who had ever had sex, nearly one-in-four became pregnant each year.[53] Teenage births outside of marriage have more than doubled between 1970 and 1988, from 30 percent of births to teen mothers in 1970 to 66 percent by 1988; this increase is due to both a marked reduction in births to married teens and a decreased tendency to legitimize non-marital pregnancies through marriage.[54] Since many teen mothers are not marrying, they are at a greater risk of having to rely on welfare to support their child.

Indicators of deterioration in children's emotional well-being and life satisfaction over time include a rising adolescent suicide rate, greater use of psychological services by children and youth, a higher proportion of children who have had seriously disturbing experiences, and increases in the proportion of students receiving or needing special educational assistance for chronic emotional problems. The suicide rate for teenagers 15 to

19 years old doubled between 1960 and 1975, from 3.6 deaths to 7.5 deaths per year per 100,000; by 1989, the rate had nearly doubled again, reaching a level of 13.9 deaths per 100,000 in 1989.[55] The rate of attempted suicide (not readily available) would probably be a better indicator of emotional distress; for each instance in which a young person succeeds in killing him- or herself, there are many more attempts at suicide that do not succeed.

The frequency with which adolescents are taken to see psychiatrists or psychologists for emotional, mental, or behavioral problems nearly doubled between the late 1960s and the early 1980s.[14] More frequent use of psychological services by young people is associated both with a growing need for such services and greater accessibility and acceptance of such services by families with teenagers than in the past.

In contrast to the negative picture provided by the suicide rate and the use of psychological services, national survey data show that the majority of today's young Americans are not anxious, depressed, alienated, or profoundly dissatisfied with their lives. On the contrary, most high school seniors seem to be reasonably happy and satisfied with their lives.[56,57] A substantial majority of high school and college students consider it very important to find the right person to marry, rear children, and have a happy family life. Survey data of young people also show a greater acceptance of maternal employment and a more equal division of labor within the family.[14] High school seniors and college freshmen of the 1980s are more concerned with material success than students of the 1960s, but a majority of today's students still endorse humanitarian values and think that American society is too materialistic.

In addition, two recent changes in marriage and childbearing patterns have positive implications for the well-being of children and youth. The first is the trend toward marriage and childbearing at later ages. Later marriages are more likely to endure than those that occur in the teenage years or early twenties.[58,59] The second positive development is the trend toward smaller family sizes and more widely spaced births. Smaller family size means that each child in the family gets a larger share of the human and material resources available to the family. Two children now constitute the most common family size.

In sum, although high school students are somewhat less likely than their elders to describe themselves as "very happy," most young people appear to be reasonably content with their families, their schools, their communities, and their lives in general. The predominant impression received from examining trends in subjective well-being from annual high school surveys is that not much has changed in the past ten years, despite the continuing changes in marital disruption, maternal employment, and other aspects of children and youth's family environments.

## FUTURE PROSPECTS

The family remains the central institution in children's lives; though changing, the family is not disintegrating. Trends in children's well-being have been mixed, with deterioration in some areas but stability and even improvement in others. Family disruption and out-of-wedlock childbearing and rearing have increased over the past three decades. Maternal employment has also increased, resulting in greater family income at least for two-parent families, as well as a greater demand for child care outside the home. Other developments in family circumstances have taken place that are clearly positive for children, such as the trend toward higher levels of parental education, later marriages, and smaller family size.

The prospects for today's children and youth are uncertain. Children have fewer siblings, more often live in a single-parent family, frequently have a working mother, and spend more time as a "latch-key kid." Although more children are in child care than in the past, there is evidence of continued, relatively high, family involvement in caring for young children and school-age children by their parents. Moreover, significant progress has been made since the 1960s in improving child health, minority educational achievement, and the economic situation of families with children. Anti-discrimination laws, equal opportunity programs, immunization drives, health and safety regulations, Medicaid, food stamps and child nutrition programs, compensatory education, and other federal and state programs have played a role in these advances. Nonetheless, a significant minority of children are being reared in less-than-optimal family environments, particularly the working poor and those in mother-only families. The challenge to policy-makers is to find ways to help these children at risk. Families and governments share the responsibility for ensuring the well-being of children by investing in education and providing a safe and wholesome environment for the next generation.

# REFERENCES

1. U.S. Bureau of the Census: U.S. Population Estimates, by Age, Sex, Race, and Hispanic Origin: 1989, Current Population Reports, Series P-25, No. 1057, Washington, DC, U.S. Government Printing Office, 1990

2. Hofferth SL: Updating children's life course. J Marriage Fam 47 no.1:93-115, 1985

3. Bumpass L: Children and marital disruption: a replication and an update. Demography 21 no.1:71-82, 1984

4. U.S. Bureau of the Census, Miller LF, Moorman JE: Married-Couple Families with Children, Current Population Reports, Series P-23, No. 162, Washington, DC, U.S. Government Printing Office, 1989

5. U.S. Bureau of Labor Statistics: Handbook Bulletin 2217 and unpublished tabulations from the Bureau of Labor Statistics

6. U.S. Bureau of Labor Statistics: Half of Mothers with Children Under 3 Now in Labor Force. News, August 20, 1986

7. Labor Force Activity of Mothers of Young Children Continues at Record Pace. News, September 19, 1985

8. Unpublished data from the March 1988 Current Population Survey

9. Desai S, Chase-Lansdale PL, Michael RT: Mother or market? Effects of maternal employment on the intellectual ability of 4-year old children. Demography 26 no. 4:545-561, 1989

10. Stafford FP: Women's Work, Sibling Competition, and Children's School Performance. Working Paper 8036, University of Michigan, Institute for Social Research, 1987

11. U.S. Bureau of the Census: Who's Minding the Kids? Current Population Reports, P-70, No. 20, Washington, DC, U.S. Government Printing Office, 1990

12. U.S. Bureau of the Census: Who's Minding the Kids? Current Population Reports, Series P-70, No. 9, Washington, DC, U.S. Government Printing Office, 1987

13. U.S. Bureau of the Census, Bruno RR: After School Care of School-Age Children: December 1984, Current Population Reports, Series P-23, No. 149, Washington, DC, U.S. Government Printing Office, 1987

14. Zill N, Rogers CC: Recent trends in the well-being of children in the United States and their implications for public policy, The Changing American Family and Public Policy. Edited by A Cherlin. Washington, DC, The Urban Institute Press, 1988, pp 31-115

15. Committee on Ways and Means, U.S. House of Representatives: Background Material and Data on Programs within the Jurisdiction of the Committee on Ways and Means, 1989 Edition, Washington, DC, U.S. Government Printing Office, 1989

16. Bane MJ, Ellwood D: One fifth of the nation's children: why are they poor? Science 245, September 8, 1989

17. Fuchs VR: Why Are Children Poor? Working Paper No. 1984, National Bureau of Economic Research, 1986

18. U.S. Bureau of the Census: Money Income and Poverty Status in the United States: 1988, Current Population Reports, Series P-60, No. 166, Washington, DC, U.S. Government Printing Office, 1989

19. U.S. Bureau of the Census: Money Income of Households, Families, and Persons in the United States: 1980 and 1987, Current Population Reports, Series P-60, Nos. 132 and 162, Washington, DC, U.S. Government Printing Office, 1982 and 1989

20. Hill CR, Stafford FP: Parental care of children: time diary estimates of quantity, predictability, and variety. J Hum Resour 15 no. 2:219-239, 1980

21. National Center for Health Statistics: Annual Summary of Births, Marriages, Divorces, and Deaths: United States, 1989, Monthly Vital Statistics Report 38, No.13, Hyattsville, MD: U.S. Public Health Service, 1989

22. National Center for Health Statistics: Advance Report of Final Natality Statistics, Monthly Vital Statistics Report, annual series

23. National Center for Health Statistics: Health: United States, 1989 and Health: United States, annual issues, Hyattsville, MD: U.S. Public Health Service

24. U.S. Bureau of the Census: Statistical Abstract of the United States, 1990, Washington, D.C., U.S. Government Printing Office, 1990

25. Centers for Disease Control: annual data from the U.S. Immunization Survey

26. U.S. Public Health Service, Centers for Disease Control, Division of Immunization: unpublished data from the annual School Entry Assessment

27. National Center for Health Statistics: Current Estimates from the National Health Interview Survey: United States, 1985, Vital and Health Statistics, Series 10, No. 160, Hyattsville, MD: U.S. Public Health Service

28. National Center for Health Statistics: Current Estimates from the National Health Interview Survey: United States, Vital and Health Statistics, Series 10, annual issues

29. Guyer B, Gallagher SS: An approach to the epidemiology of childhood injuries, Pediatr Clin North Am, 32 no.1:5-15, 1985

30. National Center for Health Statistics, Mortality Statistics Branch, Division of Vital Statistics: unpublished work tables

31. U.S. Bureau of the Census: School Enrollment - Social and Economic Characteristics of Students: October 1988 and 1987, Current Population Reports, Series P-20, No. 443, Washington, DC, U.S. Government Printing Office, 1990

32. Bianchi S: America's Children: Mixed Prospects, Population Bulletin, 45, No. 1, Washington, DC, Population Reference Bureau, 1990

33. U.S. Bureau of the Census: School Enrollment - Social and Economic Characteristics of Students: October 1986, Current Population Reports, Series P-20, No.429, Washington, DC, U.S. Government Printing Office, 1988

34. National Center for Education Statistics, U.S. Department of Education: High School and Beyond: A National Longitudinal Study for the 1980s, Two Years in High School: The Status of 1980 Sophomores in 1982, and Two Years After High School: A Capsule Description of 1980 Seniors, Washington, DC, U.S. Government Printing Office, 1984

35. National Center for Education Statistics: The Condition of Education, Vol. 1: Elementary and Secondary Education, Washington, DC, U.S. Government Printing Office, 1989

36. College Entrance Examination Board: Profiles, College-Bound Seniors, 1981-1985, News from the College Board, October 14, 1982

37. Austin GR, Garber H (eds): The Rise and Fall of National Test Scores. New York, Academic Press, 1982

38. National Assessment of Educational Progress: The Reading Report Card, Progress Toward Excellence in Our Schools: Trends in Reading Over Four National Assessments, 1971-1984, Report No. 15-R-01, Princeton, NJ, Educational Testing Service, 1985

39. National Assessment of Educational Progress (NAEP): Three National Assessments of Reading: Changes in Performance, 1970-80, Report No. 11-R-01, Denver, CO, Education Commission of the States, 1981

40. National Assessment of Educational Progress (NAEP): Changes in Mathematical Achievement, 1973-78, Denver, CO, Education Commission of the States, 1979

41. National Assessment of Educational Progress: The Third National Mathematics Achievement, Trends and Issues, Report No. 13-MA-01, Denver, CO, Education Commission of the States, 1983

42. National Assessment of Educational Progress (NAEP): Writing Achievement, 1969-79 Princeton, NJ, Educational Testing Service, 1980

43. Cook PJ, Laub JH: The (surprising) stability of youth crime rates. J Quantitative Criminology, 2 no. 3:265-277, 1986

44. Hindelang MJ, McDermott MJ: Juvenile Criminal Behavior: An Analysis of Rates and Victim Characteristics, Albany, NY, Criminal Justice Research Center, 1981

45. Zimring FE: American youth violence: issues and trends Criminal Justice: An Annual Review of Research 1. Edited by N Morris and M Tonry. Chicago and London, University of Chicago Press, 1979, pp 67-107

46. U.S. Department of Justice, Bureau of Justice Statistics: Children in Custody, Rockville, MD, Justice Statistics Clearinghouse, 1986

47. U.S. Department of Justice, Bureau of Justice Statistics: Teenage Victims: A National Crime Survey Report. Rockville, MD, Justice Statistics Clearinghouse

48. U.S. Bureau of the Census: Statistical Abstract of the United States: 1990, Washington, DC, 1990

49. National Institute on Drug Abuse: National Household Survey on Drug Abuse: 1988 Population Estimates. Rockville, MD, National Institute on Drug Abuse, 1989

50. Johnston LD, Bachman JG, O'Malley PM: National Trends in Drug Use and Related Factors among American High School Students: 1975-1986. Rockville, MD National Institute on Drug Abuse, 1987

51. National Center for Health Statistics: National Survey of Family Growth, unpublished tabulations

52. Forrest JD: calculations from National Center for Health Statistics data: Risking the Future: Adolescent Sexuality, Pregnancy, and Childbearing. Edited by SL Hofferth and CD Hayes. Washington, DC, National Academy Press, 1987

53. Hofferth SL: calculations for the Center for Population Research, National Institute for Child Health and Human Development, in Select Committee on Children, Youth, and Families, U.S. House of Representatives: U.S. Children and Their Families: Current Conditions and Recent Trends, 1987, Washington, DC, March 1987

54. O'Connell M, Rogers CC: Out-of-wedlock births, premarital pregnancies and their effect on family formation and dissolution. Fam Plann Perspect 16, no. 4:157-162, 1984

55. National Center for Health Statistics: Annual Summary of Births, Marriages, Divorces, and Deaths: United States, 1989, Monthly Vital Statistics Report 38, No.13

56. Johnston LD, Bachman JG, O'Malley PM: Monitoring the Future: Questionnaire Responses from the Nation's High School Seniors

57. Davis JA: General Social Surveys, 1972-1978: Cumulative Codebook, Chicago, IL, National Opinion Research Center, University of Chicago, 1978

58. U.S. Bureau of the Census: Household and Family Characteristics, Current Population Reports, Series P-20, annual issues

59. Cherlin AJ: Marriage, Divorce, Remarriage. Cambridge, MA, Harvard University Press, 1981

# 3

## Nutrition Priorities
## in Student Health Services

JOHANNA DWYER, DSc AND ANNE BOURGEOIS, MS, RD

This chapter reviews high-priority issues affecting the nutritional status of school and college students in the United States. It emphasizes the importance of school-based nutrition programs in addressing these concerns. Federal nutrition programs and the U.S. Public Health Service's Objectives for the Year 2000 relevant to student health, to planning, and to policy-making in school settings are highlighted and discussed.[1]

Today's health profiles of American children, adolescents, and young adults have improved dramatically since the turn of the century. However, the need for nutrition-related health promotion and attention to diet-related problems continues in student populations.

Recent national health-planning documents emphasize the great potential of school-based services.[1,2] Since students spend extensive time in school and college environments, these settings are ideal for reaching them with nutrition education and for modeling sound nutrition principles in health, food service, and exercise facilities. Moreover, school-based services provide an opportunity for delivering health care to poor students who otherwise might lack access.

## NEW ROLES IN NUTRITION
## FOR SCHOOL HEALTH PROVIDERS

The school health officer's traditional functions were chiefly in the area of primary prevention. Today the scope of health-related topics that are covered by the school health office has expanded. In addition to a focus on health promotion, prevention of infectious diseases, and identifying frank clinical signs of disease, the health officer today must screen for more subtle risks and deal with the "new morbidities." These involve social and behavioral as well as a broader spectrum of physical health risk factors, including nutrition and fitness.

However, in the past few years it has become increasingly apparent that realization of the full potential of the school health office required action and attention in additional areas, including secondary and tertiary prevention. Included in the school health officer's enlarged scope of activities is greater attention to nutrition-related treatment of problems that occur in children and adolescents and are amenable to correction in school settings.

## NUTRITION-RELATED TASKS
## OF THE SCHOOL HEALTH OFFICE

The shifting focus of school health education activities is best described by outlining the many tasks that must be dealt with by school health officers. The subsequent sections elaborate on these various activities and concentrate on the role of school-based nutrition-related programs in dealing with specific diet-related problems.

First and foremost, the school health officer must provide anticipatory guidance and promote nutritional health and fitness in later childhood and adolescence. Relevant behavioral objectives are summarized in Table 1, next page. Attention to these issues is essential in all school health activities.

A second important task of the school health officer in the nutrition area is to conduct needs assessments of which nutrition-related activities are called for in the school health office itself, in the classroom, in physical education programs, and in the school cafeteria or canteen.

A third task is to organize and conduct screening programs to identify students at high risk of various nutrition-related problems and conditions. These include undernutrition and inadequate food intake, especially among poor children and those from disrupted or chaotic families. Also important is early identification of those at high risk for eating disorders, those who are abusing drugs or alcohol, those who are pregnant and need prenatal nutrition advice, and others who have nutrition-related problems. Finally, screening is useful for identification and referral of those who have diet-related risks of chronic degenerative diseases, such as obesity, hyperlipidemia, high blood pressure, and high blood glucose. Such screening programs may be operated out of the school health office itself or

### Table 1

### Behavioral Objectives to Enhance the Health of Children, Adolescents, and Young Adults

| To Enhance Student Health In: | Help Children and Adolescents To: |
| --- | --- |
| Nutrition | – Assess their own nutritional status<br>– Monitor their own growth<br>– Understand nutrient needs and how they change with growth<br>– Adopt and maintain healthy dietary habits<br>– Ensure satisfactory iron and calcium intakes<br>– Find fulfillment of individual needs without doing violence to nutritional status<br>– Identify poor eating habits and alter them<br>– Avoid alcohol abuse |
| Fitness | – Assess their fitness and lifestyles<br>– Understand that:<br>  Fitness is important<br>    Immediate and long-term fitness benefits result<br>    Increased physical activity and exercise convey long-term advantages<br>– Added benefits result from sports training and competitive athletics<br>– Plan more physically active lives<br>– Recognize and overcome problems, fears and barriers to greater physical activity<br>– Include different types of exercise (aerobic, anaerobic, mixed) every day<br>– Emphasize positive attitudes to self, body<br>– Practice good nutrition for optimal fitness<br>– Avoid overemphasis on cosmetic aspects of fitness that have high health costs<br>– Lead physically active lives<br>– Lifelong aerobic exercise to foster cardiovascular fitness and weight control |

conducted in collaboration with the physical education or classroom teachers.

A fourth task, and one which is growing in importance in schools that have school-based clinics, is providing direct health services to high-risk children and adolescents. Such direct care services fill gaps that are still present in coverage of low-income and minority youth, whose families often lack a personal physician. When such health services are provided, it is important to include direct services in nutrition. At the very least, there should be a system of referral for dealing with nutrition problems. Direct nutrition counseling services provided in the school are probably the most helpful to the students, since they avoid the inevitable losses to follow-up that occur when many referrals are made. In our experience in inner city schools, poor minority youth are particularly receptive to the provision of such on-site services in the schools.

Other groups deserving attention and special surveillance are those who, upon screening, have been found to be at high risk (usually defined as above the 85th percentile for age and sex) on specific health indices, such as height for weight, serum lipids, blood pressure, or blood glucose levels. Although direct health services may be provided in other settings, monitoring, follow-up, and supportive services are desirable from the school health services.

A fifth task that faces the school health officer is assuring that the school environment is conducive to meeting the needs of all children, including children with special developmental and health needs. All children need an environment that promotes a healthy lifestyle. For handicapped children additional modifications may be necessary. These may include routines for dealing with acute hypoglycemic reactions in diabetes and arrangements in the school cafeteria and with the school health services to ensure that children with special eating problems, such as those with severe cerebral palsy, can eat.

The sixth set of nutrition tasks of the school health officer involves integrating nutrition more fully into all related health activities in the school. The Year 2000 Goals for the Nation provide a useful blueprint of specific activities to do this.[1,3]

School health officers must also collaborate with teachers to ensure that classroom instruction relating to health education is factually correct, skills-oriented, and targeted to the actual problems of the students as determined by the needs assessment survey. Since instruction in the classroom is not their direct responsibility, this requires a good deal of coordination and tact.

The task of integrating nutrition more completely into the school cafeteria and other school food services requires diplomacy. The ability to work closely with school food service personnel and to understand the constraints under which they operate is essential. The American School Food Service Association is a national organization that publishes many helpful materials dealing with the role of nutrition in schools and food services. It is a valuable resource for learning about what food services can and cannot do. (For a catalogue, write to American School Food Service Association, 3620 South Galapago, Englewood CO 80110.)

Integration of nutrition-related concerns into school physical education programs requires developing a good working relationship with teachers and coaches. Of particular concern is the development of programs for physical fitness that touch **all** children, not only the children who are most fit. Also needing attention, especially in the secondary schools, is the integration of sound nutrition into training regimens for high school athletes.

The final task of the school health officer is in ensuring that school health functions in nutrition are sound and up-to-date. Consultation from a registered dietitian can be helpful in accomplishing this.

## PRESENT GAPS IN NUTRITION SERVICES OF SCHOOLS AND COLLEGES

Many school health programs overlook nutrition services. At present the ability of existing personnel in the school health office to deal with nutritional issues is frequently insufficient for the task at hand. Medical and nursing professionals who staff school health clinics often lack the time, interest, or expertise to render nutrition services to students. Unfortunately, most medical schools today do not even require human nutrition as part of their curriculum, and many nursing schools have de-emphasized the subject in recent years.[2] Thus these generalists are often unfamiliar or unaware of the realities of food composition, of food practices, and of the nutrition programs that are available. Interest in the field of nutrition is helpful, but in and of itself it is not enough.

At times unbridled enthusiasm on the part of ill-informed officials has lead to nutrition programs of a faddist or otherwise unsound nature. Until medical and nursing education become more adequate in nutrition, formal consulting and referral arrangements are likely to be necessary to cover the nutritional aspects of student health services in the school setting. Otherwise, both students at high nutritional risk and those with more general nutrition needs may be unrecognized and ignored.

Consultation with knowledgeable nutrition professionals such as a registered dietitian or community nutritionist can be helpful in strengthening nutrition components in school programs. These professionals can also be used as referral sources. Consultants can be obtained from state dietetic associations and public health associations.

# Nutritional Status of Children, Youth, and Young Adults

School health providers must attend to and reinforce the nutritional aspects of health promotion, disease prevention, disease treatment, and rehabilitation in their students, especially among those at high nutritional risk.

Table 2, next page, summarizes the diet-related targets for action at the primary, secondary, and tertiary levels of prevention in schools.

## Primary Prevention (Risk Reduction) in School Settings

### Nutrition as a Basic Preventive Tool
Health promotion, risk reduction, and disease prevention are the aims of primary prevention. It involves preventing the nutrition-related problems arising from deficiencies, imbalances, and excesses of one or more nutrients in the diet. It also involves screening for diet-related risk factors for chronic degenerative diseases and conditions.

Table 3 (page 37) provides a food guide for promoting health and reducing diet-related risk factors associated with chronic degenerative disease, which incorporates these concerns.

### Major Federal Food Programs
Students from economically disadvantaged families or of ethnic minorities are at increased risk for **under-** and **malnutrition** due to shortfalls in calorie, protein, and vitamin and mineral intakes.[1] The problems of children and adolescents from poverty groups include, but are not limited to, nutrition; these are summarized in a recent publication.[4] The impacts of severe protein-calorie malnutrition and nutrient deficiencies (especially

Table 2

Primary, Secondary, and Tertiary Levels of Prevention

| Level of Prevention & Overall Intention | Method | Nutrition-Related Problems |
|---|---|---|
| **Primary Prevention:** Health promotion & disease prevention | Reduction of diet-related risk factors: Increasing awareness and education in the school classrooms, cafeterias, and exercise facilities. Recommending students adopt prudent dietary and exercise habits. Having role models, such as teachers and parents, reinforcing positive lifestyle habits. Referring high-risk individuals to health care providers and/or food assistance programs. | Undernutrition & dietary inadequacies such as iron deficiency anemia, low calcium intakes, and other forms of undernutrition. Overnutrition, imbalances, excesses, and obesity. Risks for chronic degenerative diseases including hyperlipidemia, high blood pressure, and sedentary lifestyles. Eating disorders. Teenage pregnancy. Alcohol and drug abuse. |
| **Secondary Prevention:** Control of nutritional complications from existing diseases and conditions | Modifying or eliminating one or more nutrients in the diet (therapeutic diets). Establishing these plans via individual and/or group diet instruction, education and counseling. | The overall diet, food habits and behaviors of children, adolescents & young adults who are: —Pregnant —Obese —Anorexic —Bulimic —Diabetic —Hyperlipidemic, hypertensive or who suffer from other chronic degenerative diseases —Malabsorbing nutrients or who suffer from other gastrointestinal disorders —Cachectic as a result of cancer or other chronic conditions |
| **Tertiary Prevention:** Rehabiliation, amelioration, and preservation of function and independence | Individualizing diet plans for calories, protein, and other nutrients. Modifying the texture or consistency of food. Using alternate routes for alimentation. Utilizing special adaptive equipment and feeding positions. Exercising a total team approach. | Diseases and conditions include: Disorders of the nervous system and sense organs; Disorders of bones and muscles; Congenital malformations; Mental, psychoneurotic, and personality disorders; Allergic, endocrine system, and nutritional diseases. |

iron) on growth, learning, and behavior may be significant and are reviewed elsewhere.[5,6] Their effects are most apparent in younger children with severe malnutrition. They are less clear-cut with the more moderate degree of undernutrition usually present in this country. Less severe deficits may also give rise to some problems, however.

Table 4 (page 38) highlights the federal school-based nutrition programs. These include free or reduced-price school lunch and breakfast programs, food stamps, subsidized health care and other support programs that are available for assisting poor individuals and their families to meet their nutritional needs.

## Preventing Other Nutritional Problems: Iron Deficiency Anemia

Low-income minority group members tend to exhibit more iron deficiency anemia than their more affluent peers.[1] The prevalence of iron

---

**Table 3**
**Food Guide: A Pattern for Daily Food Choices**
**Adapted for Children and Adolescents**

| Food Group | Recommended Daily Servings |
|---|---|
| Fruits<br>Citrus, melon, berries<br>Other fruits | 2-4 |
| Vegetables<br>Dark green and deep yellow<br>Starchy, including dry beans and peas<br>Other vegetables | 3-5<br><br>(Dark green vegetables and dry beans and peas several times per week) |
| Meat, Poultry, Fish, Eggs | 2-3<br>(A total of 5-7 ounces daily from lean choices) |
| Milk, Yogurt, and Cheese | 3<br>(4 servings for pregnant and nursing teenagers) |
| Grains, Breads, and Cereals | 6-11<br>(Include several servings of whole grain products daily) |
| Fats & Sweets | In moderation |
| Alcohol | None<br>No alcohol during pregnancy |

**Table 4**
**School-based Federal Nutrition Programs**

| | (NET) Nutrition Education and Training Program | (SBP) School Breakfast Program | (NSLP) National School Lunch Program | (SFSP) Summer Food Service Program |
|---|---|---|---|---|
| **Program** | (NET) Nutrition Education and Training Program | (SBP) School Breakfast Program | (NSLP) National School Lunch Program | (SFSP) Summer Food Service Program |
| **Purpose** | Provide funds to states for in-service training of teachers and food service personnel, and for dissemination of nutrition information to children | Provide breakfast to students (grades K-12) | Provide lunch to students (grades K-12) | Ensure needy students continue to receive meals when school is not in session |
| **Eligibility** | Teachers, food service personnel and children in all schools and child care facilities | All schools and residential institutions except private schools; benefits vary depending on family income. | | All public and private schools, residential camps, state and local governments |
| **Delivery** | Services usually made possible through grants | Schools are responsible for meal preparation and service. Cash reimbursements are based on the number of meals served to participants in each income group. | | Sponsor is responsible for meal preparation and service. |

deficiency among teenage girls (15-19 years) is high, reaching as much as 31 percent in young, low-income pregnant women.[1] Iron requirements are higher for females, owing to blood loss during menstruation, making them more prone to iron deficiency than males. Pregnancy and lactation further boost the nutrient requirements of the growing teenager. Lean red meats and poultry and other animal foods (with the exception of milk) are rich sources of highly bioavailable iron. Vegetable protein sources of iron include fortified and enriched breads and cereals. Ascorbic acid-rich foods enhance iron absorption. Risks of iron deficiency anemia are somewhat reduced when oral contraceptives are routinely used since menstrual losses are decreased.[7]

## Calcium intakes

Many teenagers, especially girls, fail to meet dietary recommendations for calcium.[2] The Recommended Dietary Allowance (RDA) for calcium was recently increased to 1200 mg/day for individuals 11-24 years of age since peak bone mass is probably not achieved until the end of the third decade of life.[8] Individuals who dislike, avoid, or replace milk in their diet with other beverages low in calcium usually have low calcium intakes, may have lower peak bone mass, and may be at greater risk for developing osteoporosis later in life. Those groups at especially high risk include pregnant and lactating teenagers (whose calcium needs are increased), chronic dieters, those afflicted with eating disorders, and the lactose-intolerant.

At least four servings from milk products or other calcium-rich foods such as spinach, tofu, canned salmon, or sardines (with bones) need to be consumed each day. Calcium carbonate supplements are another economic alternative to meeting calcium needs if dietary sources do not suffice. Schools and colleges should include skim and low-fat milk, cheeses, yogurt, and frozen low-fat dairy desserts in their food service operations to help meet adolescents' especially high calcium needs. A physically active lifestyle that includes weight-bearing exercise will help to maintain normal body weight and normal menstrual function. Moderation in sodium intake and not smoking are also helpful in reducing later risks of excessive bone loss.

## Obesity

The concern about overnutrition, imbalances, and excesses is increasing in the U.S. and other industrialized nations.

**Obesity** afflicts those at all socioeconomic levels, including poor minorities. Between 10 percent and 30 percent of all adolescents are obese, depending on the definition used.[9,10] Poor and minority youth are often affected with a combination of obesity, shortfalls of nutrients such as iron, and excesses of others such as saturated fat. By age 6-9 years, correlations with adult obesity are considerable. By the teen years, other risk factors such as blood pressure and blood cholesterol "track" or hold their rank well. Thus, by the teen years, action is warranted for identifying those at risk for later problems. Sedentary lifestyles aggravate development of overweight and possibly high blood pressure as well. Excessive television viewing is one culprit in fostering sedentary lifestyles.[11] Other culprits include spending time after school and on weekends engaged in physically non-taxing activities.

The impact of obesity on personal health and well-being is immediate. When severe, obesity may cause a distorted body image and sense of self-worth. The added weight of stored fat can cause exacerbations of existing handicaps, such as pain in juvenile arthritis, which may further foster sedentary lifestyles. Complications such as increased risk of coronary heart disease, hypertension, and non-insulin dependent diabetes later in life are also likely if obesity persists into adulthood. The earlier the obesity is established, the more likely it is to become a continuing and chronic problem in adulthood.[12]

School-based obesity prevention and treatment programs need to include on-going screening, diet, exercise, and nutrition education to help students. At present, unfortunately, most American schools at either the primary or secondary school level do not have such programs in place.

The treatment program for obesity needs to be nutritionally sound, provide a variety of foods with a modest caloric deficit (e.g., 100-200 calories less per day), and meet the Recommended Dietary Allowances for all nutrients except calories. It should include behavior modification, psychological support, and an exercise program so that appropriate weight can be maintained and physical activity increased. The goal is to "grow the child into his or her fatness" by slowing weight gain, rather than by encouraging actual weight loss, except in the very fattest children. At the same time school health personnel should encourage a wide range of acceptable body shapes and sizes in order to increase all students' self esteem.[13] Positive behavior change must be reinforced continually. Encouragement is vital, regardless of whether weight status has changed as desired or not. Programs must continue from primary through secondary schools if they are to have a lasting effect. Reasonably priced or free obesity control and treatment programs should be available in the school or by referral so poor minority students are not discouraged by financial barriers from seeking treatment.

## Other Risk Factors Related to Diet

Heredity and environmental factors place some students at high risk for **chronic degenerative diseases and conditions.** Modifiable risk factors, such as control of obesity, hyperlipidemia, high blood pressure, body weight, smoking, and sedentary lifestyles deserve particular attention in later childhood and adolescence.

Table 5 (pages 42 and 43) lists some common food habits of school and college students, their possible health implications, and steps that schools can take to help decrease these health risks. Excessive reliance on the present range of convenience, snack, and fast foods can negatively influence the health status of children and adolescents. Many conventional fast food items are high in calories, saturated fat, cholesterol, and sodium, and the trend is for "fast foods" to become even more a part of American cuisine.[14] Although healthier alternative food choices are slowly being incorporated into these restaurants and fast food eating styles, students need help in making informed food choices in these facilities. They also need assistance in planning other snack and between-meal eating. Nutrition education assists youth in making nutritious food choices. But schools must also lead the way by giving not only guidance but good example by providing nutritious foods in vending machines, cafeterias, and elsewhere.

**Chronic dieting** to lose weight is now common, even in primary school; it reaches epidemic proportions among high school girls. By age 18, many girls have been on diets and some have become chronic dieters.[15] Adolescent girls are particularly susceptible to social and environmental pressures to achieve thinness. Their perceptions of most-desirable female physiques are often distorted. These distortions are typified by the sometimes emaciated models seen on the covers of fashion and beauty magazines. Male perceptions of themselves and their ideals of beauty in females are fortunately somewhat less distorted.

To attain unrealistically lean bodily ideals, teenage girls often attempt restrictive and chronic dieting. This may lead to shortfalls in intakes of vitamins, minerals, and protein. In susceptible individuals with a psychological and possibly a biological predisposition, anorexia nervosa may result.[16] In other less susceptible adolescents restrained eating, associated with dieting to lose weight, may trigger binge eating.[17] Binge/purge syndromes often follow and become readily established, with fasting, laxative abuse, vomiting, or intense exercise used in attempts to control body weight in the absence of control over food intake to achieve weight loss. Unfortunately, none of these methods is efficacious for controlling weight, and eventually both cycles of self-induced vomiting and purging followed by more and more binge eating result in weight gain.

**Table 5**

**Common Food Habits of Students and Their Nutritional Implications and Steps Schools Can Take to Help Remedy Their Negative Effects**

| Food Habit | Nutritional Implications | Steps to Decrease Related Risks in Schools and Colleges |
| --- | --- | --- |
| Fast Food Use | – Many convenience and fast foods are high in fat, saturated fat, and sodium.<br>– Excesses of these nutrients are associated with increased risks for certain chronic degenerative diseases.<br>– Food choices in the school stores, cafeterias, and vending machines often are not consistent with the Dietary Guidelines for Americans. | – Schools must increase nutrition education and awareness in the classroom, cafeterias, and exercise facilities.<br>– Food service operations must offer menus that are consistent with the Dietary Guidelines for Americans (eat a variety of foods; maintain desirable weight; avoid too much fat, saturated fat, and cholesterol; eat foods with adequate starch and fiber; avoid too much sugar; avoid too much sodium; if you drink alcoholic beverages, do so in moderation). |
| Snacking | – Depends on selections made<br>– Nutrient profiles of snacks are often low in nutrient density.<br>– May lead to dietary imbalances, overnutrition, and increase risk for coronary heart disease when convenience items of poor nutritional value are consistently relied upon.<br>– Sugary sticky snacks may increase risk for dental caries if oral hygiene is poor. | – Schools should increase nutrition education and awareness in classrooms, cafeterias, and exercise facilities.<br>– Food service operations, including cafeterias, school stores, and vending machines must offer skim and low-fat milk, cheese and yogurt, fresh fruits and vegetables, more whole grain breads, plain popcorn and pretzels for quick snacks.<br>– Nutrition and dental health must be emphasized in health classes. |

**Table 5 (Continued)**

| | | |
|---|---|---|
| **Dieting** | – Adolescents with low energy intakes often fail to meet RDAs, especially for iron, calcium, B6, copper, and zinc<br>– May lead to extreme weight loss, and/or amenorrhea<br>– May trigger binge eating in some individuals<br>– Associated with eating disorders, such as anorexia nervosa and bulimia, when other factors (e.g., neurosis and disturbed family problems) are present | – Teachers and physical education instructors must teach students a healthy approach to diet and weight maintenance<br>– Students who are at high risk or who display signs/symptoms of chronic dieting, eating disorders, or weight changes must be referred to outside help for rehabilitation of eating habits |
| **Alcohol and Drug Abuse** | Alcohol is a drug as well as a food that is high in calories and little else.<br>– May replace more nutritious food in diet and increase risk for dietary deficiencies<br>– Associated with car accidents, dependency, behavior problems, cirrhosis of the liver, gastritis, pancreatitis, and adverse pregnancy outcomes | – Alcohol and drug abuse education in the classroom<br>– Sponsor and promote non-alcoholic and drug-free parties and functions<br>– Use peer counselors<br>– Refer students with substance abuse problems and treat secondary malnutrition |

School health officials need to recognize the signs of **eating disorders** before the disorders become firmly established. They also need to put anticipatory guidance programs in place to assist students in understanding how to control weight more sensibly than by these faddist methods.

**Eating disorders,** such as anorexia nervosa and bulimia, are much more common in adolescence, especially among females, than at any other time of life. Eating disorders are not solely a consequence of dieting. They result from a variety of family and individual psychological problems that foster the disorder.[16]

Nutrition counseling is important for helping the victim of eating disorders to make appropriate food selections, to alter attitudes toward food, and to adopt more healthful means of controlling weight. Assistance with realimentation is vital to overcoming anorexia nervosa-related protein-calorie malnutrition as well as the poor food habits and the obesity often associated with bulimia. Psychotherapy and family counseling are needed in eating disorders to find and treat the underlying roots of the disturbance.

Highly competitive child and teenage athletes and dancers may also attempt strict chronic dieting or other techniques in an effort to reach the low body weights they perceive as being best for optimum performance. This may give rise to chronic dieting and eating disorders together or to exercise-induced amenorrhea.

**Exercise-induced amenorrhea** is often a complication of very rigorous diet and exercise regimens among very competitive athletes and performers.[18] Limitation of food intake itself can also induce amenorrhea if it is extreme. It is particularly common in juvenile ballet dancers, gymnasts, marathon runners, swimmers, figure skaters, and others with over-zealous trainers and coaches.

**Alcohol and drug abuse** is a major cause of ill health in adolescents. Alcohol is both a food and a drug. As a food it provides little nutritive value other than calories. As a drug, acute use may result in early death due to accidents while driving under the influence of alcohol.[19] Chronic alcohol abuse gives rise to social problems, physical ill health, and powerful negative nutritional consequences (Table 5).

Substance abuse, especially chronic heroin addiction, greatly increases risks of undernutrition in teenagers. Poor minority groups are at greatest risk for such alcohol and drug abuse-related malnutrition.[1]

Steps to prevent and control substance abuse more effectively are sorely needed. Minimum drinking ages have been increased to 21 years, and drunk-driving laws have been strengthened and enforced more strictly in many states over the past decade; they need to be extended to all states. Alcohol and substance abuse education is needed in classrooms and in informal educational settings. Schools and universities also need to sponsor substance-free parties and other interventions to encourage abstinence among students.

Primary prevention steps relating to the nutritional problems associated with **teenage pregnancy** need to include nutrition education; weight-status monitoring prior to conception to achieve more closely the ideal body weight; dealing with the prevention of alcohol, drugs, or tobacco abuse; and identifying and modifying other nutrient intakes that fall short of desired levels, particularly folic acid, iron, and calcium intakes.[20] If family planning programs are included in school health activities, they should also include a nutrition component. School health personnel can also add to the classroom teaching on pregnancy and reproduction, including nutritional considerations.

## SECONDARY PREVENTION (TREATMENT) IN SCHOOL SETTINGS

Secondary prevention is directed at controlling the nutritional complications and secondary malnutrition that may arise as sequelae from pre-existing diseases or conditions. Nutrition counseling also plays a significant role in treating obesity and in following teenage pregnancy as described in the last section.

For **obesity,** the school health office should refer students for health care services for obesity treatment as well as support students in their efforts. For **pregnancy,** it is essential that all students be provided with appropriate guidance and comprehensive health and nutritional care.

Many **handicapped and chronically ill** students who previously attended special schools are increasingly being "mainstreamed" into regular schools.[21] Their presence means additional work for the school health office. In some instances, special dietary arrangements will be needed so students can adhere to their special diets at school. For diseases and conditions such as inborn errors of metabolism, diabetes mellitus, malabsorption, and other gastrointestinal disorders, nutrition counseling and arrangements relating to diet are especially important in treating the disease. Some who attend school will need additional help. Appropriate food selections improve both immediate and more long-term complications.

Nutrition education stressing a diet that is in line with the Dietary Guidelines for Americans (Table 5) and a vigorous physical activity program are especially important. They help to identify and reduce diet-related risks of chronic degenerative diseases and conditions, including hyperlipidemia, hypertension, and obesity. Schools can further help by screening and identifying those at high risk and by referring those so identified for treatment elsewhere. The school cafeteria can assist in chronic degenerative disease risk reduction by offering dietary choices that are low in fat, saturated fat, cholesterol, and sodium.

Table 6 includes a list of nutrition-related objectives for students, taken from the Year 2000 Goals for the Nation.[1] High dietary intake of fat, saturated fat, and cholesterol contribute to raising serum **cholesterol.** The

---

### Table 6
### National Nutrition Objectives for the Year 2000 Relating to the Health of Children, Adolescents, and Young Adults

**Risk Reduction**

Reduce average dietary fat intake to no more than 30 percent of calories and average saturated fat intake to no more than 10 percent of calories.

Increase participation in regular physical activity to 60 percent.

Reduce prevalence of overweight to less than 15 percent.

Increase use of sound dietary practices combined with physical activity to achieve weight loss in overweight individuals to 60 percent.

Increase consumption of calcium-rich foods (3 per day) to 60 percent.

Increase average age for first use of alcohol and marijuana by at least 2 years.

Reduce alcohol, marijuana and/or cocaine use by at least 50 percent.

Reduce occasions of heavy drinking to no more than 28 percent of high school seniors and 32 percent of college students.

Increase abstinence from alcohol, marijuana, and tobacco in pregnant women to at least 40 percent.

**Services and Protection**

At least 95 percent of school lunch and breakfast services have menus consistent with the **Dietary Guidelines for Healthy Americans.**

All states will have nutrition education as part of a comprehensive school health program.

At least 45 percent of students (K-12) participate in school physical education programs daily.

All school districts and private schools have educational programs on alcohol and other drugs as part of a comprehensive school health program.

Adapted from: U.S. DHHS, Public Health Service: Healthy People 2000: National Health Promotion and Disease Prevention Objectives. Washington, DC, U.S. Government Printing Office, 1990

Year 2000 Goals and also the recent report of the population-based panel of the National Cholesterol Education Program suggest reducing average dietary fat intakes to no more than 30 percent of calories and average saturated fat intakes to no more than 10 percent of calories for the entire U.S. population ages 2 and older.[1,22]

Obesity and high sodium intakes can contribute to **high blood pressure**. Therefore, obesity should be reduced and sodium intakes should be lowered. Physical activity should be encouraged to help students maintain appropriate body weight, reduce stress, and enhance their overall sense of well-being.

Inactivity, low fiber intakes, and inadequate fluids can contribute to **constipation** and may also be associated with hemorrhoids and possibly increased risks of diverticulosis or colon cancer. Therefore, high dietary fiber intakes, high fluid intakes, and high levels of physical activity are to be encouraged.

High sticky sugary snack or other food consumption without proper oral hygiene may increase the risk of **dental caries**. Therefore it is important to control what is sold in school vending machines and cafeterias, to ensure that oral hygiene is fostered, and to provide routine screening and anticipatory guidance for dental caries.

Students need help in making dietary changes to lower all of the diet-related risk factors mentioned above. Also, without adequate planning, their dietary intakes may fall short in several nutrients, especially during the pubertal phase of adolescence when growth is very rapid. For this reason, it is important for school health officers and teachers to provide students and family members with additional nutrition information via direct nutrition counseling and school health services. The Diet and Health Report and the National Cholesterol Education Program population-based panel offer prudent suggestions for fostering healthier eating habits.[22,23] The guide for food intake patterns for children and adolescents presented in Table 3 is in line with the recent reports from the National Academy of Sciences, the National Institutes of Health, and the Dietary Guidelines for Americans, and other expert groups.[8,21,24]

Nutrition counseling and anticipatory guidance are vital when students become pregnant. The school health service can help to refer such individuals for treatment. The potentially negative health effects of **adolescent pregnancy** include dietary intakes inadequate in energy, protein, calcium, and iron. Pregnancy-induced hypertension, iron deficiency anemia, substance abuse, and limited weight gain are common problems, especially among adolescents who are pregnant out-of-wedlock.[25] The physiologic risks are also especially common in young girls who become pregnant within one or two years of menarche or under 15 years of age. Social and psychological problems, especially when the pregnancy is out-of-wedlock, further add to risks of poor pregnancy outcomes for both mother and fetus among younger teenagers. Teenage mothers and fathers often lack the knowledge, resources, and skills for optimal parenting, including skills related to feeding and nourishing their babies. Social and financial support are also often inadequate. While schools cannot assume all of the burdens of assisting these youth to become competent parents, school health officers must provide as much help as they can to this needy group.

Table 7 (next page) lists federally-funded programs that are available to young mothers and children to help meet their nutritional needs. All pregnant adolescents need basic nutrition counseling, food, and nutrition education. The Supplemental Food Program for Women, Infants, and Children (WIC) is designed especially to help meet the nutritional needs of low-income pregnant or lactating women and children under the age of five. Adolescents are given priority. Abstinence from alcohol, cigarettes, and drugs also is stressed for all pregnant women, including adolescents, in the Year 2000 objectives.[1]

Proper nutrition is also part of the rehabilitation process for **teenage addicts and alcoholics** who are undernourished or who suffer from other forms of secondary malnutrition as a result of their untreated health problems. School health offices can assist in identifying students who are addicts, in referring them for treatment, and in providing support for abstinence when they are rehabilitated.

**Castaway, homeless, runaway, and thrown away** children need to be identified since their food situations may be precarious and their nutritional status poor. Such children and adolescents deserve particular benefit from the federal food programs in schools, and from direct health services or referrals for health so that other problems do not develop.

## TERTIARY PREVENTION (REHABILITATION) IN SCHOOL SETTINGS

Tertiary prevention centers on rehabilitation. It is particularly essential for those who are **chronically ill** or who suffer from **handicapping conditions.** These children and adolescents are increasingly being "mainstreamed" into regular classes and school settings.[21] Nutrition care plans for coping with their diet-related problems in schools need to be individualized. The school health office needs to take the lead in making such arrangements with the family and health care providers. Interventions often involve a combination of services including food, health, education, social, and physical environmental adaptations in the school setting. Those who are mentally or physically handicapped often have inadequate dietary intakes and poor growth including delayed puberty, which is secondary in part to improper feeding techniques and inadequate intakes.[26] Attention to providing food selections and supportive services in school services can often improve nutritional status, enhance growth, and help to preserve function and independence.

---

**Table 7**

**Community-based Federal Nutrition Programs Relating to Student Health**

| Program | Food Stamps | Special Supplemental Food Program for Women, Infants, and Children (WIC) | Child Care Food Program |
|---|---|---|---|
| **Purpose** | To alleviate hunger among the poorest individuals in the country | To improve the nutritional status of low-income pregnant or breast-feeding women, and children under 5 | To provide nutritious meals and snacks to children enrolled in child-care facilities or institutions |
| **Eligibility** | Individuals living at or below the poverty line | Individuals from target groups (above) who are at nutritional risk | All public and private non-profit organizations providing licensed or approved non-residential day-care service |
| **Delivery** | State health departments usually distribute food stamps for redemption at local grocery stores | Local health clinics provide food vouchers that are redeemed for specified food items | Health facilities, and sometimes their sponsoring agencies, are responsible for meal preparation and service |

Adapted from Heimendinger J: U.S. Department of Agriculture's Food Assistance Programs, Right to Grow, 1985

# IMPLICATIONS FOR PLANNING AND POLICY

## IMPLEMENTING OBJECTIVES FOR THE NATION

The health office has a great deal of potential that is as-yet unrealized in assuring that nutrition becomes a basic preventive tool in health services of children, youth, and young adults, and that the Year 2000 Objectives for the Nation are implemented.

## SCHOOL HEALTH

The traditional role of the school health office must expand to include nutrition in its broadest dimensions. Proactive interventions in the health services, classroom, physical education and sports programs, and cafeteria are needed.

## COLLEGE HEALTH

In addition to dealing with the issues required for the health of children and adolescents, the growing independence of individuals in the college health setting (who are legally adults) must also be dealt with. New morbidities, old morbidities, and nutritional planning for independent living must also be addressed.

---

## REFERENCES

1. U.S. DHHS, Public Health Service: Healthy People 2000: National Health Promotion and Disease Prevention Objectives. Washington, DC, U.S. Government Printing Office, 1990

2. U.S. Public Health Service: The Surgeon General's Report on Nutrition and Health. Washington, DC, U.S. Government Printing Office, 1988

3. Green LW: Health Education Planning: A Diagnostic Approach. Palo Alto, CA, Mayfield Publishing Co., 1980

4. National Center for Children in Poverty: Five Million Children: A Statistical Profile of Our Poorest Young Citizens. Columbia University School of Public Health, New York, NY, 1990

5. Dunger DB, Preece MA: Growth and nutrient requirements at adolescence, Pediatric Nutrition: Theory and Practice. Edited by RJ Grand, JL Sutphen, and WH Dietz. Boston, Butterworth Publishers, 1987, pp 357-371

6. International conference on iron deficiency and behavioral development. Amer J Clin Nutr, Supplement 50, 3:566-674, 1989

7. Hefnawi F, Askalani H, Zaki K: Menstrual blood loss with copper intrauterine devices. Contraception 9:133-39, 1974

8. Food and Nutrition Board, National Academy of Sciences, National Research Council: Recommended Dietary Allowances, 10th Edition. Washington, DC, National Academy Press, 1989

9. Collipp PJ: Obesity in childhood. Obesity. Edited by AJ Stunkard. Philadelphia, W.B. Saunders Company, 1980

10. Epstein LH, Valoski A: Family-based behavioral weight control in obese, young children. J Amer Diet Assoc 86 4 : 481-489, 1986

11. Dietz WH, Gortmaker SL: Do we fatten our children at the television set? Obesity and television viewing in children and adolescents. Pediatrics 75: 807-12, 1985

12. American Academy of Pediatrics Committee on Nutrition: Obesity in infancy and childhood. Pediatrics 68: 880, 1981

13. Peck E, Ulvrich H:  Children and Weight: A Changing Perspective. Berkeley, CA, Nutrition Communication Association, 1988

14. Massachusetts Medical Society Committee on Nutrition. Soundingboard fast-food fare consumer guidelines. N Eng J Med 321, 11:752-756, Sept 1989

15. Andersen AE: Practical Comprehensive Treatment of Anorexia Nervosa and Bulimia. Baltimore, The Johns Hopkins University Press, 1985

16. Brownell KD, Foreyt JP (ed): Handbook of Eating Disorders: Physiology, Psychology, Treatment of Obesity, Anorexia, and Bulimia. New York, Basic Books, Inc., 1986, pp 266-282

17. Tuschl RJ: From dietary restraint to binge eating: Some theoretical considerations. Appetite 14 :105-109, 1990

18. Slavin J, Lutter J, Cushman S: Amenorrhea in vegetarian athletes. Lancet (8392):1474-1475, 1984

19. U.S. Preventive Services Task Force: Guide to Clinical Preventive Services. U.S. DHHS, Washington, DC, U.S. Government Printing Office, 1989

20. Brown SS: Prenatal Care Reaching Mothers, Reaching Infants. Washington, DC, National Academy Press, 1988

21. Wallace HM: Organization of services for handicapped children and youth (children with special needs): Systems of care for handicapped children and youth in the United States, Maternal and Child Health Practices, Third Edition. Edited by HM Wallace, GM Ryan, Jr., and AC Oglesby. Oakland, CA, Third Party Publishing Company, 1988, pp 103-122

22. Report of the National Cholesterol Education Program Expert Panel on Detection, Evaluation, and Treatment of High Blood Cholesterol in Adults: Arch Intern Med 148:3639, 1988

23. National Research Council. Diet and Health Report: Implications for Reducing Chronic Disease Risk. Washington, DC, National Academy Press, 1989

24. U.S. Department of Agriculture and U.S. DHHS: Nutrition and Your Health: Dietary Guidelines for Americans. Second edition. Home and Garden Bulletin No. 232, Washington, DC, 1985

25. Caliendo MA: Nutrition and Preventive Health Care. New York, Macmillan Publishing Co., Inc., 1981

26. Palombo R: Feeding problems of handicapped children. Right To Grow. Edited by J Dwyer and M Egan. Boston, Frances Stern Nutrition Center, 1986, pp 2-5

# 4

# Control of Communicable Diseases

ALAN R. HINMAN, MD, MPH

Communicable diseases are among the most common health problems affecting students. Many occur in outbreaks that can be quite disruptive of school functioning. Preventive measures are available for several of the most common communicable diseases likely to be seen in school settings. These preventive measures are more effective and less troublesome than attempting to control outbreaks of disease once they occur. This chapter will focus on prevention of several diseases through immunization and prevention of transmission of sexually transmitted diseases. Specific details are beyond the scope of this chapter but important references are cited.

## GENERAL CONSIDERATIONS

Communicable diseases result from the transmission of an infectious agent from a source (an infected individual or vector) to a susceptible host in a favorable environment. Control efforts may be directed toward any one (or more) aspect of the process.[1,2] For example, assuring purity of water and food or giving appropriate therapy to infected individuals can eliminate the agent from these possible sources. Reducing the availability of susceptible hosts can be accomplished by excluding susceptible individuals from settings of risk or rendering them non-susceptible (e.g., by immunization). Finally, the environment can be rendered non-favorable for transmission, for example, by use of rubber gloves or masks.

The four principal means of transmission of communicable diseases are common vehicle, contact, airborne, and vector borne. **Common-vehicle** transmission results from contamination of a vehicle to which several susceptible individuals are exposed, such as food, water, or intravenous fluids. **Contact** transmission can occur as a result of direct physical contact (e.g., sexual intercourse) or indirect contact (e.g., sharing needles for injection of drugs, fecal-oral spread of enteric organisms, inhalation of large droplets of infected respiratory secretions). **Airborne** spread occurs when infectious droplets remain suspended in air for minutes to hours and are dispersed widely (e.g., measles has been transmitted to a patient visiting a physician's office approximately one hour after the source case had left the office[3]). **Vectors** are typically arthropods which acquire the infectious agent from feeding on an infected individual and subsequently inoculate it into a susceptible host, either as passive carriers of the organism (e.g., plague, Lyme disease) or as an integral part of the life cycle of the agent (e.g., malaria).

Each of these means of transmission can result in the spread of illness in schools, although vector-borne transmission is not as common in the United States as are the other means. Common-vehicle transmission can be curtailed by appropriate food-handling practices (e.g., assuring the quality of the food supply, washing hands, keeping cold foods cold and hot foods hot).

Contact spread and airborne spread may be more difficult to contain in the school setting. Depending on the age of the student and the setting, different forms of contact spread may be prominent. In day-care settings with children who are not toilet trained, fecal-oral spread may be common. In virtually all settings, respiratory droplet spread may cause outbreaks of diseases such as the common cold or influenza. In these situations, it may be difficult to curtail transmission since patients may become infectious before they become symptomatic and it is difficult to restrict face-to-face contact. In high school and college settings, sexually transmitted diseases may be relatively common, although their incidence is probably higher in out-of-school adolescents and young adults than it is in their age peers who are in school. Airborne spread in school settings has occurred primarily with measles and tuberculosis.

All states have laws requiring that the occurrence of certain communicable diseases be reported. School health services should check with local or state health departments to determine which conditions are reportable in their areas.[4]

## IMMUNIZATION

Vaccines are among the safest and most effective means of preventing infectious diseases.[5] Introduction and widespread use of vaccines and toxoids have brought about dramatic reductions in the occurrence of many diseases, including the worldwide eradication of smallpox, surely the most dramatic public health achievement to date. For the diseases against which children are routinely immunized, Table 1 shows the maximum number of cases reported in the United States (and the year in which that occurred), the provisional total reported in 1989, and the percent reduction achieved. For each of these diseases a reduction of more than 90 percent has been achieved. No cases of paralysis due to wild poliovirus acquired in the United States have occurred in the past 10 years. Information about disease caused by *Haemophilus influenzae* type b is not shown, since the vaccines have been so recently introduced that impact on incidence cannot yet be demonstrated.

Table 2 (next page) shows the currently recommended schedule for administration of vaccines to infants and children.[6,7] Table 3 (next page) summarizes vaccination recommendations for older children who were not vaccinated in infancy. Recommendations have also been developed for immunization of adults, who may have special needs, including hepatitis B, influenza, and pneumococcal polysaccharide vaccines.[8,9]

The combination of widespread acceptance of the utility of immunization and the enactment and enforcement of school immunization laws has led to very high levels of immunization among children of school age. In states that license day-care establishments, immunization requirements also include licensed day-care settings. In most states, the school immuni-

## Table 1
### Maximum and Current Reported Morbidity of Vaccine-Preventable Diseases in the U.S.

| Disease | Number of cases reported Maximum | (year) | 1989 (prov.) | % Reduction |
|---------|---------|--------|--------------|-------------|
| Diphtheria | 206,939 | 1921 | 2 | 99.9 |
| Measles | 894,134 | 1941 | 16,236 | 98.2 |
| Mumps[a] | 152,209 | 1968 | 5,611 | 96.3 |
| Pertussis | 256,269 | 1934 | 3,745 | 98.5 |
| Polio (paralytic) | 21,269 | 1952 | 0[e] | 100.0 |
| Rubella[b] | 57,686 | 1969 | 373 | 99.4 |
| Congenital Rubella[c] | 20,000 | 1964-5 | 3 | 99.9 |
| Tetanus[d] | 601 | 1948 | 47 | 92.2 |

[a] First reportable in 1968
[b] First reportable in 1966
[c] Estimated
[d] First reportable in 1947
[e] A few suspected cases of vaccine-associated paralysis are under investigation.

## Table 2
### Recommended Immunization Schedule for Infants and Children

| Age(s) | Vaccine/toxoid |
| --- | --- |
| 2 months | DTP #1[a], OPV #1[b], HBCV[c,d] |
| 4 months | DTP #2, OPV #2 |
| 6 months | DTP #3 |
| 12 months | HBCV[d] |
| 15 months | MMR #1[e], OPV #3, DTP #4, HBCV[c] |
| 4-6 years (school entry) | MMR #2, OPV #4, DTP #5 |
| 14-16 years | Td[f] |
| Every 10 years thereafter | Td |

[a] Diphtheria and tetanus toxoids and pertussis vaccine
[b] Oral poliovirus vaccine
Haemophilus B conjugate vaccine:
[c] HBOC is given at 2, 4, 6, and 15 months
[d] PRP-OMP is given at 2, 4, and 12 months
[e] Measles, mumps, and rubella vaccine
[f] Tetanus and diphtheria toxoids (adult)

## Table 3
### Recommended Immunization Schedule for Persons ≥7 Years of Age
### Not Immunized as Recommended in Infancy

| Timing | Vaccine/toxoid |
| --- | --- |
| First visit | Td #1[a] |
| | OPV #1[b] |
| | MMR #1[c] |
| 2 months later | Td #2 |
| | OPV #2 |
| | MMR #2 |
| 6-12 months after | Td #3 |
| Td #2, OPV #2 | OPV #3 |
| 10 years later and | Td |
| every 10 years thereafter | |

[a] Tetanus and diphtheria toxoids (adult)
[b] Trivalent oral poliovirus vaccine
[c] Measles, mumps, and rubella vaccine (if born after January 1, 1957)

zation requirements apply not only to first entry to school (kindergarten-first grade) but also to attendance at higher grade levels. In 16 states, immunization requirements include at least some college or university students. The number of states requiring proof of immunization as a condition of entry to college or university is increasing. The American College Health Association has been an important factor in this increase.[10] Table 4 (page 58) summarizes current immunization requirements for attendance in different school settings.[11] Immunization levels in those attending school settings covered by these laws are quite high, as shown in Table 5 (page 58).

Of the diseases against which children are routinely vaccinated, the ones most likely to cause significant outbreaks in school settings are measles, mumps, and rubella, particularly measles. Although 98 percent of students have records of having received measles vaccine, and between 95 percent and 98 percent of vaccinees are protected, the disease is so infectious that introduction of measles virus into a school can result in transmission of the disease if there are a significant number of susceptibles and a high frequency of contact among susceptibles (such as at high school or college). Two patterns of transmission are seen: The more common pattern involves several generations of transmission resulting from person-to-person spread (e.g., in classrooms or dormitories). The other pattern results from airborne transmission and may be reflected by a single wave of cases in which essentially all susceptibles are exposed at the same time. Faculty and staff as well as students may be affected, underscoring the need to ensure that they also are immune to measles.

The continued occurrence of measles in highly vaccinated populations has led immunization advisory bodies in both the private and public sectors to recommend that all children receive two doses of measles vaccine (combined with mumps and rubella as MMR).[12,13,14] There is some difference in the age at which the second dose is routinely recommended – the Immunization Practices Advisory Committee (ACIP) of the U.S. Public Health Service and the American Academy of Family Physicians recommend that the second dose be given at first entry to school, whereas the American Academy of Pediatrics recommends that the second dose generally be given at entry to middle or junior high school. All agree that students entering colleges or universities should receive a second dose until a cohort of two-dose recipients arrives at college age.

The increasing number of vaccines and the complexity of the immunization schedule make it increasingly important that schools at all levels require students to provide immunization records and maintain documentation of the students' immunization status.

Table 4
Number of States with Specific Immunization Requirements[a]
1989-1990 School Year

| Vaccine/Toxoid | Setting | | |
|---|---|---|---|
| | Day-care[b] | K-12[c] | College[d] |
| Diphtheria | 51 | 52 | 7 |
| H. flu b[e] | 10 | 0 | 0 |
| Measles | 51 | 52 | 16 |
| Mumps | 41 | 41 | 5 |
| Pertussis | 47 | 43 | 0 |
| Rubella | 51 | 52 | 15 |
| Tetanus | 49 | 49 | 5 |

[a] 50 States, District of Columbia, Puerto Rico
[b] Licensed day-care settings
[c] Kindergarten-12 grade, any or all grades
[d] Some or all colleges and universities
[e] *Haemophilus influenzae* type b

Table 5
Immunization Levels for Kindergarten-First Grade,
Kindergarten-Twelfth Grade, and Licensed Day-Care Facilities
Uunited States, 1988-1989 School Year

| Vaccine/toxoid | Day-care | K-1 | K-12 |
|---|---|---|---|
| DTP (3+ doses) | 94% | 97% | 98% |
| OPV (3+ doses) | 94% | 97% | 98% |
| Measles | 95% | 98% | 98% |
| Mumps | 95% | 98% | 97% |
| Rubella | 95% | 98% | 98% |

## VACCINE SAFETY AND EFFICACY

Although modern vaccines are safe and effective, they are not perfectly so. Some people who receive vaccines will not be protected and some who receive them may actually be harmed. The goal in vaccine development is to maximize both safety and efficacy. Most vaccines currently recommended for use in all children will provide protection to 90 percent or more following completion of the recommended course.

In developing recommendations for vaccine use, it is essential to consider the risks, as well as the benefits, of the vaccine. The balance between vaccine use and risk and severity of disease must continually be reassessed as it may change over time. For example, in the U.S., the risk of rare complications of smallpox vaccine outweighed the risk of complications or death associated with possible importation of smallpox even before global eradication was achieved. In consequence, routine smallpox vaccination was discontinued years before global eradication was certified.

Adverse events that follow administration of a vaccine may or may not be causally related to the vaccination; temporal association does not, by itself, prove causality. Since many of these events may occur in the absence of vaccination, it may be impossible, in a particular situation, to determine whether vaccine was responsible. Adverse events caused by vaccines may be common and minor (e.g., fever and transient rash occur 7-10 days following vaccination in 5 percent to 15 percent of measles vaccine recipients) or rare and severe (e.g., paralysis in a recipient of OPV or close contact of a recipient occurs once for every 2.7 million doses of vaccine distributed).

It is important that vaccine recipients (or their parents) be aware of the potential adverse events associated with vaccination as well as of the benefits. The Centers for Disease Control has developed Important Information Statements for use with vaccines purchased with federal funds. In addition, the National Childhood Vaccine Injury Act of 1986 (Section XXI of the Public Health Service Act), requires all vaccine providers to notify patients and parents formally of the risks and benefits of specified vaccines (diphtheria and tetanus toxoids; measles, mumps, pertussis, poliomyelitis, and rubella vaccines). Standardized Vaccine Information Pamphlets are under development and their use will be mandatory when released. The same Act also establishes a no-fault compensation mechanism for those who are injured by the specified vaccines. Those desiring further information about this mechanism should contact the National Childhood Vaccine Injury Compensation Program (Parklawn Building, 5600 Fishers Lane, Rockville MD 20857).

## SEXUALLY TRANSMITTED DISEASES

Approximately two-thirds of teenagers are sexually experienced by the age of 18 and the majority of these do not use contraceptives regularly.[15] Consequently, sexually transmitted diseases (STDs) are increasingly common communicable diseases in high school and college settings. Because of the large number of STDs and their differing manifestations, diagnosis, and management, this section will deal with the primary elements that should be present in school health services: education, diagnosis and treatment, and partner notification. (A more complete discussion of STDs is found in Chapter 5 of this volume and in Chapter 13 of volume 3.) In all aspects of STD management, **confidentiality is of the utmost importance** and must be assured.

### Education

STDs are transmitted as a result of behaviors that are usually voluntary. Students should receive accurate information about STDs and their prevention as part of a comprehensive school health education program. This should be tailored to the students' level of development and should include information about the means of reducing the risk of transmission (e.g., abstinence, avoidance of unprotected intercourse). In addition, specific materials that provide more detailed information about STDs should be available through school health services. Most state health departments and many local health departments have such educational materials.

### Diagnosis and Treatment

A high index of suspicion is one of the most important aspects of diagnosis and treatment. Availability of reliable laboratory services and knowledge of latest treatment guidelines are also essential.[16] If diagnosis and treatment services are not provided by the school health service, staff should know where and when they are available (e.g., local health department) and make arrangements with these facilities for referral of students.

### Partner Notification

A key element in controlling transmission of STDs is through the identification, examination, and appropriate treatment of sex partners of patients.[17] Notification of sex partners that they have been exposed to an STD can be done by the patient him- or herself or by the health care provider. Provider referral may be beyond the scope of many school health services; if so, arrangements must be made with local STD-control programs to ensure that partner notification occurs.

# CONCLUSION

Communicable diseases are the most common health problems affecting students. Many occur in outbreaks that can be quite disruptive of school functioning. Prevention of many such diseases is possible through immunization. School health authorities should take all steps necessary to ensure that students (and faculty and staff) are fully protected with vaccines. The occurrence of sexually transmitted diseases can also be affected by a mix of education and service delivery.

## REFERENCES

1. Last JM (ed): Maxcy-Rosenau Public Health and Preventive Medicine. Twelfth edition. Norwalk, Appleton-Century-Croft, 1986

2. Benenson AS (ed): Control of Communicable Diseases in Man. Fifteenth edition. Washington, American Public Health Association, 1990

3. Bloch AB, Orenstein WA, Ewing WM et al: Measles outbreak in a pediatric practice: Airborne transmission in an office setting. Pediatrics 75:676-683, 1985

4. Chorba TL, Berkelman RL, Safford SK et al: Mandatory reporting of infectious diseases by clinicians. JAMA 262:3018-3026, 1989

5. Plotkin SA and Mortimer EA, Jr. (eds): Vaccines. Philadelphia, W.B. Saunders, 1988

6. Centers for Disease Control: Recommendations of the Immunization Practices Advisory Committee (ACIP). General Recommendations on Immunization. MMWR 38:205-214, 219-227, 1989

7. American Academy of Pediatrics: Report of the Committee on Infectious Diseases. Twentieth edition. Elk Grove Village, American Academy of Pediatrics, 1988

8. Centers for Disease Control: Recommendations of the Immunization Practices Advisory Committee (ACIP). Adult Immunization. MMWR 33(Suppl.):1S-68S, 1984

9. American College of Physicians: Guide for Adult Immunization. Philadelphia, American College of Physicians, 1990

10. American College Health Association: Position statement on immunization policy. J Am Coll Health 32:7-8, 1983

11. Centers for Disease Control: State Immunization Requirements, 1989-1990. Atlanta, Centers for Disease Control, 1989

12. Centers for Disease Control: Recommendations of the Immunization Practices Advisory Committee (ACIP). Measles prevention. MMWR 38(Suppl.):1-18, 1989

13. Committee on Infectious Diseases, American Academy of Pediatrics: Measles: Reassessment of the current immunization policy. Peds 84:1110-1113, 1989

14. American Academy of Family Physicians: Immunization Guidelines, Part 2. Kansas City MO, American Academy of Family Physicians, 1990

15. Pratt WF, London KA, Mosher WD: Reproductive behavior in the United States, 1988: Findings from the National Survey of Family Growth, Cycle IV. Popul Bull (in press)

16. Centers for Disease Control: Sexually Transmitted Diseases Treatment Guidelines, September 1989. MMWR Recommendations and Reports 38(S-8), September 1, 1989

17. Rothenberg RB, Potterat JJ: Strategies for management of sex partners, Sexually Transmitted Diseases, Second edition. Edited by KK Holmes et al. New York, McGraw Hill, 1990, pp. 1081-1086

# Sexually Transmitted Diseases and Student Health

WILLARD CATES, JR., MD, MPH

Sexually transmitted diseases (STDs) are a major health problem among adolescents and young adults in the United States.[1] As a result, they account for a sizeable share of visits to student health services.[2,3,4]

During the last two decades, both the number of sexually active students and the incidence of STDs in this group were growing to epidemic levels.[1] A recent representative survey of first-year Canadian college students showed high levels of both coital activity and sexual risk-taking. For example, one in five men and one in eleven women reported having had ten or more sexual partners.[5] In addition, inaccurate self-perceptions of STD risk among sexually active college students lead to inadequate planning for safer sex practices.[6,7]

This chapter addresses the epidemiology and prevention of STDs in students. It includes the magnitude of the problem in the student-age population, types of prevention approaches employed to reduce STDs in communities, and implications of STDs for future directions in adolescent health.

## EXTENT OF THE PROBLEM

### GONORRHEA

Because of the large numbers and the reporting stability, trends in gonorrhea provide the best estimates of STD patterns in students.[8,9] Between 1975 and 1989, the total number of gonorrhea cases reported to CDC decreased from approximately 1 million to 750,000, a 25 percent decline.[10] This favorable trend was temporally associated with the initiation of a national gonorrhea control program in the early 1970s to detect people with infection and interrupt transmission of the organism.[11] Teenagers shared in this overall numerical decrease. In 1989, approximately 175,000 cases of gonorrhea were reported in teenagers, compared to over 200,000 in 1975.

However, while the **number** of gonorrhea **cases** declined among those of student age, the **rates** of gonorrhea declined more slowly in students than in older age groups.[9] This apparent contradiction reflects both demographic and behavioral factors. First, the size of the teenage population, especially the white teenage population, began to shrink by the mid-1970s. Conversely, the 25 to 44 year olds, the tail-end of the "baby boom" cohorts, constituted an increasing population base. Second, as described earlier, high-risk teenage sexual behaviors continued to escalate in the 1980s.

During the 1980s, gonorrhea rates in both teenage males and teenage females had the dubious distinction of increasing their standing compared to rates in other age groups (Figures 1 and 2, next page). The incidence of gonorrhea in males ages 15-19 rose during the decade, whereas for all other age groups the incidence declined. Females ages 15-19 assumed the highest age-specific gonorrhea rate in 1984, and widened the gap over the next several years.

Racial differences are also apparent in gonorrhea trends among teenagers of both genders.[12] Among white males, steady declines in gonorrhea occurred in all age groups, yet those 15-19 years of age had the slowest decline. Similarly, white teenage females also had a slower decline than older ages; their gonorrhea rate went from the second highest in 1981 to the highest in 1989. Unlike their white counterparts, gonorrhea rates for black teenagers actually **increased** between 1981 and 1989. The incidence in black males showed a pattern of gradual increase during the 1980s, whereas for black females the levels peaked in 1986 and then fell slightly in the next three years. Nonetheless, rates for young black females were still higher in 1989 than at the beginning of the decade.

The effect of these temporal trends has further widened the gonorrhea gap between black and white American teenagers. In 1981, the gonorrhea rates in black male and female teenagers were twelvefold and ninefold, respectively, higher than whites. By 1989, these differences had risen to 44-fold and 16-fold. Various hypotheses have been offered to account for the worsening patterns: 1) STD primary prevention messages, especially those aimed at HIV, have been more successful in white communities; 2) STD clinical care in public clinics has been overwhelmed by an increasing

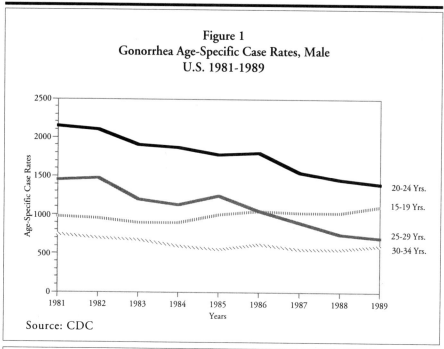

**Figure 1**
**Gonorrhea Age-Specific Case Rates, Male**
**U.S. 1981-1989**

Source: CDC

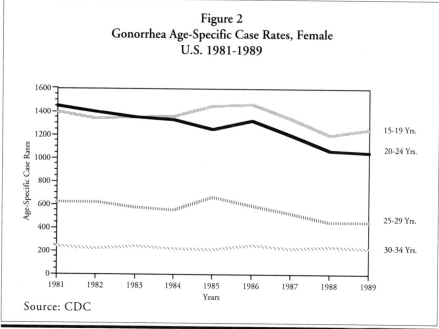

**Figure 2**
**Gonorrhea Age-Specific Case Rates, Female**
**U.S. 1981-1989**

Source: CDC

spectrum of responsibilities, which has a greater negative impact on the minority populations who disproportionately rely on these clinics; 3) STD interviewing and partner notification activities have been gradually shifted from gonorrhea to chlamydia and syphilis, again affecting gonorrhea control in minorities; and 4) STD risk behaviors fueled by illicit drugs have created an increasing STD "core" group among low-income heterosexual minorities.[13,14] Because of marked geographic variation, each of these hypotheses probably played a role to a greater or lesser degree throughout the country.

## SYPHILIS

Syphilis is the other traditional STD about which we have consistent data to measure trends. During the 1980s, syphilis rates decreased among white males, presumably because of safer sexual behaviors in response to HIV prevention messages.[15] However, these gains have been more than offset by rapid rate increases since 1985 in black heterosexuals, in part due to riskier sexual and health care seeking behaviors associated with illicit drugs. By 1989, syphilis in the United States was at its highest level since World War II.

Students as a group apparently have suffered less from this syphilis epidemic than older age groups, in part because the mean age of those with syphilis is older than those with gonorrhea.[16] Nonetheless, the rate of syphilis in minority teenage women has been increasing. If they become pregnant, this leads to heightened risks of congenital syphilis, especially if prenatal care is minimal. Moreover, the genital ulcers of syphilis have been associated with increased risks of HIV infection if sex occurs with an infected person.[17]

## CHLAMYDIA

*Chlamydia trachomatis* causes more lower genital tract infections among students than gonorrhea.[18,19] Unlike gonorrhea, however, chlamydial infections are not reportable conditions in all 50 states, and national surveillance of chlamydia is based on pilot projects. Thus, consistent trends for this infection in teenagers are not available. The prevalence of cervical chlamydia is between 8 percent and 40 percent of young women cultured during pelvic examinations.[19] Most investigations of adolescent females have found cervical chlamydia to be at least two times more common than gonorrhea.[18,19]

Similar ratios occur in urethral specimens from asymptomatic, sexually active adolescent males.[20] In virtually all studies, teenage women appear to have an increased risk of chlamydial infections compared to older age groups.[19] Whether this higher percentage of chlamydia in teenagers is a result of social/behavioral factors or an increased biologic susceptibility remains unclear.

## GENITAL HERPES AND GENITAL WARTS

Trends in sexually transmitted viral infections among teenagers have followed the same course as their bacterial counterparts.[21,22] Based on consultations for genital herpes and genital wart infections in office-based fee-for-service practices, the number of visits for females aged 15-19 years increased for both these viral STDs during the past two decades. For genital herpes, the increase went from 15,000 yearly visits in 1966 to over 125,000 visits by 1989. Similarly, for genital warts, caused by the human papillomavirus (HPV), the number of visits for teenagers rose from approximately 50,000 in 1966 to nearly 300,000 in 1989. Student health authorities find genital warts to be the most prevalent symptomatic STD among their population.[2]

For both these viral STDs, visits to private clinicians represent only the symptomatic tip of the iceberg. As physician awareness and availability of diagnostic methods have increased, subclinical herpes and papillomavirus infections of the male and female genital tract are becoming increasingly recognized. Serologic examination of a representative sample of Americans using herpes simplex virus (HSV) type 2 antibody showed evidence of widespread asymptomatic infection.[23] By the end of their teenage years, approximately 4 percent of whites and 17 percent of blacks have been infected with HSV-2. Most HSV transmission occurs from asymptomatic persons.[24,25] Similarly, for HPV, cervical cytologic evidence indicates at least threefold more females have asymptomatic cervical HPV infection than report external genital warts.[26] This ratio increases several fold when more sensitive indicators (e.g., molecular probes, polymerase chain reaction) are used. Because of their potential implications for future neoplasia, asymptomatic infections of HSV and HPV in adolescents need to be better documented.

## HEPATITIS B VIRUS (HBV) INFECTIONS

Nationwide, the incidence of hepatitis B has increased steadily over the last decade in spite of effective blood screening programs and the availability of a vaccine. By 1990, most HBV infections in the United States with known routes of transmission resulted from sexual and/or drug-related exposure. Unfortunately, our vaccination programs have not reached the risk groups that account for the most cases – IV drug users, people acquiring the disease through heterosexual exposure, and homosexual men.

The behavior changes of homosexual men to reduce their risk of HIV have simultaneously led to striking decreases in the number of hepatitis B cases (along with the other STDs) among this group. However, the number of cases of hepatitis B caused by heterosexual exposure has increased over the past several years, not surprisingly, primarily among inner city minority heterosexuals.[27] Approximately 30 percent of hepatitis B cases occur among student-age populations. Moreover, an estimated 5 percent of people 24 years of age or younger have been infected with HBV. Clearly, students must be a priority for vaccination programs addressing high-risk populations.

## PREVENTION OF STDS

### PRIMARY PREVENTION

Primary prevention of STDs involves preventing people from being exposed to infections and/or preventing acquisition of infection if exposure occurs. Regarding preventing exposure to STDs, two behavioral approaches are possible: first, sexual abstinence either through postponing the initial sexual involvement or by encouraging abstinence among sexually experienced people. Despite the increasing awareness of the risks of HIV and AIDS, the 1980s saw an increasing percentage of teenagers having sex at earlier ages. By 1988, over one-quarter of both black and white 15-year-olds had experienced coitus; moreover, by age 19, over four-fifths of both races were sexually experienced.[28] This has led to some creative school education programs emphasizing peer-led discussion groups that have had moderate success in encouraging high school students to postpone their sexual involvement.[29]

Second, exposure can also be prevented by ensuring that coitus occurs with an uninfected partner. Mutual lifetime monogamy is one approach to this end. However, only a small minority of couples have each had only one sex partner their entire lives. Another approach is through asking potential sex partners about their prior sexual, drug, and STD history. While some individuals will lie to have sex with others, most will not.[30] Thus, routinely asking will serve some protective function, even though not foolproof.

Once teenagers have chosen to be sexually active, preventing infection through use of barrier prophylaxis provides another tier of primary prevention. With teenagers and older students, the recent data on condom use are hopeful, but not ideal. Depending on the survey, as well as the population studied, between 38 percent and 66 percent of sexually active teenagers reported using condoms at the last coital episode.[31-34] These percentages are two to three times higher than those reported in the 1970s. However, recency of use is not the same thing as consistency of use. In every survey where the question was asked, less than half of teenagers who used condoms did so all the time.

Finally, primary prevention can occur through vaccination. However, the only STD for which we have a vaccine – hepatitis B – has had a dismal vaccination record in the high-risk, student populations. In the future, as additional vaccines become available, those concerned with providing student health services will need to routinely screen and immunize susceptible individuals for all vaccine-preventable conditions, including those transmitted sexually.

## SECONDARY PREVENTION

Secondary prevention of STDs involves identifying infected individuals and treating them before their infection either causes more costly complications or can be further transmitted within the community. Achieving secondary STD prevention requires 1) screening asymptomatic people, 2) diagnosing those with symptoms, 3) providing appropriate treatment for bacterial infections, and 4) notifying partners who have been exposed.

Screening people for an STD can serve several purposes: early case detection and treatment, referral for clinical evaluation, changing high-risk behaviors, safety for health care providers, and documentation of STD prevalence. Most STD screening of teenagers occurs either in student health services or in public clinics (STD, family planning, maternal and child health, adolescent health). Screening tests in these settings should have high sensitivity, to allow detection of as many infections as possible. Confirmatory testing can eliminate false-positives. For teenagers, non-invasive screening techniques may be most effective. For example, use of urine samples to detect evidence of genital inflammation or STD antigens would encourage participation.[35,36,37]

Diagnosing a particular STD usually occurs because of genital symptoms or notification of exposure to an STD. Presumptive diagnoses often form the basis for treatment, since most confirmatory diagnoses cannot be performed during a typical patient visit. Algorithms for approaching typical STD syndromes have been developed as a way of facilitating diagnosis.[38]

Early and adequate treatment of STDs is an effective way of preventing their spread within student populations. Ideally, therapies should be inexpensive, simple, safe, and effective. Usually treatment is provided for specific infections or symptoms. In addition, based on epidemiologic indications, antibiotics can be administered to high-risk individuals when infection is considered likely, in the interest of public health. This approach prevents complications that might occur between the time of testing and treatment, ensures treatment for infected individuals with false-negative laboratory tests, and guarantees treatment for those who might not return when notified of positive tests.

Notification of the sex partners of people with infection is a traditional part of STD control programs in the U.S. The privacy of original patients and partners is rigorously protected. Two types of partner notification are possible: 1) patient referral and 2) provider referral (i.e., contact tracing). The latter service is more labor-intensive, time consuming, and expensive. Therefore, provider referral is restricted to high-yield cases or to high-risk "core" environments. As part of student health services, partner notification can be arranged through collaboration with the local health department.

## IMPLICATIONS FOR ADOLESCENT HEALTH

Preventing STDs among the student population will require the enlistment of the entire spectrum of STD strategies, including behavioral, clinical, educational, and health promotional activities. First, we need renewed efforts both to learn more about, and also to influence, teenage sexual behavior. For example, what modifiable determinants of teenagers' lives will help deter premature sexual activity? How can we influence peer values so that it is socially acceptable to postpone sexual activity and socially unacceptable to avoid using condoms if sexually active?

Second, we need better ways to detect and treat STDs in students. For example, using urine samples from males undergoing athletic physical examinations to screen for urethral chlamydia and gonorrhea has been encouraging. Testing these specimens with leukocyte esterase,[37] enzyme immunoassay,[36] and simplified probes for specific genetic material may have some future role. Regarding treatment, antibiotics taken twice a day, such as doxycycline, may promote better compliance than those requiring four times a day administration such as tetracycline.[39] Better yet, single-dose treatment for chlamydia would be ideal.

Third, we need continued efforts to reach health care providers, especially those concerned with adolescent health care. Clinicians providing student health services must learn the recommended approaches to diagnosing and treating the vast spectrum of STDs.[40] Several opportunities for clinical training currently exist. The Centers for Disease Control (CDC) sponsors eleven regional prevention/training centers that provide one-to-two-week refresher courses at no cost to the participant. A simplified wall chart also is available from CDC that describes the symptoms, signs, laboratory approaches, therapy recommendations, and counseling messages for each of the 15 most prevalent STDs.[41] The University of Washington has developed an up-to-date manual on a variety of STD syndromes, together with easily followed algorithms for clinical management.[38]

Fourth, we need increased STD school education programs, especially if offered within an environment of peer-led training and skills-building, backed up by service availability. Most teenagers want to know more about STDs. Stimulated by recent concerns about AIDS, prototype school curriculum materials, using a self-instructional format and emphasizing behavioral messages, have been developed and field-tested for both teachers and students in grades 6 through 12.[42] Additionally, successful programs led by students themselves have helped teenagers resist peer pressures to initiate sexual activity;[29] we must build on this momentum.

Finally, we need to make better use of the mass media to convey effective health promotion messages to students. Because they spend an average of 23 hours a week listening to radio or watching television, teenagers are a special audience for these electronic approaches.[43] Messages should be aired to encourage condom use in high-risk settings or to publicize hotline numbers for further questions about STDs.

## REFERENCES

1. Cates W Jr, Rauh JL: Adolescents and sexually transmitted diseases: An expanding problem. J Adolesc Health Care 6:257-61, 1985

2. Budell JW: Health problems in a university student health service. Emory J Med 4:122-4, 1990

3. Patrick K: Student health: Medical care within institutions of higher education. JAMA 260:3301-5, 1988

4. Fingar AR: Patient problems encountered at a student health service. J Am Coll Health 38:142-4, 1989

5. MacDonald NE, Wells GA, Fisher WA et al: High-risk STD/HIV behavior among college students. JAMA 263:3155-9, 1990

6. Hernandez JT, Smith FJ: Inconsistencies and misperceptions putting college students at risk of HIV infection. J Adolesc Health Care 11:295-7, 1990

7. Manning D, Balson PM, Barenberg N et al: Susceptibility to AIDS: What college students do and don't believe. J Am Coll Health 38:67-73, 1989

8. Mascola L, Cates W Jr, Reynolds GH et al: Gonorrhea and salpingitis among American teenagers, 1960-1981. MMWR CDC Surveillance Summaries 32(3SS):25SS-30SS, 1983

9. Rice RJ, Aral SO, Blount JH et al: Gonorrhea in the United States 1975-1984: Is the giant only sleeping? Sex Transm Dis 14:83-7, 1987

10. Centers for Disease Control: Division of STD/HIV Annual Report 1989. Atlanta, Centers for Disease Control, 1990

11. Cates W Jr: Epidemiology and control of sexually transmitted diseases: Strategic evolution. Infect Dis Clin North Am 1:1-23, 1987

12. Gershman KA, Rolfs RT: Diverging gonorrhea and syphilis trends in the 1980s: Are they real? Am J Public Health 81(10) 1263-7, 1991

13. Rolfs RT, Goldberg M, Sharrar RG: Risk factors for syphilis: cocaine and prostitution. Am J Public Health 80:853-7, 1990

14. Fullilove RE, Fullilove MT, Bowser BP et al: Risk of sexually transmitted disease among black adolescent crack users in Oakland and San Francisco, Calif. JAMA 263:851-5, 1990

15. Rolfs RT, Nakashima AK: Epidemiology of primary and secondary syphilis in the United States, 1981 through 1989. JAMA 264 (11) 1432-7, 1990

16. Moran JS, Aral SO, Jenkins WC et al: The impact of sexually transmitted diseases on minority populations in the United States. Public Health Rep 104:560-5, 1989

17. Pepin J, Plummer FA, Brunham RC et al: The interaction of HIV infection and other sexually transmitted diseases: An opportunity for intervention. AIDS 3:3-9, 1989

18. Shafer M-A, Prager V, Schalwitz J et al: Prevalence of urethral *Chlamydia trachomatis* and *Neisseria gonorrhoeae* among asymptomatic, sexually active adolescent boys. J Infect Dis 156:223-4, 1987

19. Shafer M-A, Moscicki AB: Sexually transmitted diseases, Understanding and Facilitating Biological, Behavioral, and Social Development. The Health of Adolescents. Edited by WR Hendee and B Wilford. San Francisco, Jossey-Bass, 1991

20. Braverman PK, Biro FM, Brunner RL et al: Screening asymptomatic adolescent males for chlamydia. J Adolesc Health Care 11:141-4, 1990

21. Becker TM, Stone KM, Cates W Jr: Epidemiology of genital herpes infections in the United States: The current situation. J Reprod Med 31:359-64, 1986

22. Becker TM, Stone KM, Alexander ER: Genital papillomavirus infection: A growing concern. Obstet Gynecol Clin North Am 14:389-96, 1987

23. Johnson RE, Nahmias A, Madger LS et al: A seroepidemiologic survey of the prevalence of herpes simplex virus type 2 infection in the United States. N Engl J Med 321:7-12, 1989

24. Mertz GJ, Coombs RW, Ashley RL et al: Transmission of genital herpes in couples with one symptomatic and one asymptomatic partner: A prospective study. J Infect Dis 157:1169-77, 1988

25. Brock BV, Selke S, Benedetti J et al: Frequency of asymptomatic shedding of herpes simplex virus in women with genital herpes. JAMA 263:418-20, 1990

26. Stone KM: Epidemiologic aspects of genital HPV infection. Clin Obstet Gynecol 32:112-6, 1989

27. Alter MJ, Hadler SC, Margolis HS et al: The changing epidemiology of hepatitis B in the United States: Need for alternative vaccination strategies. JAMA 263:1218-22, 1990

28. Aral SO, Cates W Jr: The multiple dimensions of sexual behavior as a risk factor for STD: The sexually experienced are not necessarily sexually active. Sex Transm Dis 16:173-7, 1989

29. Howard M, McCabe JB: Helping teenagers postpone sexual involvement. Fam Plann Perspect 22:21-26, 1990

30. Cochran SD, Mays VM: Sex, lies, and HIV (letter). N Engl J Med 322:774-5, 1990

31. Hingson R, Strunin L, Berlin B: AIDS transmission: Changes in knowledge and behaviors among adolescents, Massachusetts Statewide Surveys 1986-1988. Pediatrics 85:24-9, 1989

32. Kegeles SM, Adler NE, Irwin CE: Sexually active adolescents and condoms: Changes over one year in knowledge, attitudes, and use. Am J Public Health 78:460-1, 1988

33. Sonenstein FL, Pleck JH, Ku LC: Sexual activity, condom use and AIDS awareness among adolescent males. Fam Plann Perspect 21:152-60, 1989

34. Weisman CS, Nathanson CA, Ensminger M et al: AIDS knowledge, perceived risk, and prevention among adolescent clients of a family planning clinic. Fam Plann Perspect 21:213-7, 1989

35. Adger H, Shafer M-A, Sweet RL et al: Screening for *Chlamydia trachomatis* and *Neisseria gonorrhoeae* in adolescent males: Value of first-catch urine examination. Lancet ii:944, 1984

36. Getts AG: Diagnosing *Chlamydia trachomatis* urethritis by first-catch urine enzyme immunoassay in adolescent males. J Adolesc Health Care 10:209-11, 1989

37. Sadof MD, Woods ER, Emans SJ: Dipstick leukocyte esterase activity in first-catch urine specimens. JAMA 258:1932-4, 1987

38. Stamm WE, Kaetz SM, Beirne MB et al: The practitioner's handbook for the management of STDs. Seattle, University of Washington, 1988

39. Jordan WC: Doxycycline versus tetracycline in the treatment of men with gonorrhea: The compliance factor. Sex Transm Dis 8(Suppl):105-9, 1981

40. Gilchrist MJR, Rauh JL: Office microscopic examination for sexually transmitted diseases: A tool to lower costs. J Adolesc Health Care 6:311-20, 1985

41. Centers for Disease Control: Sexually transmitted diseases summary, 1990. Atlanta, Centers for Disease Control, 1990

42. Yarber WL: Curriculum for integrated STD/AIDS teaching. Bloomington, University of Indiana, 1989

43. Strasburger VC: Adolescent sexuality and the media. Pediatr Clin North Am 36:747-73, 1989

# 6

# HIV, AIDS, and Adolescents

Diana Abramo and Karen Hein, MD

## Extent of the Problem

In the United States there are nearly as many cases of AIDS in adolescents ages 13-21 as there are in children under 13, although many people are not yet aware of this. As of March 1990, there were 1429 reported cases among adolescents.[1] While it represents only a small fraction of AIDS cases in the U.S., this is probably a function of the long incubation period of HIV. There is, on average, over twelve years' latency between the time of infection with the virus and subsequent illness, which may be even longer in adolescents.[2] Thus, for the approximately 20 percent of U.S. cases of AIDS that occur among those in their twenties,[3] it is likely that many of these people became infected in their teens. Furthermore, the number of reported cases of AIDS in adolescents is doubling every 14 months.[4] Studies of seroprevalence in different adolescent populations found rates from 0.1 percent for military recruits,[5] 1-10 percent for adolescent mothers and babies,[6] to 7 percent for those entering a youth shelter.[7]

The average age of first intercourse in the U.S. is 16 years, and in some adolescent subpopulations the average age of first intercourse is 12. Furthermore, sexually active adolescents have the highest rates of STDs of any age group,[8] and very few of them consistently use barrier methods of contraception.[9] A final reason for intervening with this group is that teens are forming patterns of behavior about sex and drugs that are likely to persist as they grow older.

The profile of the AIDS epidemic is different in adolescents. Compared to adults, proportionately more cases of AIDS occur in females, among minority group members, and through heterosexual transmission.

75

In addition, crack and other non-IV drugs, including alcohol, may play a more important role by affecting judgment and leading to unsafe sexual behavior.

Fifty-four percent of adolescents with AIDS are minority group members compared to 41 percent among adults over 30.[10] The male-to-female ratio for AIDS cases among adolescents in New York City is 3:1, compared to 7:1 for those over 21. Elsewhere in the U.S., the ratio is 7:1 for adolescents and 15:1 for those over 21.[4] Among seropositive Job Corps applicants aged 16-18, the ratio is 1:1.[11] And compared to adults, proportionately more adolescents with AIDS in NYC reported heterosexual contact as the transmission route. Fifty-two percent of AIDS cases among female teens in NYC and 47 percent in the rest of the U.S. resulted from heterosexual intercourse (compared to 29 percent for female adults).[4] In addition, while IV drug use among adolescents is proportionately much less of a risk factor,[12] crack use is believed to be a significant risk.[13]

## WHO IS AT RISK?

In the first years of the AIDS epidemic, risk for contracting HIV was usually conceptualized in terms of "risk groups": gay men, hemophiliacs, and later, intravenous drug users (IVDUs) and their sex partners. However, AIDS educators have begun to urge that we adopt a model dealing with risk behaviors and not risk groups. Research has shown that self-described sexual orientation is not a reliable guide to sexual behavior, as many people have had sexual experiences outside of their primary sexual orientation.[14] For example, among male teens who engage in prostitution with men, many do not self-identify as homosexual, while many self-identified gay male teens have not yet had sexual intercourse.[15] Similarly, a study of urban adolescent females found that 26 percent of those who were sexually experienced had engaged in anal intercourse, a very high-risk behavior.[16] Thus, the risk-group model can lead professionals to target those whose behaviors do not put them at high risk, or to overlook the needs of those whose behaviors are in fact high risk. But this model can also cause motivational problems for those at whom these messages are aimed. The heterosexual female may hear that she is not in a "risk group" and believe she does not need to take precautions; the gay male may conclude that his risk is so high that precautions would be pointless.

While all youth who have had unprotected intercourse or use drugs (IV or non-IV) are at risk, special attention should be paid to the needs of males who have sex with males (many of whom, especially among minority groups, do not identify themselves as gay); out-of-home youth, who may support themselves by exchanging sex for money or shelter; those with substance abuse problems, who may exchange sex for drugs, or experience loss of judgment when intoxicated; those who have been sexually abused, who may later exhibit unselective voluntary sexual activity; youth with hemophilia or other conditions requiring multiple transfusions; and the developmentally disabled, who require very explicit, concrete demonstration of AIDS-prevention behaviors. Adolescents with a history of STDs or unplanned pregnancy should be targeted as well, as this is evidence of unprotected intercourse, and HIV rates are known to be higher in those with other STDs.

## PREVENTION

In order to practice AIDS-preventive behaviors (APBs), adolescents must have correct information, the belief that they are personally vulnerable but can protect themselves, and the appropriate skills and resources to practice these behaviors. AIDS education interventions limited to giving information are not sufficient. For example, it was found that condom use by teens decreased over a year in which media and school education increased their knowledge that condoms effectively prevent HIV transmission.[17]

**Information** that teens need to practice sexual APBs includes: reviewing how HIV is and is not transmitted, correcting misconceptions about casual contact; underscoring the fact that someone with HIV may look and feel perfectly healthy for many years; emphasizing risk behaviors and not risk groups; pointing out that many effective methods of birth control, such as oral contraceptives, are not effective against STDs including HIV; describing alternative forms of personal intimacy such as hugging, massage, and masturbation, which have no risk; and emphasizing the need to use a condom or dental dam for **all** forms of intercourse (oral, vaginal, and anal). Teens need to learn what behaviors **don't work:**[18] avoiding casual contact; unprotected monogamous sex (adolescent relationships are short-lived); unprotected sex with "nice" people you know well; unprotected sex with fewer partners; abstinence in the absence of appropriate plans for the time when sexual activity will begin. They also need to be told that even intermittent use of alcohol or drugs (IV or non-IV) can impair judgment and lead to AIDS-related risk behaviors, and the ability to refuse substance use should be taught through skills exercises.

To avoid HIV transmission through needles, adolescents need to learn that transmission can occur through sharing needles for any activity, including steroid injection, tattooing, ear- or nose-piercing, as well as IV drug use. They need to be informed that needles sold on the street as new are often used, and IV users who cannot stop their use should be shown how to use bleach to clean their injection equipment. However, these interventions are not sufficient to offset the continuing lack of age-appropriate drug treatment facilities for adolescents, especially crack users.

**Skills** that teens need in order to practice APBs include: decision-making; assertiveness training; defending decisions that are unpopular with one's social network; negotiating with a potential partner concerning sexual intercourse and condom use; where and how to buy condoms; using condoms and dental dams; and cleaning needles. As it is believed that many people may be less likely to practice safe sex in a committed relationship, exercises should emphasize communication in this situation. One popular exercise involves writing all the substeps in condom use on cards, giving each student one card, and then asking them to decide together how to line themselves up in the correct order. This is effective because it facilitates communication about sensitive issues, teaches a specific skill in a hands-on fashion, and creates the expectation that other students are aware of safe sex. This and many other age-appropriate exercises for learning about safer sex are described in *Teaching Safer Sex*. (See Publications list at the end of the chapter.)

**Presentation.** Lack of skills, not information, is implicated in much HIV-related risk behavior. Skills training is much more effective in demonstration or workshop form, rather than didactic presentation.[19] As adolescents tend to engage in concrete thinking, exercises should be participatory, allowing them to use their sense of sight and touch. Students should be given a chance to practice the skills in role plays, preferably over several sessions, as complex new behaviors are not learned immediately. Take-home exercises can also be used, such as asking the students to buy condoms and report on their experiences at the next session. Motivation can be enhanced by having adolescents help plan the presentation. Group rather than individual sessions can be effective, as they can help create a norm in the student's social network for the new kind of behavior.[20]

In addition, the credibility of the presenter appears to be an important factor.[21] A person who is perceived to be "like" the students, preferably of similar ethnicity, may function as a role model and thus be a more effective presenter or co-presenter. Similarly, it may be preferable to have the presenter be the same gender as the audience, if possible, with a male-female team for coed audiences. Slightly older peers are believed to be effective, and many programs are experimenting with trained peer educators.[22] In any case, the presenter should be knowledgeable about AIDS, adolescents, and the ethnic culture and values of the audience;[23,24] be nonjudgmental; be aware of his or her own biases; and be comfortable using the same terms for body parts and sexual acts as does the target audience.

**Resources** needed include materials that permit adolescents to act on their information and skills (for example, condoms, clean needles, confidential information, and appropriate educational materials). In general, educational materials should be illustrated with pictures matching the age and ethnicity of the target audience, be at the appropriate reading level, use both "street" language and technical terms, show sex in a positive light, be sensitive to different sexual orientations, and describe what to do as well as what not to do. The National AIDS Information Clearinghouse (1-800-458-5231) provides free information on age-appropriate educational materials. Other educational resources are referenced at the end of this chapter.

## TREATMENT OF HIV-INFECTED YOUTH

### ENGAGING IN CARE

Outreach is essential to engaging adolescents in care. Adolescents must overcome many external barriers to care, including payment, confidentiality, and the right to consent to treatment.

Networking should be done with local adolescent community centers, runaway services or shelters, pregnancy prevention and drug treatment programs, gay and lesbian organizations, and residential treatment centers, among others. Some programs (such as group homes, Job Corps, the military) may require HIV testing as part of the application process. Adolescents who are found to be HIV-positive may not be accepted to the program and are often not linked with age-appropriate care. Arranging follow-up care is essential before notification of positive test results. Services should be set up to identify and engage HIV-positive adolescents, and to accommodate and encourage participation by their sexual partners and families.

## ISSUES FOR SCHOOL AND COLLEGE HEALTH SERVICES

If the sexual partner of a seropositive student is a student attending the same medical service, the clinician may have a contractual relationship with that partner. This contract affects confidentiality with the index patient. This should be clarified in counseling and testing before blood is drawn; ideally, it should be part of a broader discussion of confidentiality at the first visit. Policies and procedures should be developed to deal specifically with partner notification, contact tracing, and extent of confidentiality, particularly in dealing with minors.

Health service policies should reflect state laws regarding sex-related health care for minors, parental consent, and confidentiality. In addition, the service should assess its ability to provide on-site reproductive health services, and HIV counseling and testing. If referral is necessary, agencies should be assessed for their ability to provide adolescents with age-specific services.

## CONFIDENTIALITY AND CONSENT

Teenagers, parents, and health care providers must be aware of their own state's laws regarding care of minors, since they vary at this time.[25] As of May, 1990, at least nine states authorize minors to consent to HIV testing (CA, CO, DE, FL, IA, MI, NM, NY, RI) and two authorize minors to consent to HIV-related treatment (CO, MI). In all states, laws permit minors to consent to services for one or more of the following conditions: pregnancy, STDs, HIV or AIDS, substance abuse, mental health problems, and sexual assault. In all states, laws permit one or more of the following categories of minors to consent to most medical care: those who are emancipated, or live apart from their parents, or are parents, or are mature, or are high school graduates, or are pregnant. Idaho, Kentucky, and Washington authorize minors to consent to diagnosis and treatment of an STD, including HIV. In addition, AL, NC, PA, VA, CA, MT, OK, and TX authorize minors to consent to diagnosis and treatment of reportable diseases, including AIDS.

## TESTING

At the first invitational National Conference on AIDS and Adolescents, held in 1988, recommendations were developed for counseling and testing, and reported in a special edition of the Journal of Adolescent Health Care.[26] In summary, their recommendations state that: testing should be done only if it is expected to benefit the adolescent; counseling should be age-appropriate, and not limited to single pre- and post-test session; supportive-adult participation should be sought but not required; those able to give informed consent should be able to consent to HIV testing; special care should be taken regarding confidentiality in institutions such as detention centers; mandatory testing should not be a prerequisite for program admission; anonymous, unlinked seroprevalence testing is helpful for program planning; and that further research is needed on adolescent-appropriate test counseling and its impact.

The decision to have an HIV antibody test should not be made without consideration of all the consequences. Some of the specific questions pertaining to adolescents are listed in Table 1 (next page), reprinted from AIDS: Trading Fears for Facts.[27] This may also serve as a guide to some specific issues for which policies should be developed.

Drawbacks to testing have been noted.[28,29] Testing should be limited to those who can act on the results of a positive test, that is, gain access to treatment, monitor their health status, and be motivated to change their risk behaviors. Poor, minority youths, who are over-represented among HIV-positive youth at this time, may face more serious consequences, such as exclusion from group homes and shelter systems in many cities. Youth with a prior history of suicide attempts should not be tested unless proper supports are in place. A small study of disenfranchised youth[30] found no increase in suicide attempts after notification of HIV-positive test results, although there was some increase in suicidal ideation.

## CLINICAL AND LABORATORY ASSESSMENT

Staging classifications and criteria for the diagnosis of AIDS were not developed specifically for adolescents, and so have limited applicability, especially for females.

There are important differences in the appropriate history, physical exam, and normal laboratory values for HIV-positive adolescents. For example, the case definition for AIDS does not include any signs or symptoms referable to the female genitourinary tract, yet vaginitis and pelvic inflammatory disease are both common problems in adolescents with HIV disease.[31]

## RANGE AND STRUCTURE OF SERVICES NEEDED

Many HIV-positive youth are among the most vulnerable members of our society, and may require a wide variety of services. In contrast to adults, they are often unable to produce documentation needed for entitlements such as Medicaid, and generally do not have sufficient money to pay for medical services on their own. In contrast to those with other medical conditions, HIV-positive youth may need access to entitlements, housing, food, legal services, drug treatment, and assistance in obtaining medications. They may need a variety of mental health services, including support

### Table 1
### Specific AIDS Questions Pertaining to Adolescent HIV Testing

|  | Yes | No |
|---|---|---|
| Will you give the results to my employer? | ___ | ___ |
| Will you give the results to my future employer? | ___ | ___ |
| Will you give the results to my parents' insurance company? | ___ | ___ |
| Will you help me talk to my parents, sex partner(s), or other people whom I might want to tell? | ___ | ___ |
| Will you give the results to my insurance company in the future? | ___ | ___ |
| Will someone explain to me both the advantages and the disadvantages of HIV testing? | ___ | ___ |
| Do you give counseling before and after I take the test? (If the answer is yes, be sure to ask how long the counseling session will be. You need a place that can give you a lot of time.) | ___ | ___ |
| May I come back more than once to talk about whether or not to have the test? (You should be able to take your time making this decision.) | ___ | ___ |
| How long will I have to wait for an appointment? | _____ | |
| How long does it take to get the test results? | _____ | |
| How will I be told the results? | _____ | |
| Do you usually take care of people 10 to 21 years old? | ___ | ___ |
| Do my parents or another adult have to come with me? | ___ | ___ |
| Do I need my parents' or another adult's permission to have the HIV test? | ___ | ___ |
| Will my parents or another adult be told the results whether I want them to be told or not? | ___ | ___ |
| Can I get the test for free? | ___ | ___ |
| If not: | | |
|    How much will it cost? | _____ | |
|    Do I have to pay before I get the test? | ___ | ___ |
|    Do you give teenagers who can't afford the price a reduced rate? | ___ | ___ |
| Will a bill be sent in the mail for the lab test and for the office visit? | ___ | ___ |
| Would you put the test results in my medical record? | ___ | ___ |
| Will you put the test results in my medical records in the future? | ___ | ___ |
| Will you automatically give the results to my school? | ___ | ___ |
| Will you automatically give the results to my school if it asks for them? | ___ | ___ |
| Will you notify my sex partner(s) if I want you to? | ___ | ___ |
| Will you notify my sex partner(s) if I don't want you to? | ___ | ___ |

Reprinted with permission from Hein K and DiGeronimo T: AIDS: Trading Fears for Facts. NY, Consumer Reports Books, 1989, pp 104-5.

for decision-making regarding disclosure of their HIV status, sexual behavior, future childbearing, and risk reduction. In cases where a youth is served by more than one agency, provision should be made for inter-agency case management, with a designated case manager.

There are five major approaches to organizing these services. HIV-related services can be added to categorical programs serving adolescents, such as family planning clinics, drug treatment or prevention programs, teen pregnancy programs, or STD clinics. However, this can result in fragmented care. A second approach is to integrate HIV-related health services with other youth services on one site, as is done by The Door in New York and The Bridge in Boston. A third approach is to add adolescent services to pre-existing HIV service agencies geared toward children or adults. However, without adolescent-appropriate staff training, outreach, and services, HIV-infected youth are unlikely to enroll or continue in such programs. The fourth approach is an Adolescent AIDS specialty program, such as the one at Montefiore Hospital in the Bronx, combining clinical care, clinical research, and advocacy for HIV-positive and high-risk youth. Finally, a number of networks coordinating HIV and adolescent issues across education, social service, and health care agencies have been developed successfully. In the past few years, regional networks have been organized in San Francisco, Washington DC, New York, Chicago, Miami, Houston, and Los Angeles.[32]

In addition to the difficulties experienced in funding any HIV services, such programs must contend with funding difficulties specific to those serving adolescents. Most out-of-home youth and one-quarter of those living with their families are uninsured or cannot produce necessary documentation for entitlement programs to cover the cost of health care visits or medications. Reimbursement mechanisms do not currently exist for the range of outreach or ambulatory activities provided by those now caring for high-risk or HIV-infected youth. Since most monies are allocated to either pediatric or adult programs, adolescents tend to "fall through the cracks." And even when funding is available, adolescents tend to be viewed as small adults or large children, so that services are often age-inappropriate.

## CONCLUSION

The AIDS epidemic has an impact on today's adolescents whether or not they are personally at risk for acquiring the virus. Fear and misinformation are still prevalent even as we enter the second decade of the epidemic. The developmental tasks of adolescence include getting to know oneself and others, including physical intimacy. This is now more difficult, particularly due to mixed messages about sex (e.g., mass media images that glorify sex and AIDS education that tell teens to "just say no").

For those who are uninfected, the goal should be to provide them with the means to stay uninfected – but to keep their compassion for others who may be at risk or infected. For those who are not aware that they are infected, the goal should be to get them into age-appropriate care and to help them deal with issues such as disclosure. For those who are infected and in care, the goals should not be limited to early intervention and care, but include keeping them on track regarding school, friends, employment, and independent living.

Significant progress has been made in our ability to treat the medical aspects of HIV-related illness. The urgent need now is to find ways to match that progress in prevention, access to care, and treating the social aspects of this epidemic.

## REFERENCES

1. Sondheimer D, NICHD: personal communication

2. Goedert JJ, Kessler CM, Aledort LM: A prospective study of human immuno-deficiency virus type 1 infection and the development of AIDS in subjects with hemophilia. N Engl J Med 321:1141-1148, 1989

3. National Research Council: AIDS and adolescents, AIDS: The Second Decade. Edited by HG Miller, CF Turner, LE Moses. Washington, DC, National Academy Press, 1990, p.152

4. Vermund SV, Hein K, Gayle H et al: AIDS among adolescents in NYC: Case surveillance profiles compared with the rest of the U.S. Am J Dis Child 143:1220-1225, 1989

5. Brundage JF, Burke DS, Gardner LI et al: HIV infection among young adults in the New York City area: Prevalence and incidence estimates based on antibody screening among civilian applicants for military service. NY State J Med 88:232-235, 1988

6. Novick LJ, Glebatis D, Stricof R et al: HIV infection in adolescent child-bearing women. Abstract WA08. Presented at the Vth International AIDS Conference, Montreal, June 1989

7. Kennedy J: Testimony before the Presidential Commission on the HIV epidemic. May 1988

8. Bell T, Hein K: The adolescent and sexually transmitted diseases, Sexually Transmitted Diseases. Edited by KK Holmes et al. New York, McGraw-Hill, 73-84, 1984

9. Kahn JR, Rindfuss RR, Guilkey DK: Adolescent contraceptive method choices. Demography 27(3)323-35, 1990

10. National Research Council: AIDS and adolescents, AIDS: The Second Decade. Edited by HG Miller, CF Turner, LE Moses. Washington, DC, National Academy Press, 1990, p.160

11. St. Louis ME, Hayman CR, Miller C et al: HIV infection in disadvantaged adolescents in the U.S.: Findings from the Job Corps screening program. Presented at the Vth International Conference on AIDS, Montreal, June 4-9, 1989. Abstract MDPl

12. National Research Council: AIDS and adolescents, AIDS: The Second Decade. Edited by HG Miller, CF Turner, LE Moses. Washington, DC, National Academy Press, 1990, p.162

13. Fullilove RE, Fullilove MT, Bowser BP et al: Risk of sexually transmitted disease among black adolescent crack users in Oakland and San Francisco, CA. JAMA 263:6: 851-855, 1990

14. Reinisch JM, Sanders SA, Ziemba-Davis M: The study of sexual behavior in relation to the transmission of human immunodeficiency virus. Am Psychol 43:921-927, 1988

15. Remafedi G: Adolescent homosexuality: Psychosocial and medical implications. Pediatrics 79:331-337, 1987

16. Jaffe LR, Seehaus M, Wagner C et al: Anal intercourse and knowledge of acquired immunodeficiency syndrome among minority-group female adolescents. J Pediatr 112:1005-7, 1988

17. Kegeles SM, Adler NE, Irwin CE Jr: Sexually active adolescents and condoms: Changes over one year in knowledge, attitudes and use. Am J Public Health 78:460-461, 1988

18. Rotheram-Borus MJ, Koopman C: HIV and adolescents. Leukefeld CG and Battjes R (eds). J of Primary Prevention, Special Issue on Preventing the Spread of AIDS and HIV. (in press)

19. U.S. General Accounting Office: AIDS Education: Reaching Populations at Higher Risk. GAO/PEMD-88-35, September, 1988

20. Fisher JD: Possible effects of reference group-based social influence on AIDS-risk behavior and AIDS prevention. Am Psychol 43:914-920, 1988

21. U.S. Congress, Office of Technology Assessment: How effective is AIDS Education? Washington, DC, May 1988

22. Center for Population Options, Peer Education: Teens Teaching Teens about AIDS and HIV Infection Prevention. Washington, DC, 1989

23. Peterson JL, Marin G: Issues in the prevention of AIDS among Black and Hispanic men. Am Psychol 43:871-877, 1988

24. Mays VM, Cochran SD: Issues in the perception of AIDS risk and risk reduction activities by Black and Hispanic/Latina women. Am Psychol 43:949-957, 1988

25. Sondheimer D, English A, Hein K et al: Legal, Ethical and Social Complexities in Conducting HIV-Related Research Involving Adolescents. Presented at VI Int'l Conference on AIDS, San Francisco, California, June 1990. Abstract No. Th.D. 888

26. English A (ed.): AIDS testing and epidemiology for youth: Recommendations of the work group. J Adolesc Health Care 10:52S-57S, 1989

27. Hein K, DiGeronimo T: AIDS: Trading Fears for Facts. A guide for young people, Consumer Reports Books, New York, June 1989

28. Rotheram-Borus M, Koopman C: Protecting children's rights in AIDS research, Social Research on Children and Adolescents: Ethical Issues. Edited by B Stanley, R Thompson, J Sieber. Newbury Park, Sage Publications, 1991

29. Rotheram-Borus M, Koopman C: Children and AIDS: Clinical Practice #19. Edited by M Stuber. Washington, DC , Am Psychiatric Association Press, 1991

30. Futterman D, Hein K, Kipke M et al: HIV-positive Adolescents: HIV Testing Experiences and Changes in Risk Related Sexual and Drug Use Behavior. Presented at the VIth Int'l Conference on AIDS, San Francisco, California. Abstract No. S.C.663

31. Futterman D, Hein K: Medical management of adolescents, Pediatric AIDS: The Challenge of HIV Infection in Infants, Children, and Adolescents. Edited by P Pizzo and C Wilfert. Baltimore, Williams & Wilkins, 1991

32. Hein K: Fighting AIDS in adolescents, Issues in Science and Technology. Washington, DC, National Academy of Sciences, 7,3, pp 67-72, April 1991

# RESOURCES

The National AIDS Information Clearinghouse, P.O. Box 6003, Rockville, MD 20850, 1-800-458-5231

National Center for Youth Law, 1663 Mission Street, 5th floor, San Francisco, CA 94103, 415-543-3307

National Association of State Boards of Education. 1012 Cameron Street, Alexandria, VA 22314, 703-684-4000

Center for Population Options/AIDS Adolescents Initiative. 1025 Vermont Ave. N.W., Ste 210, Washington, DC 20005, 202-347-5700

Hetrick Martin Institute for Gay and Lesbian Youth. 401 West St., New York, NY

National Network of Runaway and Youth Services, 1400 I N.W., Suite 330, Washington, DC 20005, 202-682-4114

Society for Adolescent Medicine, 19401 East 40 Highway, Suite #120, Independence, MO 64055, 816-795-TEEN

American College Health Association, P.O. Box 28937, Baltimore, MD 21240-8937, 410-859-1500

Black Americans and AIDS Project of the National Urban League. 105 East 22nd Street, New York, NY 10021, 212-674-3500

Hispanic AIDS Forum. 121 Avenue of the Americas, New York, NY 10013, 212-966-6336

Sex Information and Education Council of the U.S. 32 Washington Place, New York NY 10003, 212-673-3850

# PUBLICATIONS

National Academy Press. AIDS and adolescents, AIDS: The Second Decade. Edited by HG Miller, CF Turner, and LE Moses. Washington, DC, National Academy Press, 1990

Quackenbush M, Sargent P: Teaching AIDS: A Resource Guide on Acquired Immune Deficiency Syndrome. Santa Cruz, Network Publications, a division of ETR Associates, 1988

Girls Clubs of America, Inc: Keeping Healthy, Keeping Safe: Effective strategies for AIDS and HIV prevention among girls and young women. Girls Clubs of America's AIDS Education Project, 1989

Brick P, Cooperman C: Positive Images: A New Approach to Contraceptive Education. The Center for Family Life Education. Planned Parenthood of Bergen County, Inc, 1987

Brick P, Charlton C, Kunins H et al: Teaching Safer Sex. The Center for Family Life Education, Planned Parenthood of Bergen County, Inc, 1989

Post J, McPherson C: Into Adolescence: Learning About AIDS. Santa Cruz, Network Publications, a division of ETR Associates, 1988

Hein K, DiGeronimo T: AIDS: Trading Fears for Facts. A guide for young people, Consumer Reports Books, New York, June 1989

AIDS and Adolescence: Exploring the Challenge, Special Issue of J Adolesc Health Care 10:3, May, 1989

American College Health Association: General Statement of Institutional Response to AIDS. AIDS Record. 2:8-9, 16-19, April 8, 1988

# 7

# Prevention of Injuries to Children and Adolescents

FREDERICK P. RIVARA, MD, MPH

Twenty years ago the National Academy of Sciences called injuries "the neglected disease of modern society."[1] Two decades and 2.5 million trauma deaths later, the Academy issued a similar report stating: "Injury is the principal public health problem in America today; it affects primarily the young and will touch one of every three Americans this year."[2]

Why is the death toll from injuries so great, and why has it not experienced a decline similar to that of deaths from other causes? More importantly, how can losses be reduced? Where should efforts and expenditures be placed? The purpose of this chapter is to examine who is injured in the population, where these injuries occur, and which agents are repeatedly involved in producing injuries.

First, the terms used in the article are defined and the magnitude of the injury problem outlined. The body of the article is devoted to considering injuries within an epidemiologic framework of how the host, environment, and agent influence the risk of injury.

## INJURY VS ACCIDENT

Before examining patterns of injury in the population, just what is it we are talking about? Throughout this chapter, injuries refer to "damage resulting from acute exposure to physical or chemical agents." The term **accident** will be avoided; it is an inaccurate anachronism reflecting unscientific attitudes toward injuries. The term **injury** focuses scientific attention on the problem – the damage to the person.

## SCOPE OF THE PROBLEM

About 57 million Americans require medical treatment for injuries every year and 143,000 die. From before the first birthday through age 44, injuries are the leading cause of death in the United States. For children from one to four years of age, injuries are responsible for nearly one-half of all deaths and cause three times more deaths than the next leading cause – congenital anomalies. Throughout the rest of childhood and adolescence, injuries cause more deaths than all other causes combined. The major causes of fatal injuries clearly vary with age, as shown in Table 1. Motor vehicle injuries lead the list, as they do throughout childhood. Deaths from fires and burns are particularly a problem in young children, who along with the elderly, represent the group at greatest risk of dying from this cause. Drownings, many of which occur in pools and not infrequently in bathtubs, constitute a large hazard for young children.

Among the young school-age (5-9 year old) child, pedestrian injuries constitute the most common cause of death from trauma, and are second only to cancer as a cause of death in this age group. Drowning and deaths from fires and burns continue to take a major toll in this age.

As children enter the teenage years, motor vehicle occurrences become increasingly important as a cause of serious and fatal injury. In these adolescent years, suicide and homicide take a large toll, and as discussed below, firearms play an important role in these tragedies.

Mortality statistics, however, illustrate only one part of the problem. Nonfatal injuries constitute a large burden on the health care system.

Table 1
Violent Deaths in Children and Adolescents in the United States, 1986

|  | Age in Years | | | | |
|  | <5 | 5-9 | 10-14 | 15-19 | Total |
|---|---|---|---|---|---|
| All Injuries | 4607 | 2133 | 2776 | 12895 | 22411 |
| Motor Vehicle: |  |  |  |  |  |
| Occupant | 658 | 397 | 643 | 5714 | 7412 |
| Pedestrian | 500 | 502 | 285 | 500 | 1787 |
| Drowning | 754 | 326 | 323 | 659 | 2062 |
| Fire and Burns | 859 | 321 | 177 | 262 | 1619 |
| Homicide | 660 | 134 | 245 | 1838 | 2877 |
| Suicide | 0 | 5 | 250 | 1896 | 2151 |

Population-based studies indicate that 247 per 1000 children and adolescents 0-19 years of age receive medical care for an injury each year.[3] Of these, 2.5 percent require hospital admission for care and 55 percent have at least short-term, temporary disability as a result of their injuries.

The cost of these injuries is enormous – amounting to $157.6 billion in 1985.[4] Children accounted for $13.8 billion, a relatively small proportion of the total because the cost for care of an injured child is 15-20 percent of the cost of care for an injured older adult.

## CAUSES OF INJURY AND PREVENTIVE OPTIONS

Much of the prior work on injury prevention has focused on trying to change the host – the child or the parent. Modern injury-control efforts have met with much greater success by concentrating on the agent or the environment.

For many years, study of the host factors has centered around attempts to pinpoint the "accident-prone" child; those innate characteristics of a child that result in greater frequency of injury. Most serious scientists involved with injury research have now discounted the theory of "accident proneness."[5,6] The concept of "accident proneness" is counterproductive in that it shifts attention away from potentially more modifiable factors, such as the product or the environment. Although factors such as young maternal age,[7] single parenting,[8] high household stress,[9] and low maternal education[10] are associated with increased risk of childhood injury, the final common pathway for all of these factors is most likely poverty. An analysis of child and adolescent deaths in Maine found that poor children were 2.6 times more likely to die from trauma than non-poor children.[11] Death from motor vehicle injuries was more than twice as common among poor children, who were also four times more likely to die from drowning and five times more likely to die from fire. Similar high risks for the poor have been found for residential fires[12,13] and pedestrian injuries.[14,15]

How can injury prevention efforts be best focused? First, one must be specific when either giving advice about injury prevention or setting up an intervention. For too long, pediatricians have been telling parents to "be careful," "supervise your child." This has done little good. Only when parents are given specific advice such as to buy and use a car seat, to get a bicycle helmet for the child, and not let young children cross streets alone, is the advice effective.

In general, injury-prevention strategies that are passive, i.e., work automatically, are more effective than those that require repeated behavior change on the part of the individual, so-called active measures. Air bags are more effective than seat belts because they work automatically, which in turn is more effective than telling people to drive more carefully.

## MOTOR VEHICLES

Any discussion of specific causes of traumatic deaths in children and adolescents must begin with motor vehicle crashes. Motor vehicle injuries are the leading cause of serious and fatal injuries for individuals of all ages. In order to understand accurately the characteristics of these injuries and the strategies for prevention, it is important to consider the main components of these crashes: motor vehicle occupants, including drivers and passengers; bicycle-motor vehicle collisions; and pedestrian-motor vehicle collisions.

### Passengers

Injuries to passenger vehicle occupants are the predominant cause of motor vehicle deaths among children and adolescents, with the exception of the 5-9 age group, in which pedestrian injuries make up the largest proportion of that total. The peak injury and death rates for both males and females of all ages are reached in the years 16-19.

In the past few years, much attention has been given to child occupants less than four years of age. Use of child-restraint devices in this age group can be expected to reduce fatalities by 71 percent and risk of serious injuries by 67 percent.[16] All 50 states and the District of Columbia have laws mandating their use. Overall, use in 1988 was up to 84 percent, an outstanding pediatric injury-control success story.

A number of approaches have been used in conjunction with legislation to increase use. Handouts given to parents by physicians, emphasizing the positive benefits of child seat-restraint use have been successful in improving parent acceptance. Additionally, careful studies have shown that toddlers who normally ride restrained behave better during car trips than children who ride unrestrained.

Unfortunately, child safety seat misuse is common. One recent study found a 65 percent misuse rate of child seats.[17] Common errors include seats facing in the wrong direction, safety belts improperly routed around the safety seat, and misuse of toddler seat harnesses and shields.

Children graduating from child seat restraints must still be restrained adequately. The problem of restraints in the older child is an important one. Many children in this age group are not adequately restrained and those who are, usually find themselves in back seats with lap belts only. Unfortunately, the increased use of these belts has been associated with a marked rise in seat belt-related injuries, especially Chance fractures of the lumbar spine and hollow viscus injuries of the abdomen.[18] Equipping rear seats with a lap-shoulder harness will not solve the problem entirely – most children in the 4-8 age group are too small to use the shoulder harness comfortably and safely. Redesign of these rear seat restraints is necessary.

## Teenage Drivers

Drivers ages 15-17 have 2.5 times the rate of collisions per 1000 registered drivers as motorists 18 years of age and older.[19] One past strategy to decrease the rate of crashes, and presumably injuries, was driver education. However, carefully done studies in Connecticut have failed to find differences in the crash experience of drivers who had driver education and otherwise similar drivers who have not.[20] In fact it has been found that the more driver education taught in schools, the higher the percentage of 16- and 17-year-old licensed drivers on the road. Because driver education is not associated with lower crash fatality rates among those who take it, and because it permits 16 and 17 year olds to drive, the net result is that the more driver education is provided, the higher are the fatality rates in the 16- and 17-year-old population.[21]

Research has also indicated possible injury reduction payoff from restricting 16 and 17 year olds to daytime driving. Almost half of the fatal crashes involving drivers under the age of 18 occur in the four hours before and the four hours after midnight.[19] In states imposing night-time driving curfews on teenagers under 18 years, there has been a significant decrease in crash involvement and fatalities.[22]

Finally, the problem of alcohol abuse and driving in teens is a major one with approximately half of all deaths from motor vehicle crashes in this age group involving alcohol. It is clear that impairment of driving occurs with blood alcohol concentrations as low as 0.05 grams/ml.[23] The combination of inexperience in driving and inexperience with alcohol may be a particularly dangerous one in teenagers.

## Bicycle Injuries

Bicycles are a ubiquitous part of growing up for most children. However, each year in the U.S., approximately 600 children and adolescents die from injuries incurred from riding bicycles. Bicycles are one of the most common reasons children with trauma visit emergency rooms, accounting for some 300,000 visits annually.[24] Several recent studies indicate that the majority of severe and fatal bicycle injuries involve head trauma.[25,26]

A logical step in the prevention of these head injuries is the use of helmets. A recent case-control study from Seattle indicates that bicycle helmets are very effective in the prevention of bicycle injuries – reducing the risk of head injury by 85 percent and brain injury by 87 percent.[27]

Health care professionals can be an effective source of advice to parent and child on the need for a bicycle helmet and should incorporate such advice into their anticipatory guidance schedules. Appropriate helmets are those with a firm polystyrene liner and should bear a label indicating that they are approved either by the Snell or ANSI testing organizations.

Promotion of helmets can and should be extended beyond the office. Community education programs spearheaded by a coalition of physicians, educators, bicycle clubs, and community service organizations have been successful in promoting the use of bicycle helmets.[28] In Seattle, such a coalition increased helmet use from 5 percent to 16 percent in the first three years[29] and to 25 percent by the fourth year.

## Pedestrian Injuries

One area that has been relatively neglected by the injury-prevention community is that of pedestrian injuries. Approximately 6600 people per year are killed as pedestrians and 100,000 are injured.[30] Children and the elderly are clearly the groups at the greatest risk, and in fact, for 5- to 9-year-old children, pedestrian injuries are the **single** most common cause of traumatic death.

Examination of the epidemiology of pedestrian injuries may suggest areas for intervention, as well as delineate areas where changes would have little impact on the problem.

Few children are injured at night; most of the injuries occur during the day, with peaks in the after-school period. Improved lighting or retrore-flective clothing would therefore not be expected to prevent injuries. Most of the injuries occur on arterials, indicating that speed bumps on residential streets are not the answer. Surprisingly, approximately 30 percent of pedestrian injuries occur while the individual is in a marked crosswalk. It appears that children in particular get a false sense of security when in a crosswalk, while few drivers routinely stop and look for children when approaching such crosswalks.

One important risk factor for childhood pedestrian injuries is simply the developmental level of the child. Careful studies indicate that few children under the age of nine or ten have the developmental skills to negotiate traffic successfully 100 percent of the time.[31,32] Children have a poor ability to judge the distance and speed of traffic and are easily distracted by playmates or by other factors in the environment. Many parents, however, are not aware of this potential mismatch between the abilities of the young school-age child and the skills needed to negotiate traffic safely.

Prevention of pedestrian injuries is difficult, but should consist of a multi-factorial approach. Engineering changes in roadway designs are extremely important as passive prevention measures and include one-way street networks, proper placement of transit or school bus stops, sidewalks in urban and suburban areas, edge stripping in rural areas to delineate the edge of the road, and curb parking regulations.[33]

Legislation and police enforcement are important components of any campaign to reduce pedestrian injuries. Right-turn-on-red laws increase the hazard to pedestrians.

Education of children in pedestrian safety has long been a mainstay of many programs. However, rigorous evaluations of these programs have produced conflicting and confusing results.[30] In addition, the children in most need of protection – those in the 5-7 age group – are the least likely to benefit from this instruction.

## FIRE- AND BURN-RELATED INJURIES

Fire- and burn-related injuries and deaths are extremely important problems in the U.S.; about 6000 burn-injury deaths occur each year. A number of interventions for specific types of fire- and burn-related deaths have proved to be effective, whereas others have been shown to be relatively ineffective.

One of the first effective interventions involved flammable fabrics. Flame burns resulting from ignition of clothing were a common, serious burn injury in small children. At least one-third of those injuries involved infant sleepwear. The extent of these burns was on the average 30 percent of the body surface, requiring hospitalization for an average of 70 days. In 1967 the Federal Flammable Fabrics Act was passed, requiring children's sleepwear to be flame retardant. As a result of this and similar state legislation, clothing ignition burns now account for only a small fraction of burns in children.[34]

Reduction in injury rates from tap-water scalds is another example of hazard modification resulting in a substantial reduction. Scald burns account for 40 percent of the burn injuries in children requiring hospitalization, at least 25 percent of which involve tap water. A study in Seattle showed that 80 percent of residences surveyed had hot tap water temperatures greater than 130° F.[35] The risk of full-thickness burns increases geometrically at temperatures above 130° F. An effective preventive maneuver is simply to turn down the water heater temperature to 125° F. At this setting, dishwashers and washing machines will still operate effectively, but the risk of serious scald injury is greatly reduced.

Nearly 70 percent of all fire deaths in the United States occur in private dwellings. Of these deaths, 60 percent are caused by smoke asphyxiation and not flame burns. Smoke detectors provide an inexpensive but effective method of preventing the majority of these deaths. They are small, inexpensive, and easily installed by the homeowner. Studies have shown that by offering information on smoke detectors in their offices, health care providers can alter parental behavior and increase smoke detector use.[36]

Cigarettes are estimated to cause 45 percent of all fires and 22 to 56 percent of deaths from house fires.[37] Most cigarettes made in this country contain additives in both the paper and tobacco that allow them to burn for as long as 28 minutes, even if left unattended. Studies indicate that fire-safe or self-extinguishing cigarettes are feasible. If such cigarettes replaced present types, nearly 2000 deaths and more than 6000 burns would be prevented annually.[38]

## POISONING

Deaths by poisoning among children have decreased dramatically over the last two decades, particularly for children less than five years. In 1970, 226 poisoning deaths of children less than five occurred, compared to only 55 in 1985. Poisoning prevention is one of the success stories of pediatrics and represents the effectiveness of passive strategies – child-resistant packaging and dose limits per container. The Poison Packaging Prevention Act presently includes 16 categories of household products, including nearly all prescription drugs. This law has been remarkably effective in reducing poisoning deaths and hospitalizations.[39] However, compliance with the law by pharmacists is only 70 to 75 percent at present.[40] In addition, difficulty using child-resistant containers is an important cause of poisoning in young children today. A survey by the Centers for Disease Control found that 18.5 percent of households in which poisoning occurred to children less than five years old had replaced the child-resistant closure and 65 percent of the ones used did not work properly.[41] Nearly one-fifth of ingestions occur from drugs owned by grandparents, a group that has difficulty using traditional child-resistant containers. There is a need for better child-resistant closures that do not require manual dexterity or strength greater than the capabilities of older adults.

Other poisoning interventions such as "Mr. Yuk" stickers are far less effective. They do not deter young children from ingesting labeled medications and may in fact be attractive to children under three years.[42]

## DROWNING

In 1986, 2122 drownings, associated primarily with recreational activities, occurred to children and adolescents in the U.S. For children, drowning ranks second only to motor vehicle injury as a cause of traumatic death. Although no precise data exist on the number of water-related injuries, it is estimated that 140,000 occur annually from swimming activities alone.

The proportion of drowning deaths that are pool-related varies by region of the country. In Los Angeles, half of all drownings take place in residential pools. This rate is similar to that of other areas with pools, but much higher than in areas without a large number of pools.[43]

Clearly the most effective way to prevent childhood pool drownings is through fencing. To be most protective, these barriers should restrict entry to the pool from yard and residence, use self-closing and self-latching gates, be at least five feet high, and have no vertical openings more than four inches wide. Ordinances to require appropriate fencing have been demonstrated to be effective. Many people have advocated "water-babies" and other swimming instruction for young children. The efficacy of such techniques is untested. The potential exists for both parent and child to become less vigilant around water, possibly with tragic consequences.

Among adolescents and young adults, alcohol and drug use have been found to be involved in nearly one-half of all drowning deaths. The restriction of the sale and consumption of alcoholic beverages in boating, pool, harbor, marina, and beach areas may combat this dangerous combination of activities.

More restrictive licensing of boat owners should also be considered. Coast Guard data show that although only 7 percent of boats involved with mishaps lacked available personal flotation devices, they accounted for 29 percent of the boating fatalities.

## FIREARM INJURIES

Injuries to children and adolescents involving firearms occur in three different situations: non-intentional injury, suicide attempt, and assault. In each case, the injury induced may be fatal or may result in permanent sequelae.

Among children under the age of 18 years, firearms are the fifth-ranking cause of death from non-intentional trauma in the United States. Five hundred children die each year from non-intentional gunshot wounds. An additional 8000 children and adolescents are left with permanent sequelae, not including emotional and psychological problems.[44]

Non-intentional firearm injuries generally occur in a family dwelling; 85 percent of firearm deaths occur in the home. In gunshot fatalities in children under 16 years of age, poverty is more closely related to shooting deaths than race or population density. Urban whites have the lowest death rate, rural whites are intermediate, and urban black children have the highest fatality rate.

Suicide is now the third most common cause of death in teenage males and the fourth for females. During the period from the 1950s to 1982, the rates for children and adolescents have more than doubled.[45] As with homicides, firearms have played an important role in this increase and are now the most common means of suicide in males of all ages. The difference in the rate of suicide between males and females is related less to number of attempts than to method. Women die less often in suicide attempts because they use less lethal means, mainly drugs. The use of firearms in a suicidal act usually converts an attempt into a fatality.

Homicides are second only to motor vehicle crashes among causes of death in teenagers over the age of 15 years. In 1985, more than 2900 children and adolescents were homicide victims; nonwhite teenagers accounted for almost half the total, making homicides the most common cause of death among this group. At present almost 95 percent of homicides among males involve firearms, 75 percent of which are handguns.

In the U.S. today there are an estimated 210 to 220 million firearms. During the last two decades, over six million firearms were sold annually. Handguns account for only about 20 percent of the firearms in use today, yet they are involved in 90 percent of criminal and other firearm misuse.

A series of studies done in Seattle emphasize the risks to household members  from private ownership of firearms. For every firearm death committed in self-defense, there were 1.3 non-intentional firearm deaths,

4.6 firearm homicides, and 37 firearm suicides involving guns kept in the home.[46] Comparisons of Seattle to Vancouver, British Columbia, a very similar city 140 miles away, but in a country with restrictive gun control laws, indicate that homicides were 1.63-fold greater in Seattle than in Vancouver, a difference due entirely to a 4.8-fold greater rate of handgun homicides in Seattle.[47] Similarly, among 15-24 year olds, suicide rates were 1.38-fold greater in the Seattle area, again due to a tenfold greater rate of suicide by handgun.[48]

The data seem to indicate that, of all firearms, handguns pose the greatest risk to the health of children and adolescents. Regulations and elimination of handguns, rather than all firearms, would appear to be the most appropriate focus of efforts to reduce shooting injuries in children and adolescents.

One approach that has been tried in the past is information and education campaigns in firearm safety. No data exist to support the effectiveness of such programs in decreasing the number of gunshot wounds in children. Regardless of the merits of safety education, firearms around the home pose a risk to children and adolescents, who have not yet developed adequate judgment for the safe handling of these weapons. Elimination of these weapons from the environment of children and adolescents is the necessary key to reduction in firearm fatalities and injuries. Furthermore, safety education will have no effect on the use of firearms in homicides and suicides. Most homicides are between relatives or acquaintances and are acts of rage. Elimination of handguns would certainly not eliminate arguments, but it would decrease the likelihood of a fatal conclusion; in an assault, the chance of a death is five times greater with a firearm than with a knife. As recently stated in a New England Journal of Medicine editorial: "Injury from firearms is a public health problem whose toll is unacceptable. The time has come for us to address this problem in the manner in which we have addressed and dealt successfully with other threats to the public health."[49]

## CONCLUSION

The magnitude of the injury problem need not lead to paralysis of action. The involvement of the health care community as described above can represent realistic goals for the medical community. The directions for educational and legislative action are clear, as well as the areas requiring further research and injury countermeasure development. As the prime health problem among children today, injuries can no longer be ignored or dealt with ineffectively.

# REFERENCES

1. National Academy of Sciences: Accidental Death and Disability: The Neglected Disease of Modern Society, Washington, DC, National Academy Press, 1966

2. National Academy of Sciences: Injury in America: A Continuing Public Health Problem, Washington, DC, National Academy Press, 1985

3. Rivara FP, Calonge N, Thompson RS: Population-based study of unintentional injury incidence and impact during childhood. Am J Public Health 79:990-94, 1989

4. Rice DP, MacKenzie EJ and Associates: Cost of Injury in the United States: A Report to Congress. San Francisco, CA: Institute for Health and Aging, University of California and Injury Prevention Center, The Johns Hopkins University, 1989

5. Langley J: The "accident prone" child - the perpetuation of a myth. Australian Paediatrics 18:243-46, 1982

6. Sass R, Cook G: Accident proneness: Science or nonscience. Int J of Health Serv 11:175-90, 1981

7. Taylor B, Wadsworth J, Butler NE: Teenage mothering, admission to the hospital, and accidents during the first five years. Archives Dis Child 58:6-11, 1983

8. McCormick MC, Shapiro S, Starfield BH: Injury and its correlates among 1-year-old children. Am J Dis Child 135:159-63, 1981

9. Daniels JH, Hampton RL, Newberger EH: Child abuse and accidents in black families. Am J Orthopsychiatry 48:595-603, 1983

10. Beautris AL, Fergusson DM, Shannon DT: Childhood accidents in a New Zealand birth cohort. Australian Paediatrics 18:238-42, 1982

11. Nersesian WS, Petit MR, Shaper R, et al: Childhood death and poverty: A study of all childhood deaths in Maine, 1976 to 1980. Pediatric 75:41-50, 1985

12. Federal Emergency Management Agency: Fire in the U.S. Washington, DC, 1982

13. Mierley MC, Baker SP: Fatal house fires in an urban population. JAMA 249: 1466-68, 1983

14. Rivara FP, Barber M: Sociodemographic determinants of childhood pedestrian injuries. Pediatrics 76:375-81, 1985

15. Pless IB, Verreault R, Arsenault L et al: The epidemiology of road accidents in childhood. Am J Public Health 77:358-60, 1987

16. Kahane CJ: An evaluation of child passenger safety. The effectiveness and benefits of safety seats (summary). Washington, DC, National Highway Traffic Safety Administration, 1986; DOT Publication No. (DOT HS) 806-889

17. Ziegler PN: Child safety seat misuse. Washington, DC, National Highway Traffic Safety Administration. Research Note, 1985

18. Reid AB, Letts RM: Pediatric Chance fractures and intra-abdominal injuries. J Trauma (abst); 29:1303, 1989

19. Robertson LS: Patterns of teenaged driver involvement in fatal MV crashes: Implications for policy choice. J Health Politics, Policy, Law 6:303-14, 1981

20. Robertson LS, Zador PL: Driver education and fatal crash involvement of teenaged drivers. Am J Public Health 68:959-65, 1987

21. Robertson LS: Crash involvement of teenaged drivers when driver education is eliminated from high schools. Am J Public Health 70:599-603, 1980

22. Preusser DF, Williams AF, Zador PL et al: The effect of curfew laws on motor vehicle crashes. Law Policy 6:115-28, 1984

23. AMA Council on Scientific Affairs: Alcohol and the Driver. JAMA 255:522-27, 1986

24. Bicycle-related injuries: Data from the National Electronic Injury Surveillance System. MMWR 36:269-71, 1987

25. Fife D, Davis J, Tate L et al: Fatal injuries to bicyclists: The experience of Dade County, Florida. J Trauma 23:745-55, 1983

26. Guichon DMP, Myles ST: Bicycle injuries: One-year sample in Calgary. J Trauma 15:504-506, 1975

27. Thompson RS, Rivara FP, Thompson DC: A case-control study of the effectiveness of bicycle safety helmets. N Engl J Med 320:1361-67, 1989

28. Bergman AB, Rivara FP, Richards DD et al: Anatomy of a children's bicycle helmet campaign. Am J Dis Child 144:727-31, 1990

29. Diguiseppi CG, Rivara FP, Koepsell TD et al: Bicycle helmet use by children: Evaluation of a community-wide helmet campaign. JAMA 262:2256-61, 1989

30. Rivara FP: Child pedestrian injuries in the United States: Current status of the problem, potential interventions, and future research needs. Am J Dis Child 144:692-96, 1990

31. Young DS, Lee DN: Training children in road crossing skills using a roadside simulation. Accid Anal Prev 19:327-41, 1987

32. Rothengatter T: A behavioral approach to improving traffic behavior of young children. Ergonomics 27:147-60, 1984

33. Zeeger CV: Feasibility of roadway countermeasures for pedestrian accident experience. Warrendale, PA, Society of Automotive Engineers 104-14, 1984

34. McLoughlin E, Clarke N, Stahl K et al: One pediatric burn unit's experience with sleepwear-related injuries. Pediatrics 60:405-409, 1977

35. Feldman KW, Schaller RT, Feldman JA et al: Tapwater scald burns in children. Pediatrics 62:1-7, 1978

36. Reisinger KS, Blatter MM, Wacher F: Pediatric counseling and subsequent use of smoke detectors. Am J Public Health 72; 392-93, 1982

37. Mierley MC, Baker SP: Fatal house fires in an urban population. JAMA 249:1466-68, 1989

38. Maguire A: There's death on the block, there's hope in Congress. J Public Health Policy 8:451-54, 1987

39. Walton W: An evaluation of the Poisoning Packaging Prevention Act. Pediatrics 69:363-70, 1982

40. Dole EJ, Czajka PA, Rivara FP: Evaluation of pharmacists' compliance with the Poison Packaging Prevention Act. Am J Public Health 76:1335-36, 1986

41. CDC: Unintentional ingestions of prescription drugs in children <5. MMWR 36 (9):125-32, 1987

42. Fergusson DM, Horwood LJ, Beautris AL et al: A controlled field trial of a poisoning prevention method. Pediatrics 69:515-20, 1982

43. O'Carroll P, Alkon E, Weiss B: Drowning mortality in Los Angeles county. JAMA 100:380-83, 1988

44. Jagger J, Dietz P: Deaths and injuries by firearms. Who cares? JAMA 255:314, 1986

45. Boyd JH, Mosciki EK: Firearms and youth suicide. Am J Public Health 76:1240-42, 1986

46. Kellermann AL, Reay DT: Protection or peril? An analysis of firearm related deaths in the home. N Engl J Med 314:1557-60, 1986

47. Sloan JH, Kellermann AL, Reay DT et al: Handgun regulations, crime, assaults and homicide. A tale of two cities. N Engl J Med 319:1256-62, 1988

48. Sloan JH, Rivara FP, Reay DT et al: Firearm regulations and rates of suicide: A comparison of two metropolitan areas. N Engl J Med 322:369-73, 1990

49. Mercy J, Houk V: Firearm injuries: A call for science. N Engl J Med 319:1283-84, 1988

# Suicide

Patrick W. O'Carroll, MD, MPH,
Linda E. Saltzman, PhD, and Jack C. Smith, MS

Suicide is not a new problem, but its prevention among the young has become increasingly urgent. From 1950 to 1980,[1] suicide rates among persons 35 years of age and older generally declined, but during the same period the suicide rate tripled in persons 15 to 24 years of age.[2] Suicide rates are much higher among 15 to 24 year olds than among younger persons, but marked increases in the rate of suicide have also been reported for those 10 to 14 years of age. In this age category, from 1960 to 1987, the suicide rate doubled for males and tripled for females.[3,4] We do not know what factors are responsible for these trends.

In this chapter, we describe the extent and nature of suicide among young children, adolescents, and young adults of college age (20-24 years). We also review pertinent risk factors for suicide in this population and discuss present obstacles to suicide prevention, as well as the implications for school health professionals.

## THE EXTENT OF THE PROBLEM

Health officials generally agree that a child less than 5 years of age cannot commit suicide, although the age at which a child understands the finality of death and the implications of suicide certainly varies from child to child.[5,6] In any case, the suicide rate is very low during early childhood and does not really increase significantly until after age 10. After the first decade of life, age-specific suicide rates climb dramatically, increasing a hundredfold during the teenage years (Table 1, next page). For the period 1981 to 1987, the average annual suicide rate for 19 year olds was 12.7 per

100,000,[a] which was higher than the total suicide rate for all ages in 1984 (12.4). The suicide rate among persons age 20 to 24 years is approximately twice the rate among persons 15-19 years of age.[7]

After age 8, suicide rates among males are greater than rates among females at every age, a pattern that continues throughout life but which is especially strong during adolescence and young adulthood (Figure 1, next page). During the teenage years, suicide rates among males are from three to five times greater than suicide rates among females; among persons 20 to 24 years of age, rates among males are approximately five times greater than suicide rates among females. A racial pattern also emerges during the teenage years and also persists throughout life: Suicide rates for whites are

Table 1
Average Annual Suicide Rates* for Persons 5-24 Years of Age by Sex and
Single Year of Age, United States, 1981-87

| Age | Male | Female | Both |
|-----|------|--------|------|
| 5 | 0.0 | 0.0 | 0.0 |
| 6 | 0.0 | 0.0 | 0.0 |
| 7 | 0.0 | 0.0 | 0.0 |
| 8 | 0.1 | 0.0 | 0.0 |
| 9 | 0.1 | 0.0 | 0.1 |
| 10 | 0.3 | 0.0 | 0.1 |
| 11 | 0.7 | 0.1 | 0.4 |
| 12 | 1.3 | 0.3 | 0.8 |
| 13 | 2.4 | 0.8 | 1.6 |
| 14 | 4.3 | 1.7 | 3.0 |
| 15 | 6.9 | 2.6 | 4.8 |
| 16 | 11.8 | 3.5 | 7.7 |
| 17 | 15.7 | 3.9 | 9.9 |
| 18 | 20.0 | 3.9 | 12.0 |
| 19 | 20.9 | 4.4 | 12.7 |
| 20 | 22.5 | 4.1 | 13.4 |
| 21 | 25.8 | 4.6 | 15.2 |
| 22 | 25.7 | 5.3 | 15.6 |
| 23 | 26.2 | 5.1 | 15.6 |
| 24 | 26.8 | 5.8 | 16.3 |

Source: National Center for Health Statistics detailed mortality tapes, and
U.S. Bureau of the Census Current Population Reports
*Rates per 100,000 population

[a] Average annual rates for single years of age are calculated as follows: 1) the number of deaths for persons of a given age during the 7-year period 1981 to 1987 were summed; 2) this sum was divided by 7 to get the average annual number of deaths for that age; and then 3) this average was divided by the population of that age in 1984, the middle year of the 7-year period. This procedure lends stability to rates for single years of age.

consistently 1.5 to 2 times greater than suicide rates for blacks. Rates for non-black minorities are generally quite similar to rates for blacks.

The methods by which suicide is committed vary by age during the teenage and young adult years. Among 10 to 12 year olds, more than half (54.2 percent) of the victims commit suicide by hanging. With advancing age, however, firearms increasingly become the preferred method of suicide. The proportion of suicides committed with firearms increases from 31 percent among children age 10 and younger to 61 percent by age 24. This pattern is somewhat more pronounced for males than for females.

## TRENDS

As noted previously, in the 25-year period 1960 to 1985 suicide rates among teenagers and young adults increased markedly (Table 2, next page). The suicide rate more than doubled among males 10 to 14 years of age and among both males and females 15 to 19 years of age. Among

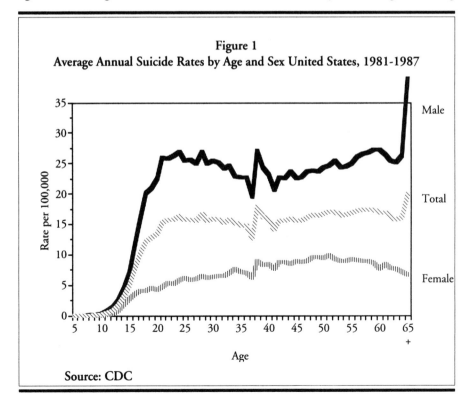

**Figure 1**
**Average Annual Suicide Rates by Age and Sex United States, 1981-1987**

Source: CDC

**Table 2**
**Suicide Rates\* for Persons 5-24 Years of Age, by Age Group and Sex for Various Years, United States, 1960-1985**

| Both sexes Age Group | 1960 | 1965 | 1970 | 1975 | 1980 | 1985 |
|---|---|---|---|---|---|---|
| 5-9 | 0.0 | 0.0 | 0.0 | – | 0.0 | 0.0 |
| 10-14 | 0.5 | 0.5 | 0.6 | 0.8 | 0.8 | 1.6 |
| 15-19 | 3.6 | 4.0 | 5.9 | 7.6 | 8.5 | 10.0 |
| 20-24 | 7.1 | 8.9 | 12.2 | 16.5 | 16.1 | 15.6 |
| **Males** Age Group | 1960 | 1965 | 1970 | 1975 | 1980 | 1985 |
| 5-9 | 0.0 | – | 0.0 | – | 0.0 | 0.0 |
| 10-14 | 0.9 | 0.9 | 0.9 | 1.2 | 1.2 | 2.3 |
| 15-19 | 5.6 | 6.1 | 8.8 | 12.2 | 13.8 | 16.0 |
| 20-24 | 11.5 | 13.8 | 19.3 | 26.4 | 26.8 | 26.2 |
| **Females** Age Group | 1960 | 1965 | 1970 | 1975 | 1980 | 1985 |
| 5-9 | 0.0 | 0.0 | – | – | – | – |
| 10-14 | 0.2 | 0.2 | 0.3 | 0.4 | 0.3 | 0.9 |
| 15-19 | 1.6 | 1.9 | 2.9 | 2.9 | 3.0 | 3.7 |
| 20-24 | 2.9 | 4.3 | 5.7 | 6.8 | 5.5 | 4.9 |

Source: Vital Statistics of the United States, Vol II – Mortality (various years)
\*Rates per 100,000

females 10 to 14 years of age, the suicide rate increased fourfold. Between 1960 and 1985, among 20- to 24-year-old males, the suicide rate more than doubled, and the rate for females increased 1.5 times. In contrast to the rates among persons 15 to 19 years of age, between 1975 and 1985 suicide rates among persons 20 to 24 years of age decreased slightly among males, and remained essentially the same among females. The magnitude of the suicide rates among persons less than age 15 is quite low when compared with rates during later life. Nevertheless, the overall trend of increasing suicide rates among persons 10 to 24 years of age is consistent from one period to the next, and thus merits concern.

Trends in the methods of suicide have also been observed. Among persons 15 to 24 years of age, the proportion of suicides committed with firearms has steadily increased. In 1970, 47.2 percent of all suicides in this age group were committed with firearms. By 1980, this proportion had increased to 57.5 percent.[2] The same pattern was noted for both males and females, but the increasing proportion of firearm suicides was most evident for females. In 1970, only one-third (32.3 percent) of suicides among females aged 15 to 24 were committed with firearms, but by 1980, almost half (45.4 percent) of them were.

## Factors Playing a Role

People commonly say that a person committed suicide because he or she was mentally ill, or could not cope with stressful life events. There are many factors, however, that contribute to any given death from suicide. Certain psychiatric illnesses are, of course, both extremely important and well-recognized as risk factors for suicide. In particular, affective disorders have been clearly shown in both retrospective case-control studies and prospective cohort studies to markedly increase the risk of suicide.[8,9]

After clinical depression, alcoholism is the most commonly reported mental illness associated with suicide.[10-13] Certain personality disorders (in particular, borderline and antisocial personality disorders) have also been shown to be correlated with suicidal behavior.[14] There is an increasing body of literature addressing putative genetic and biological risk factors for suicide. Meta-analyses of twin studies strongly suggest a genetically based risk for mental illness and suicide. Several Danish-American adoption studies suggest that this genetic risk may be inherited independently of major psychiatric illness, perhaps as an inability to control impulsive behavior.[15]

Certain neurotransmitter metabolites have been convincingly associated with an increased risk of suicide.[16] In particular, a clear relationship has been demonstrated between low concentrations of the serotonin metabolite 5-hydroxyindoleacetic acid (5-HIAA) in cerebrospinal fluid (CSF) and an increased incidence of attempted and completed suicide among psychiatric patients. The mechanism that accounts for the relationship between a disturbed or inadequate serotonin system and suicidal behavior is not clear.

Recent suicide clusters among teenagers and young adults have suggested that suicides may sometimes be caused by "contagion," that is, by exposure to the suicide or the suicidal behavior of others.[17,18] There is ample anecdotal evidence to suggest that, in any given suicide cluster, suicides occurring later in the cluster often appear to have been influenced by suicides occurring earlier in the cluster.[19,20] Despite uncertainty about contagion as a risk factor for suicide, many believe that it is prudent to recognize the possibility of a contagious effect of suicide and to institute measures to minimize potential contagion in the context of an apparent suicide cluster.[21]

There are a variety of situational risk factors for suicide. Stressful life events, such as the death of a loved one or the recent loss of employment, often appear to be clear precipitants of suicide[22] and may elevate the background risk of suicide by a factor of 5 to 10.[23] The loss or disruption of normal social support mechanisms also increases the risk of suicide. Divorce, unemployment, and migration from one community to another are but three examples of factors that may lead to some disruption of social support networks; all three have been shown to be related to increased suicide rates.[8,24] Absent or inadequate social support networks presumably increase the risk of suicide through interaction with other suicide risk factors, such as clinical depression and recent stressful life events.

A recent investigation addressed two of the above risk factors – mobility and contagion – in a freshman college student population.[25] Students who reported having attempted suicide within the past 12 months were significantly more likely to have been exposed to past suicidal behavior among relatives and friends than students who had not attempted suicide. Moving from one city to another in the 12 months before the survey was strongly associated with the risk of attempted suicide; this association was stronger as the number of moves increased. Although limitations in the study design preclude a definitive interpretation of these findings, results of this study suggest that recent mobility and exposure to the suicidal behavior of others may at least serve as markers for an increased risk of suicidal behavior among college students.

Another situational risk factor of potentially great importance is the ready accessibility of firearms. Unlike drug ingestions, carbon monoxide poisoning, and many other methods of suicide, a suicide attempt with a firearm is often immediately lethal, leaving little or no opportunity for rescue after the attempt. The accessibility of a firearm may both limit the pre-attempt opportunity for intervention by others and facilitate impulsive suicidal acts.[26,27] Theoretically, at least some proportion of impulsive decisions to commit suicide might never be acted on if substantial efforts were needed to arrange for a method of suicide. The factors that determine the choice of suicide method are complex, however, and careful research is needed to determine whether accessibility to firearms increases the risk of suicide.

Finally, several risk factors for suicide are useful for delineating high-risk groups, although these factors do not appear to be "causal" in the traditional sense. Being male, for example, or being elderly, identifies one as belonging to a high-risk group. Having a past history of attempted suicide has also been clearly shown to increase the risk of future completed suicide.[8] These markers for increased suicide risk presumably correlate with other, causal risk factors for suicide. A past history of attempted suicide, for example, may correlate with impulsivity or with a vulnerability to affective illness.

## PAST APPROACHES TO PREVENTION

For many years, the typical suicide victim was an older, depressed white male. It was reasoned, therefore, that doing a better job of diagnosing and treating depression was the most appropriate way to prevent suicide. This may well have been true and, although suicide rates among older males have increased in recent years, the generally decreasing rates of suicide among older people during the 1960s and 1970s may be due in part to this approach. Unfortunately, this strategy does not seem to be as appropriate for preventing suicide among the young. Depression, as clinically defined by psychiatrists, remains an important risk factor for suicide in this age group. Suicides attributable to clinical depression, however, seem to account for a much lower proportion of suicide among the young than among people in older age groups. New approaches to identifying adolescents at high risk of suicide are urgently needed, and a great deal of research is under way in an effort to identify and evaluate the importance of a number of putative risk factors.

Other approaches to suicide prevention are based on the notion that many suicides could be prevented if suicidal individuals just had someone with whom to talk. Suicide crisis centers and suicide hotlines represent two logical manifestations of this reasoning. Despite the intuitive appeal of these approaches, however, there is very little scientific evidence demonstrating their effectiveness. It may be that hotlines and crisis centers are used primarily by those who would have attempted – but not completed – suicide, whereas those intent on committing suicide eschew these potential avenues of aid. Evaluating crisis centers, hotlines, and other interventions is another urgent priority for suicide prevention research.

## OBSTACLES TO PREVENTION

One of the most fundamental theoretical obstacles to suicide prevention is the validity, or lack thereof, of the data used to calculate the magnitude and trends of suicide rates. It is widely recognized that many suicide deaths are misclassified by coroners and medical examiners, usually as deaths due to unintentional injuries ("accidents").[28,29] It is not clear, however, what proportion of all suicide deaths are so misclassified. It is generally believed that the magnitude of misclassification is not such that it threatens the validity of conclusions drawn from general analyses of existing suicide data.[30,31] Nevertheless, various social, religious, financial, and political factors may make coroners and medical examiners reluctant to arrive at a determination of suicide in equivocal cases. These factors may be especially influential in cases of suicide among children, adolescents, and young adults. In response to these concerns, a group of individuals from an array of professional organizations related to death certification has developed operational criteria for the determination of suicide.[32] It is hoped that the use of these criteria during the investigation of an equivocal death will increase the validity of suicide mortality data.

Another difficulty in preventing suicide among the young is that, except for certain psychiatric disorders, our knowledge of risk factors for suicide in this group is limited. Many potential risk factors have been suggested, including mobility, coming from a broken family, suicide contagion, and substance abuse.[33] Unfortunately, few of these potential risk factors have been confirmed through studies in which suicide cases have been carefully compared with a control population. If we are to identify risk factors that distinguish young people at high risk of suicide from all other people, these comparisons must be rigorously performed. In other words, it is of little use in focusing suicide prevention resources to say that most teenaged suicide victims have had problems in school, with their parents, or with their girlfriend/boyfriend. Such a description might fit most teenagers and college students.

It is well documented, however, that people who have attempted suicide once are more likely than others both to attempt suicide again and to complete suicide.[34,35] This risk factor – a history of a past suicide attempt – might be very useful in bringing those at high risk of suicide in touch with existing suicide prevention resources. For example, in the context of an apparent suicide cluster, students who are known to have attempted suicide in the past might be given a screening interview by a school counselor to determine whether they were dangerously affected by the recent suicides. These students might be referred for special counseling as appropriate, or advised of helping resources available in the community (hotlines, crisis centers, etc.). At present, school counselors and health professionals are doing very little to systematically identify those students who have attempted suicide, although such information might be invaluable in the early stages of responding to an apparent cluster of youth suicides.

Focusing resources on suicide attempters raises an issue that has yet to be resolved: the relationship between suicide attempters and suicide completers. Apparently, these two groups are composed of different, but overlapping, populations. In other words, not all suicide attempters go on to complete suicide, but many suicide victims have had previous suicide attempts. From a prevention standpoint, however, this is a moot point. Attempted suicide is a morbid health event that should be prevented in its own right. Moreover, attempted suicide may be an indicator of other problems that need to be addressed, such as alcoholism, depression, or victimization from physical abuse.

The most formidable obstacle to suicide prevention may well be the prevailing assumption among many health professionals that either nothing can be done to prevent suicide (except perhaps among those now suicidal) or that only mental health professionals can prevent suicides. There is no reason to accept either assumption. Mortality from infant diarrhea, for example, has been reduced in many places largely by providing clean water and educating mothers about the proper techniques for countering dehydration in their children. Suicide may not yield as readily to such social and environmental interventions, but it would be uncharacteristically fatalistic for health professionals to assume from the outset that no such interventions can be devised to prevent suicide.

## THE ROLE OF SCHOOL HEALTH PROFESSIOANLS IN PREVENTING SUICIDE

The causes of suicide are clearly multifaceted, and this public health problem is not likely to be solved by any single approach or any single discipline. But this has been true of many causes of childhood mortality and morbidity. The previous review of the epidemiology of suicide among the young suggests numerous potential avenues for intervention; some have already been alluded to. For example, the predominance of firearms as a method of suicide suggests some possible intervention strategies. The ready availability of lethal weapons, such as handguns, may be the final ingredient that turns an impulsive decision to harm oneself into an irrevocable tragedy. Indeed, recent evidence suggests that the availability of firearms may increase the risk of suicide among people 15 to 24 years of age, although this effect was not noted in older age groups.[27] There are clearly contentious political as well as public health dimensions to any consideration of limiting access to firearms. Nevertheless, this fact should not prevent us from exploring the hypothesis that the ready availability of lethal weapons increases the risk of suicide among adolescents and young adults. Careful scientific research on this matter is urgently needed.[36]

But what role, in particular, can school and college health professionals play in preventing suicide? Obviously, one important role would be in identifying and properly treating and referring those who are currently suicidal. School health professionals might also explore attitudes and beliefs regarding suicide with adolescents and their parents. Many may not know or believe that occasional thoughts of or impulses toward suicide are normal – and transient. Such assurances, when appropriate, may increase the chances of communication should suicidal feelings arise. Finally, we should take advantage of simple environmental modifications that may decrease the likelihood of suicide. For example, parents of disturbed or depressed adolescents should be made aware that firearms and potentially lethal doses of medications should not be readily available to their children.

Clearly, none of these measures will prevent all suicides. We are still a long way from being able to prescribe proven preventive interventions. Nevertheless, health professionals cannot and should not ignore this important cause of injury and death among the population whose health they are dedicated to safeguarding and improving. In the absence of definitive answers, we should do whatever seems reasonable and appropriate to prevent these tragic deaths. In the meantime, let us acknowledge that progress has been made in recognizing suicide as a public health problem. Including a chapter on suicide in this textbook is evidence of that progress.

## REFERENCES

1. Centers for Disease Control: Suicide Surveillance, 1970-1980. Atlanta, CDC, 1985

2. Centers for Disease Control: Youth Suicide in the United States, 1970-1980. Atlanta, CDC, 1986

3. U.S. Department of Health, Education, and Welfare, Public Health Service: Vital Statistics of the United States, 1960. Vol. II - Mortality, Part A. Washington, DC, U.S. Government Printing Office, 1963

4. National Center for Health Statistics: Unpublished final data. Hyattsville, MD, DHHS, Public Health Service, NCHS

5. Paulson MJ, Stone D, Sposto R: Suicidal potential and behavior in children ages 4 to 12. Suicide Life Threat Beh 8:225-69, 1978

6. Rosenthal PA, Rosenthal S: Suicide among preschoolers: Fact or fallacy. Children Today 12:22-24, 1983

7. Saltzman LE, Levenson A, Smith JC. Suicides among persons 15-24 years of age, 1970-1984. CDC Surveillance Summaries, February 1988. MMWR 37(No. SS-1):61-68, 1988

8. Monk M: Epidemiology of suicide. Epidemiol Rev 9:51-69, 1987

9. Hagnell O, Lanke J, Rorsman B: Suicide rates in the Lundby study: Mental illness as a risk factor for suicide. Neuropsychobiology 7:248-53, 1981

10. Murphy GE:  Problems in studying suicide. Psychiatr Dev 1(4):339-50, 1983

11. Miles CP: Conditions predisposing to suicide: A review. J Nerv Ment Dis 164(4):231-46, 1977

12. Roy A, Linnoila M: Alcoholism and suicide. Suicide Life Threat Beh 16(2):244-73, 1986

13. Kendall RE: Alcohol and suicide. Subst Alcohol Actions Misuse 4(23):121-27, 1983

14. Frances A, Blumenthal S: Personality as a predictor of youthful suicide, Risk factors for youth suicide. Report of the Secretary's Task Force on Youth Suicide. Volume 2. Alcohol, Drug Abuse, and Mental Health Administration. DHHS Pub. No. (ADM)89-1624. Washington, DC, U.S. Government Printing Office, 160-71, 1989

15. Roy A: Genetics and suicidal behavior. Risk factors for youth suicide. Report of the Secretary's Task Force on Youth Suicide. Volume 2. Alcohol, Drug Abuse, and Mental Health Administration. DHHS Pub. No. (ADM)89-1624. Washington, DC, U.S. Government Printing Office, 247-62, 1989

16. Asberg M: Neurotransmitter monoamine metabolites in the cerebrospinal fluid as risk factors for suicidal behavior. Risk factors for youth suicide. Report of the Secretary's Task Force on Youth Suicide. Volume 2. Alcohol, Drug Abuse and Mental Health Administration. DHHS Pub. No. (ADM)89-1624. Washington, DC, U.S. Government Printing Office, 193-212, 1989

17. Robbins D, Conroy C: A cluster of adolescent suicide attempts: Is suicide contagious? J Adolesc Health Care 3:253-55, 1983

18. Davidson L, Gould MS: Contagion as a risk factor for youth suicide. Risk factors for youth suicide. Report of the Secretary's Task Force on Youth Suicide. Volume 2. Alcohol, Drug Abuse and Mental Health Administration. DHHS Pub. No. (ADM)89-1624. Washington, DC, U.S. Government Printing Office, 88-109, 1989

19. Centers for Disease Control: Cluster of suicides and suicide attempts—New Jersey. MMWR 37:213-16, 1988

20. O'Carroll PW: An investigation of a cluster of suicide attempts, Combined Proceedings of the Twentieth Annual Meeting of the American Association of Suicidology and the Nineteenth Annual Congress of the International Association of Suicide Prevention. Edited by RI Yufit. San Francisco, American Association of Suicidology, 262-64, 1987

21. O'Carroll PW, Mercy JA, Steward JA: CDC recommendations for a community plan for the prevention and containment of suicide clusters. MMWR 37(suppl. no. S-6):1-12, 1988

22. See, for example, Paykel ES, Prusoff BA, Myers JK: Suicide attempts and recent life events: A controlled comparison. Arch Gen Psychiatry 32:327-37, 1975

23. Paykel ES: Stress and life events, Risk factors for youth suicide. Report of the Secretary's Task Force on Youth Suicide. Volume 2. Alcohol, Drug Abuse and Mental Health Administration. DHHS Pub. No. (ADM)89-1624. Washington, DC, U.S. Government Printing Office, 110-30, 1989

24. Platt S: Unemployment and suicidal behavior: A review of the literature. Soc Sci Med 19:93-115, 1984

25. Meehan PJ, Lamb JA, Saltzman LE et al: Suicide Attempts Among Young Adults. Presented at the Epidemiologic Intelligence Service Conference, CDC, Atlanta, April 1990

26. Boyd JH: The increasing rate of suicide by firearms. N Engl J Med 308:872-74, 1983

27. Sloan JH, Rivara FP, Reay DT et al: Firearm regulations and community suicide rates: A comparison of two metropolitan areas. N Engl J Med 322:369-73, 1990

28. Sainsbury P: Validity and reliability of trends in suicide statistics. World Health Stat Q 36:339-48, 1983

29. Litman LE: Psychologic-psychiatric aspects in certifying modes of death. J Forensic Sci 13:46-54, 1968

30. Sainsbury P, Jenkins JS: The accuracy of officially reported suicide statistics for purposes of epidemiologic research. J Epidemiol Community Health 36:43-48, 1982

31. O'Carroll PW: A consideration of the validity and reliability of suicide mortality data. Suicide Life Threat Beh 19(1): 1-16, 1989

32. Rosenberg ML, Davidson LE, Smith JC et al: Operational criteria for the determination of suicide. J Forensic Sci 32(6):1445-55, 1988

33. U.S. DHHS: Report of the Secretary's Task Force on Youth Suicide. Volume 2. Risk factors for youth suicide. DHHS Pub. No. (ADM)89-1622. Washington, DC, Supt. of Docs., U.S. Government Printing Office, 1989

34. Motto JA: Suicide attempts: A longitudinal view. Arch Gen Psychiatry 13:516-20, 1965

35. Dahlgren KG: Attempted suicide—35 years afterward. Suicide Life Threat Beh 7:75-79, 1977

36. Mercy JA, Houk VN: Firearm injuries: A call for science. N Engl J Med 319(19):1283-85, 1988

# 9

# Homicide and
# Violence in Youth
DEBORAH PROTHROW-STITH, MD AND HOWARD R. SPIVAK, MD

Interpersonal violence and its most devastating outcome, homicide, are endemic in urban black areas with low socioeconomic indicators. The United States stands out among industrialized countries as having very high homicide rates. The rate of approximately 10 per 100,000 is five times that of Canada and twenty times that of the Netherlands.[1] Those who are most affected are young and male. Homicide is the leading cause of death for black men ages 15-24 years at a rate of 72.5 for every 100,000[2] and for black men ages 25-44 years at a rate of 125 for every 100,000.[3]

Non-fatal interpersonal violence occurs at rates that are at least a magnitude higher than homicide and likely represents an even greater overall cost to society. There are less adequate data on non-fatal interpersonal violence. Emergency room and school data are the best sources of rates for non-fatal interpersonal violence. However, these rates are underestimations because many episodes of interpersonal violence are neither treated in emergency rooms nor reported in schools. The Northeastern Ohio Trauma Study measured the incidence of cause-specific trauma by collecting emergency room data for the year 1977. The study reported an assault rate of 862 per 100,000 population.[4]

School-based data are equally compelling. During the 1969-70 school year, Seattle Public Schools had four assaultive injuries per 1,000 students.[5] In the U.S. generally there are approximately 75,000 assaultive injuries to teachers a year at a rate of 35 per 1,000.[6] A November 1983 publication from the Boston Commission for Safe Schools[7] reported a survey of four public high schools revealing that 50 percent of the teachers and 38 percent of the students reported being victims of a school-based crime during the year.

Weapon-carrying behavior was also reported in this Boston survey. Seventeen percent of the girls and 37 percent of the boys reported bringing a weapon to school at some time during the school year.

Urban blacks are over-represented among all the indicators of violence, emergency room use rates, arrest rates, school suspension rates, and homicide rates. Socioeconomic factors are thought to account for this. In a recent study of domestic homicide in Atlanta, data that were corrected for socioeconomic status, using the number of people per square foot of housing, no longer showed a racial bias.[8] Urban blacks are over-represented among the poor[9] and are over-represented among the victims of fatal and non-fatal violence.

The severity and urgency of the problem for young Americans dictates the use of appropriate and effective prevention strategies. The possibilities for such prevention strategies were greatly enhanced by the acceptance of interpersonal violence as a public health problem, markedly demonstrated in the words of ex-Surgeon General Koop: "Violence is as much a public health issue for me and my successors in this country as smallpox, tuberculosis, and syphilis were for my predecessors in the last two centuries."[10]

Traditionally, violence was understood as only a law enforcement problem. This is an understanding that limits the professional expertise, the variety of institutions involved, and the emphasis on prevention. The criminal justice approach is not prevention. It is triggered by a violent episode and is expert at establishing blame, inflicting punishment, and more recently providing victim protection. It is not a vehicle for primary prevention. Public health strategies are those aimed at ascertaining risk factors and reducing those risk factors. It is prevention independent of specific violent episodes, but informed by the epidemiology of such episodes.

Such strategies include the application of a multi-institutional and interdisciplinary model to change knowledge, attitudes, and behavior. This model has been applied to other public health initiatives. The national campaign to reduce smoking is an example of such an initiative. The media, health care institutions, public schools, job sites, health fairs, and county fairs become the source of education, information, and incentives. Product labeling and advertisement restrictions are a part of the effort. This approach is applicable to interpersonal violence prevention as well when it is understood as a public health problem. We have raised children on a very glamorous portrayal of violence through television and movie heroes. These characters choose violence as a first response, they are always successful, they are always rewarded, and they are never hurt badly. In addition, adults often encourage children to fight. Parents do not want children to be wimps, so they do not routinely teach or encourage alternative behavior.

## THE ADOLESCENT

Designing violence-prevention strategies that are effective with adolescents requires an understanding of adolescence and a knowledge of issues of race and poverty.

Adolescence is the period of dynamic physical and psychosocial maturation that is the transition from childhood to adulthood. The physical changes are the growth and development of puberty. The psychosocial changes include both cognitive maturation from concrete to abstract thinking and the mastering of specific developmental tasks. The major developmental tasks are:

1.  individuation from family with the development of same-sex and opposite-sex relationships outside the family;
2.  adjustment to the physical changes of puberty with the development of a healthy sexual identity;
3.  development of a moral character and a personal value system; and
4.  preparation for future work and responsibility.

Failure to accomplish these tasks can result in significant dysfunction for adolescents, which can further impair them as adults. The tasks are accomplished simultaneously and are the major requisites for healthy adulthood. The experience of poverty and of racism can significantly hinder the accomplishment of these essential tasks. The development of a healthy self-identity requires a sense of self-esteem and a healthy racial identity, both of which can be undermined by poverty and racism. Preparing for future work and responsibility is a meaningless enterprise when unemployment rates are astonishingly high. Developing a sense of moral character and a functional personal value system is not easy when television and the street are the main sources of values.

## WHAT IS "NORMAL"?

One of the most difficult problems facing service providers for adolescents is that of defining normal behavior. Normal behavior for adolescents includes a variety of experimental behaviors that would be abnormal at other developmental stages. Defining normal is even more difficult in cases where there is a subcultural experience. Claude Brown in his literary work, *Manchild in the Promised Land,* describes such an experience:

> "Throughout my childhood in Harlem, nothing was more strongly impressed upon me than the fact that you had to fight and that you should fight. Everybody would accept it if a person was scared to fight, but not if he was so scared that he didn't fight."[11]

The example clearly illustrates the dilemma. How much fighting is too much? When is it problematic? Many would agree that violence in self-defense is appropriate; yet, if a homicide results, would running not have been a better response? On the other hand, in a violent world, is it not healthier to defend oneself rather than be beaten or harassed?

## NARCISSISM AND SEXUAL IDENTITY

There are several characteristics of adolescence that make a teenager more prone to violence. One such characteristic is narcissism. Narcissism helps the adolescent make the transition from family to the outside world. Yet, this narcissism is also responsible for the extreme self-conscious feelings of adolescents that make them extremely vulnerable to embarrassment. They feel that they are always in the limelight and on center stage. Adolescents are particularly sensitive to verbal attack, and it is nearly impossible for them to minimize or ignore embarrassing phenomena.

Peer pressure is the single most important determinant of adolescent behavior.[12] This vulnerability to peer pressure is a normal part of adolescence. It is a necessary product of the separation from family and the development of a self-identity. Yet it is a characteristic of adolescence that enhances the predisposition for violence. If fighting is the expectation of peers, as illustrated in Claude Brown's quote, then an adolescent is most unable to disregard those expectations.

Erikson[13] describes a moratorium from social responsibility that is necessary during adolescence to allow the requisite experimental behavior to occur without compromise of future options. Thus, the adolescent is able to experiment with a variety of roles without making a commitment. There is debate as to whether this moratorium occurs at all, yet many agree that in the situation of poverty, it does not. The adolescent in poverty struggles with developmental tasks without the protection of a social moratorium.

The black adolescent has to develop a healthy racial identity, in addition to the listed developmental tasks. Contact with racism results in anger that appears to contribute to the over-representation of black youth in interpersonal violence. Psychologist Lewis Ramey, Ph.D., used "free-floating anger" to describe anger not generated by a specific individual or event but from global factors such as racism and limited employment options.[14] This anger is the excess baggage that an individual brings to an encounter that lowers his threshold for directed anger and violence. This concept is helpful in that it attempts to account for the environmental and socioeconomic factors and not label the individual as deficient. The anger is normal and appropriate. Violence prevention is therefore designed to achieve a healthier response to anger, not to eliminate the anger itself.

Violence-prevention programs that are appropriate for adolescents developmentally and that have a realistic cultural context can be expected to be effective. Developmentally appropriate programs utilize peers in education and counseling and reflect an understanding of the stages of adolescent development. The cultural context has to acknowledge the violence, racism, and classism that many such adolescents experience.

The problem of interpersonal violence has been long appreciated by frontline health providers, school administrators, teachers, and counselors. And despite an incomplete understanding of the causal factors, prevention and intervention programs have been developed with moderate success. The majority of these prevention programs are either based in a school or linked to a school because of the captive audience. Most are interdisciplinary and multi-institutional.

## THE BOSTON EXPERIENCE

The Violence Prevention Project of the Health Promotion Program for Urban Youth[15] (Boston Department of Health and Hospitals) is an effort to reduce the incidence of violent behavior and associated social and medical hazards for adolescents. Through outreach and education this community-based primary prevention effort is endeavoring to change individual behavior and community attitudes about violence. A supportive network of secondary therapeutic services and a hospital-based secondary prevention service project directed toward patients with intentional injury supplement the primary prevention activities to provide a comprehensive program. The project is modeled after other prevention initiatives that have focused on individual behavior modification through risk communication and education. This community-based model has been used successfully in the prevention of heart disease and hypertension.[16,17]

## THE VIOLENCE PREVENTION CURRICULUM

The curriculum[18] is designed:

1. to provide statistical information on adolescent violence and homicide;
2. to present anger as a normal, potentially constructive emotion;
3. to create an awareness in the students of alternatives to fighting by discussing the potential gains and losses from fighting;
4. to have students analyze situations preceding a fight and practice avoiding fights by using role play and videotape; and
5. to create a classroom ethos that is non-violent and values violence-prevention behavior.

The prevention curriculum is aimed specifically at raising the individual's threshold for violence by creating a non-violent ethos within the classroom and by extending the student's repertoire of responses to anger. It acknowledges the existence of societal and institutional violence and the existence of institutional racism. Students are taught not to become passive agents, but to claim anger and become intentional and creative about their responses to it.

Anger is presented as a normal, essential, and potentially constructive emotion. Creative alternatives to fighting are stressed. The classroom discussion during one session focuses on good and bad results of fighting. The students list the results. The list of bad results is invariably longer than the good list; thus, the need for alternatives. This exercise emphasizes that fighting or not fighting is a choice and that the potential consequences are important to consider when making the choice.

In addition to providing education on handling anger, the schools (at all levels) are appropriate for mediation activities. These usually involve the use of peer mediators and teachers who are trained to recognize the signs of an escalating conflict and to interject mediation techniques. These programs have been implemented successfully at elementary (using 4th and 5th graders), high school, and college levels.

# HEALTH CARE PROVIDERS

Peer violence, family and domestic violence, and to some extent stranger violence, are promoted by society's glamorous portrayal of violence. Some are more at risk, particularly those who have been victims or witnesses of violence as children. This learned violent behavior can be changed, and public health, including health care providers, has a role to play.

Individual clinicians have many opportunities to incorporate violence prevention in their medical care. One such opportunity involves raising the issue of violence prevention as part of anticipatory guidance.[19] Because we know that violence is a learned behavior, parents can be enlisted to help to prevent violent behavior in their children. Parents have daily opportunities to teach their children how to handle anger, such as encouraging verbal rather than physical expression of angry feelings. With some guidance, parents can play an active, conscious role in teaching their children positive, nonviolent strategies in directing and resolving their anger. Pediatric health providers can facilitate this process. Issues, such as styles of discipline, regulating television viewing, and negotiating conflicts between siblings also can be addressed during pediatric encounters.

Beyond the level of primary prevention, clinicians have the opportunity to play an important role in the early identification of youth at high risk for violent behavior. The work that has been done around identifying characteristics of people who are victims or perpetrators of violence can be used to recognize potentially violent youth. Screening of children and youth for a history of family or peer violence, substance abuse, depression and low self-esteem, carrying of weapons, and history of central nervous system injury or pathology can lead to the identification of youth who may be able to be helped by referral to and earlier intervention from mental health and other related services.

This effort of primary care health providers must, of course, be linked to the increased development and availability of intervention services directed toward violent behavior. Merely identifying high-risk youth without appropriate referral resources would lead to considerable frustration on the part of clinicians. Educational, mental health, and support services for adolescents need to be enhanced, and intervention strategies addressing the underlying emotional and behavioral components of violent behavior must be developed.

Of equal importance is the need to modify the response of health care professionals to youth with intentional injuries. Health care institutions, particularly emergency departments, are the major site of contact with people with violence-related problems. Diagnostic and intervention services for such events as rape, child and sexual abuse, and suicide attempts are well established in the medical setting, and the extent of support services for children and families displaying these categories. These generally are managed from the perspective of treating the injury itself without investigating or responding to the circumstances of the injury or the underlying issues and behaviors that may have led to the injury. Suturing a superficial stab wound and sending a patient home will not reduce the risk for future injury. Such patients present a double risk in that some people who present as victims may be assailants in the future. Intentional-injury victims often explicitly express their intent to seek revenge.[20] In addition, there is evidence that victims were not necessarily passive in creating the violent encounter and may in fact have displayed provocative behaviors that led to the injury-related event.[21] Routine and adequate assessment of intentional-injury victims is of extreme importance. At the minimum, this assessment should include investigation of the following factors:

1.  circumstances of the injury event,
2.  victim's relationship to the assailant,
3.  use of drugs or alcohol,
4.  presence of underlying emotional or psychosocial risk factors (especially violence in the family),
5.  history of intentional injuries or violent behaviors,
6.  predisposing biological risk factors, and
7.  intent to seek revenge.

In many cases, this information can help to identify a need for referral to appropriate intervention and support services that may reduce the risk of further problems.

Increased awareness, understanding, and attention to violence by health care providers can contribute in a significant way to addressing this problem. "Violence" needs to be incorporated into the health care system agenda.

## REFERENCES

1. Wolfgang ME: Homicide in other industrialized countries. Bull NY Acad Med 62(5):400-12, 1986

2. Centers for Disease Control: Violent deaths among persons 15-24 years of age - United States, 1970-78. MMWR 32(35):453-57, 1983

3. Alcohol, Drug Abuse, and Mental Health Administration: Symposium on homicide among black males. Public Health Rep 95(6):549, 1980

4. Barancik JI: Northeastern Ohio trauma study: I. Magnitude of the problem. Am J Public Health 73(7):746-51, 1983

5. Johnson CJ et al: Student injuries due to aggressive behavior in the Seattle public schools during the school year 1969-70. Am J Public Health 64:904, 1974

6. Baker SP, Dietz PE: Injury Prevention—Interpersonal Violence. Healthy People: The Surgeon General's Report on Health Promotion and Death Prevention Background Papers: U.S. Department of Health Education and Welfare Publication No. 79-55071 A: 71-4, 1979

7. The Boston Commission on Safe Public Schools: Making Our Schools Safe for Learning. November, 1983, pp. 12-16

8. Centerwall B: Race, socioeconomic status and domestic homicide, Atlanta 1971-72. Am J Public Health 74:1813-15, 1984

9. Joint Center for Policy Studies: A fighting chance for black youth. Focus 13(9):4, 1985

10. Koop CE: Surgeon General's Workshop on Violence and Public Health Report. Leesburg VA, Oct 1985

11. Brown C: Manchild in the promised land. New York, Macmillan, 1965

12. Jessor R, Jessor SL: Problem Behavior and Psychosocial Development: A Longitudinal Study of Youth. New York, NY, Academic Press, 1977

13. Erikson E: Identity, Youth and Crisis. New York, NY, WW Norton, 1968

14. Akbar N: Homicide among black males: Causal factors. Public Health Rep 95(6):549, 1980

15. Prothrow-Stith D, Spivak H, Hausman AJ: The violence prevention project: A public health approach. Science, Technology, and Human Values 12(3&4):67-69, 1987

16. Farquhar J: The community-based model of life style interventions. Am J Epidemiol 108:103-11, 1978

17. Tuomilehto J, Nissinen A, Salonen J et al: Community programme for control of hypertension in North Karelia, Finland. Lancet ii:900-903, 1980

18. Prothrow-Stith D: Interdisciplinary interventions applicable to prevention of interpersonal violence and homicide in black youth. Surgeon General's Workshop on Violence and Public Health. U.S. DHHS, Publication No. HRS-D-MC 86-1:35-43, 1986

19. Stringham P, Weitzman M: Violence counseling in the routine health care of adolescents. J Adolesc Health Care, 1990

20. Dennis RE: Homicide among black males: Social costs to families and communities. Public Health Rep 95:556, 1980

21. Wolfgang ME: Patterns in Criminal Homicide. New York, John Wiley & Sons, 1958

# 10

# Abuse

RICHARD D. KRUGMAN, MD

## NATURE AND SIGNIFICANCE OF THE PROBLEM

While the physical and sexual abuse of children has been occurring for centuries,[1] it is only within the past three decades that significant public and professional concern has been paid to the problem, marked by many with the coining of the phrase "battered child syndrome" in 1962 by Kempe.[2] This landmark paper led to the rapid growth and development of the multidisciplinary field of child abuse and neglect, which now includes more than the recognition and care of battered children. Included in modern definitions of abuse are:

1. Physical abuse: The non-accidental injuring of a child or adolescent by a caretaker or (usually) older individual.

2. Sexual abuse: The engaging of a child in sexual activities the child does not understand, to which the child cannot give informed consent, which are developmentally inappropriate and/or which violate the laws or taboos of society.

Other forms of child maltreatment include emotional abuse and neglect,[3] physical neglect,[4] medical care neglect,[5] and Munchausen syndrome by proxy.[6] The reader is referred to cited reviews for information on these issues.

Physical and sexual abuse of children can occur in intrafamilial and extrafamilial settings. The widespread nature of the problem, and its significant sequelae should make the recognition, treatment, and above all, prevention, of all forms of abuse and neglect of children a national priority.

## EXTENT OF THE PROBLEM

By estimates, there were 302 hospitalized cases of battered children in 1962.[1] Between 1965 and 1968 states passed legislation requiring that professionals report suspected abuse and in 1974 with the passage of PL 93-247 and subsequent amendments, federal funds were tied to expanded definitions that included mental injury, neglect, and sexual abuse. By 1979, a reported 669,000 cases of abuse and neglect were received by county and state child protective services agencies.[7] By 1986 (the last year official data were collected) that figure had tripled to 2.1 million reports.[8] There have been substantial problems in the collection of accurate, reliable data on the incidence of abuse. Definitions vary, as do the criteria used in different states to substantiate reports. Inexplicably the federal government has historically contracted this task of measuring and monitoring incidence to non-governmental entities. The most recent studies, however, suggest that approximately 1.6 percent to 2.5 percent of children are abused and neglected annually in the U.S.[9] – a figure dramatically higher than most other health problems affecting school-age children. Approximately 40 percent of the over 2.1 million reports are substantiated on a national basis although wide variation exists from state to state. Approximately 25 percent of cases are physical abuse, 20 percent sexual abuse, and 55 percent are neglect.[9]

## FACTORS KNOWN TO PROMOTE THE PROBLEM

The physical and sexual abuse of children should be viewed in an ecological perspective.[10] There are individual,[11] social,[12] and cultural[13] factors that contribute to the problem. Although nearly all abusers of children were inadequately parented in their childhood and were often abused as they abuse children,[11] this does **not** mean that all abused children will grow up to be abusive adults. Most do not repeat the cycle, although their risk is higher than non-abused children.[14] Reduced socioeconomic status, family violence, unemployment, substance abuse, and adolescent parenting have been associated with physical abuse; substance abuse, family violence, concomitant physical abuse, pornography, and cult or satanic behavior have been associated with sexual abuse, but none of these are particularly helpful associations to the practitioner dealing with an individual case.

## RECOGNITION

The recognition of abuse as a problem is dependent on the willingness of the practitioner to entertain the possibility that the condition exists.[15] There is much societal and professional denial of the existence of child abuse, especially sexual abuse, which has been called a "hidden pediatric problem."[16]

Physical abuse may be recognized when one obtains a discrepant history – that is, the history of what the caretaker said happened to the child does not fit with medical findings.[17] The discrepancy may not be obvious to the practitioner without other information generally available only to those making a site visit, such as a child protective services (CPS) worker, public health nurse, or law enforcement officer. For example, we may believe the history that a child's bruises resulted from a fall down a flight of stairs, but if we know there is no flight of stairs at the house, we might suspect abuse. Kempe often said that no child ever died of a social work evaluation; many have died because we didn't get one. Other features found in the multidisciplinary evaluation of physical abuse are listed in Table 1.[18] There are also visual clues to the diagnosis, bruises and burns being most common. Certain bruises are more suspicious – such as those resembling belts, cords, pinch marks, slap marks, cigarette burns, or scald-immersion burns.

In addition, spiral fractures of the long bones in nonambulatory children, and intracranial hemorrhage, duodenal intramural hematomas, or pancreatic injury in any child in the absence of a history of major trauma is suspicious for abuse.[17]

---

**Table 1**
**Features Differentiating Accidental and Nonaccidental Trauma**

1. Discrepant History
2. Delay in Seeking Care
3. Crisis in Abuser's Life
4. Triggering Behavior by Child
5. Prior History of Abuse in Childhood of Abuser
6. Social Isolation
7. Unrealistic Expectations for the Child
8. Pattern of Increased Severity of Injury Over Time
9. Use of Multiple Hospitals or Providers

---

Sexual abuse has a variety of presentations, most of which are nonspecific (Table 2).[19] The most specific symptom of all these relatively nonspecific findings is sexual acting-out behavior. The diagnosis of sexual abuse is generally made on the history. Physical findings are usually not helpful except in the acute sexual assault, although certain hymenal changes in prepubertal children have been associated with a history of sexual abuse.[20,21,22] Certain sexually transmitted diseases can be presenting signs of sexual abuse. Gonorrhea and syphilis in prepubertal children are diagnostic of sexual abuse; chlamydia, trichomonas, herpes 2, and condyloma acuminata are suspicious for sexual abuse.[23]

---

**Table 2**
**Presentations of Sexual Abuse**

Early Warnings
    General Statements
    Sexualized Play
Direct Statements
Behavioral Changes
    Sleep Disturbances (e.g., Nightmare, Night Terrors)
    Appetite Disturbance (e.g., Anorexia, Bulimia)
    Neurotic or Conduct Disorders
    Phobias; Avoidance Behavior
    Withdrawal, Depression
    Guilt
    Temper Tantrums, Aggressive Behavior
    Excessive Masturbation
    Runaway Behavior
    Suicidal Behavior
    Hysterical or Conversion Reactions
Medical Conditions
    Genital or Urethral Trauma
    Genital Infection
    Sexually Transmitted Diseases
    Recurrent Urinary Tract Infections
    Abdominal Pain
    Enuresis
    Encopresis
Pregnancy
School Problems
Promiscuity or Prostitution
Substance Abuse
Perpetration to Others

When any behavior, discrepant history, or physical finding makes the practitioner suspicious of any form of abuse, it must be reported to the agency mandated to accept reports. Many worry about "being wrong" in the report. As long as it is done in good faith, there is immunity from successful suit. Failure to report is a misdemeanor and may also lead to a malpractice action. In a time when so many children are cared for by caretakers other than their parents, it is critical that practitioners remember that the person who brings the child for care may not be the abuser. Thus, whenever it is suspected, an approach could be: "There are a number of potential causes for this finding, including abuse. Is that a possibility?" A report can follow, with the practitioner being available for follow-up.

## Sequelae of Abuse

There are both survivors and casualties – physically and emotionally – of child abuse. As previously noted, not all abused children repeat the cycle as adults, but certainly the risks are significantly higher for this group compared to the general population.[14] It is less the physical injury (except for the sequelae of brain injury) or the sexual acts that are harmful to children as it is the emotional context of the injury or sexual relationship being perpetrated by a family member or someone in a position of trust.

The degree of "survivability" is dependent on a number of factors. In general, the longer the abuse persists, the younger the child at the age of onset, the closer the relationship of the abuser to the child, and the more severe (physical) or intrusive (sexual) the abuse, the worse the prognosis. The sequelae of physical abuse have been suggested by retrospective analyses of high-risk or pathologic populations. They include in children and adolescents: aggressive to violent behavior, juvenile delinquency, suicide, homicide, and runaway behaviors, in addition to a risk of physical abuse to other children.[24] The sequelae of sexual abuse include all those listed below "Behavioral Changes" in Table 2; and in older adolescents and adults: depression, difficulty with relationships, drug or alcohol addiction, adolescent pregnancy, multiple divorces, sexual dysfunction, and a higher risk of abusing **or** neglecting (e.g., a baby with non-organic failure to thrive) one's own children have been described.

While child abusers are increasingly recognized by primary care providers for children, those caring for adolescents and young adults may not consider the late sequelae in their differential diagnosis. Such behaviors should trigger a referral to a competent mental health provider.

# Types of Effective Approaches

## Treatment

Any child who is a victim of abuse should be evaluated for the need for treatment. Combinations of individual and group, professional and self-help groups may be useful. Whether the child is abused within or outside the family, siblings and parents may also benefit from therapy.[25] In extrafamilial abuse the young child may recover more quickly than the parents, especially if the parents have a history of abuse in their childhood that has never been addressed. In intrafamilial cases, court-ordered treatment may be more effective than voluntary approaches.[26] The coexistence of substance abuse, sociopathy, or psychosis makes outcomes less likely to be positive.

Regrettably, the child protective services system is episodic and case-oriented, as is the mental health system. There are, therefore, no prospective longitudinal outcome data to guide in treatment. It is the health system that has the tradition of continuity of care, and therefore practitioners are urged to maintain follow-up and surveillance on their patients who have been abused, since adolescents who were abused in childhood have a much higher incidence of health-risk behaviors than nonabused peers.[24] There may be multiple times during the life cycle in which waves of symptoms may well up in prior abuse victims; e.g., adolescence with the onset of sexual activity, marriage, childbearing, divorce, or even the watching of a television show on abuse.

## Prevention

The prevention of physical abuse is possible. Studies have shown clearly that it is possible to predict with reasonable accuracy who is at high risk for physical abuse and, by providing either a lay[27] or public health nurse[28] home visitor, prevent the physical abuse of children. Other modalities such as parenting classes, hotlines, and crisis nurseries have had some success as well.[29]

The prevention of sexual abuse is more difficult. Most strategies depend on the development of resistance by the child and "telling someone." Few programs of this nature for children have been evaluated, and none are fully effective (they seem to be better at identifying existing cases than preventing new ones).[30] More attention needs to be paid to the adult components of abusive behavior and what leads to the motivation to abuse children sexually.[31]

# COMMENTARY

The last three decades have seen dramatic growth in the public and professional awareness of abuse and neglect. The past decade, however, has been marked by a steady erosion of our ability to protect abused children. Child welfare services have become less supportive of families and more investigative in nature as the number of reported cases has risen to over two million nationally. The mental health system has been flooded with the chronically deinstitutionalized mentally ill and has been unable to absorb many of the hundreds of thousands of abused children and families who need services. Further, what used to be supportive public health nursing agencies to young mothers and infants have evolved into home health care agencies that are caring primarily for children with diseased organs and, preferably, insurance. We may be the only civilized nation in the world that has no idea where all its children between two days and six years of age are.

School and college health practitioners have four main roles when it comes to abuse and neglect. Recognition and reporting of cases is the first and has been discussed. Schools can be sites of prevention activities as well, often in elementary and secondary schools, with the cooperation of parent teacher organizations. The third role is less appreciated, but for many abused children, schools are their only safe place. Many adult survivors have remarked that teachers were their best role models. Schools should be sure that children who are abuse victims get the best, most nurturing teachers. Too often there is a tendency to put these children into the classes of harsh disciplinarians so they can "shape up" these children. There is no evidence that this is helpful.

Finally, teachers in schools and colleges need to avoid their contribution to the problem. A small percentage of these (and all) professionals abuse their students – physically, sexually or emotionally.[32] It is up to each profession to monitor the behavior of its own professionals.

In an age when there are more cases than can be handled by the overburdened child protective services system, it is critical for the health system – and especially the school and college health systems, which provide continuity of care – to get involved with these children and adolescents. Physical and sexual abuse are major etiologic agents in the new morbidity facing our youth. It is incumbent on all professionals to get involved on behalf of children.

# REFERENCES

1. Radbill SX: Children in a world of violence: A history of child abuse, The Battered Child. Fourth Edition. Edited by R Helfer and R Kempe. Chicago, The University of Chicago Press, 1987

2. Kempe CH, Silverman F, Steele BF et al. The battered child. JAMA 181:17-24, 1962

3. Garbarino J, Guttman E, Seeby J et al: The Psychologically Battered Child. Jossey-Bass Social and Behavioral Sciences Series in Strategies for Identification Assessment and Intervention. San Francisco, Jossey-Bass, 1986

4. Helfer RE: The litany of the smoldering neglect of children, The Battered Child. Fourth Edition. Edited by R Helfer and R Kempe. Chicago, The University of Chicago Press, 1987

5. Bross DC: Medical care neglect. Child Abuse Negl 6:375-381, 1982

6. Rosenberg DA: The web of deceit. Child Abuse Negl 11:547-563, 1988

7. American Humane Association: Highlights of official child neglect and abuse reporting. Denver, CO, 1979

8. American Humane Association: Highlights of official child neglect and abuse reporting. Denver, CO, 1986

9. U.S. DHHS: National Study of the Incidence of Child Abuse and Neglect. Washington, DC, U.S. Government Printing Office, 1988

10. Garbarino J: A preliminary study of some ecological corretabs of child abuse: The impact of socioeconomic stress on mothers. Child Dev 47:178-85, 1976

11. Steele B: Psychodynamic factors in child abuse, The Battered Child. Fourth Edition. Edited by R Helfer and R Kempe. Chicago, The University of Chicago Press, 1987

12. Straus MA, Kantor GK: Stress and child abuse, The Battered Child. Fourth Edition. Edited by R Helfer and R Kempe. Chicago, The University of Chicago Press, 1987

13. Korbin JE: Child abuse and neglect: The cultural context, The Battered Child. Fourth Edition. Edited by R Helfer and R Kempe. Chicago, The University of Chicago Press, 1987

14. Widom CS: The cycle of violence. Science 244:160-166, 1989

15. Sgroi SM, Porter FS, Blick LC: Validation of child sexual abuse, Handbook of Clinical Intervention in Child Sexual Abuse. Edited by SM Sgroi and Z Chap. Lexington, MA, D.C. Heath, 1982

16. Kempe CH: Sexual abuse: Another hidden pediatric problem - The 1972 C. Anderson Aldrich Lecture. Pediatrics 42(2):382-389, 1978

17. Schmitt BD: The visual diagnosis of non-accidental trauma and failure to thrive. Slide series available from the C. Henry Kempe National Center, Denver, CO, 1980

18. Krugman R: The assessment process of a child protection team, The Battered Child. Fourth Edition. Edited by R Helfer and R Kempe. Chicago, The University of Chicago Press, 1987

19. Krugman RD: Recognition of sexual abuse in children. Pediatr Rev 8(1):25-30, 1986

20. Cantwell HB: Vaginal inspection as it relates to child sexual abuse in girls under thirteen. Child Abuse Negl 7(2):171-176, 1983

21. White ST, Ingram DL, Lyna PR: Vaginal introital diameter in the evaluation of sexual abuse. Child Abuse Negl 13(2):217-225, 1989

22. Paradise JE: Predictive accuracy and the diagnosis of sexual abuse: A big issue about a little tissue. Child Abuse Negl 13(2):169-177 1989

23. Committee on Child Abuse and Neglect: Guidelines for the evaluation of child sexual abuse. Pediatrics 87:254-260, 1991

24. Riggs S, Alavo AJ, McHorney C: Health risk behaviors and attempted suicide in adolescents who report prior abuse. J Pediatr 116(5):815-821, 1990

25. Jones DPH, Alexander H: Treating the abusive family within the family care system, The Battered Child. Fourth Edition. Edited by R Helfer and R Kempe. Chicago, The University of Chicago Press, 1987

26. Wolfe DA, Aragona J, Kaufman K et al: The importance of adjudication in the treatment of child abusers: Some preliminary findings. Child Abuse Negl 14:127-135, 1980

27. Gray J et al: Prediction/prevention of child abuse and neglect. J Soc Issues 35(2):127-139, 1979

28. Olds DL et al: Preventing child abuse and neglect: A randomized trial of nurse home visitation. Pediatrics 78(1):65-78, 1986

29. Wilson AL: Our national priorities for prevention, The Battered Child. Fourth Edition. Edited by R Helfer and R Kempe. Chicago, The University of Chicago Press, 1987

30. Fryer GE, Kerns KS, Miyoshi T: Measuring actual reduction of risk to child abuse: A new approach. Child Abuse Negl 11:173-179, 1987

31. Finkelhor D, Williams LM: Nursery Crimes, Sexual Abuse in Day Care. Newbury Park, Sage Publications, 1988

32. Krugman MK, Krugman RD: Emotional abuse in the classroom. The pediatrician's role in diagnosis and treatment. Am J Dis Child 138(3):284-286, 1984

# Teenage Pregnancy

LAURIE S. ZABIN, MD

In the United States, a country with a history of early childbearing, there is a strong belief that the present high rate of adolescent pregnancy and childbearing represents a serious problem. The nature of that problem is variously defined as moral, social, economic, or medical, often depending more on the bias of the judge than the evidence at hand. Similarly, the etiology of adolescent sexual and fertility behavior is also differently interpreted. There are, however, many reliable studies that suggest the dimensions of the problem and cast some light on the complex issues of consequences and causality.

Rapid changes in the level of coital activity were documented in the 1970s with the biggest increases among younger girls and among the majority white population.[1] Thus, there was an approximate 50 percent increase in the percentage of girls who were sexually active by age 15, from 14.4 percent to 22.5 percent between 1971 and 1979. There has been some evidence of a leveling off in subsequent years,[2] but large differences remain between the U.S. and other industrialized Western nations, whose rates of conception and childbearing among teenage women are significantly lower than the U.S. even when their ages of sexual onset are similar.[3]

A lowering of the age of menarche over a period of 100 years, ending a generation ago,[4] and increases in the age of marriage allow many more years of exposure to premarital pregnancy. There is a documented relationship between age of maturation and sexual onset, with the effect of maturational age greatest in early teen years,[5] and there is evidence of coital activity, especially among young boys, even before puberty. Thus, those who deliver services to young people during the middle school years must be prepared to address issues of sexuality and reproductive health, issues for which they may not be well prepared.

Although the vast majority of adolescent conceptions are described as unintended by young women themselves, a greater acceptance of unwed motherhood has resulted in a much smaller proportion of out-of-wedlock conceptions being legitimated by marriage before birth. The availability of contraception has averted a large number of unwanted conceptions,[6] and the availability of abortion has averted numerous unwanted births, but the numbers are still high and the individual and social consequences unacceptable.

These consequences are complex, and difficult to understand because the direction of causality is not always clear (see reference 2 for a summary discussion of consequences). Thus, although there is a documented relationship between adolescent motherhood and school termination before graduation, there is evidence that many young women who bear children in their teens have already suffered educational deficits or have lower academic aspirations than those who do not. Many have already dropped out of school before they conceive.[7] Nonetheless, an independent contribution of early childbearing has been documented,[8,9] as well as an association of early motherhood with economic deficits,[10] single parent households,[11] increased dependency,[12] and a more rapid pace of future childbearing.[13] The fact that, with time, many young women overcome these deficits is testament to their investment in their own futures,[14] but the toll on their offspring and their families, as well as on the young mothers themselves, suggests that too-early conception has consequences that demand early intervention.

The issue of medical consequences is equally complex. It seems clear that the incidence of low birth weight is greater and infant mortality rates higher among babies of adolescent mothers, but that phenomenon appears to be largely social and economic rather than biological in origin.[15] The degree to which good, prompt prenatal services mediate these outcomes and the success of case-managed interventions that provide high-risk care, social support, nutritional supplements, and education to young pregnant girls[16] suggests that it is the association of early childbearing with deprivation that is responsible for many of the adverse outcomes of adolescents' pregnancies. Access to prenatal care is often socially, not medically, determined. However, whether the higher incidence of morbidity is social, economic, or medical in origin, the needs among pregnant adolescents for optimal medical intervention are clear.

## POINTS OF INTERVENTION

Adolescent childbearing is the end product of an entire series of choices and behaviors. There are, then, many potential points of intervention depending upon the stage in a young person's sexual history at which it is determined to focus social attention. Depending upon where one seeks to intervene, the number of young people who become the target of the intervention differs. Thus, if the objective is to prevent the onset of sexual activity during the teen years, the target population must be all adolescents despite the fact that only about half of them will, in the absence of intervention, initiate coital activity. All, however, need education and all need to understand the role of sexuality in their lives. Hence the importance of good curricula in human sexuality for all young people, regardless of the rates of childbearing among them.

If the objective is to prevent conception and sexually transmitted disease among the subset who are sexually active, the availability of optimal clinical services for young people who are engaging in, or intend to engage in, coitus is indicated. If the intention is to offer those whose contraceptive regimens fail the option of pregnancy termination or the option of prompt prenatal care, easily accessible pregnancy testing facilities with appropriate in-depth counseling components are crucial. The medical safety of abortion to teenagers has been documented[17] as has its psychological safety;[18] its availability to those who must rely on public funding is, unfortunately, very limited. If healthy outcomes among those who carry to term are to be achieved, optimal facilities for their care, more comprehensive than those required by adult and married women, appear necessary.[15,16] Finally, because the immaturity of young people often is reflected in behavioral and emotional characteristics that are detrimental to good parenting, continuing programs to assist young mothers are vital to their offspring's well-being.[19,20]

We will discuss below the problems involved in the delivery of services at each of these points of intervention and will report aspects of some service models that appear to have demonstrated success. We will explore these issues in the context of our understanding of the special needs of the adolescent age group.

## ADOLESCENTS AND ADOLESCENCE

Although there is some debate about how clearly the maturation process is defined into developmental stages, it seems clear that all young people develop physically, cognitively, and emotionally in sequences that are quite well described. Complicating our understanding of adolescents, however, is the fact that these developmental processes move along separate tracks: maturity in one dimension does not imply maturity in another. Thus, the young person whose intellectual development is far ahead of his emotional maturity does not resemble his contemporary whose physical and emotional maturity have outstripped his cognitive development. As the age of physical maturation has become younger, as described above, a discontinuity has grown between physical development on the one hand and the capacity to manage the sexual and fertility implications of physical maturity on the other. That discontinuity presents a real challenge to those who would educate, counsel, and deliver medical services to young men and women in their early teen years.

Some well-described constructs of adolescence have obvious implications for the design of appropriate interventions. In early adolescence, young people are only beginning to develop the capacity for abstract thinking, for comprehending the ways in which their current behavior may affect their futures.[21] They are inclined to believe that they are invulnerable: the "personal fable"[22] implies that even those risks they understand intellectually, will not appear to endanger them. This belief is predicated on the younger adolescent's perception of him- or herself as "unique," an egocentrism that tends to weaken over the teen years.

During these same years the young person is forming an identity of his own,[23] a value system and a self-concept separate from that of his family and often more closely related to his peers. The behaviors that are adopted during these years may "depart from the regulatory age norms defining what is appropriate at that age or stage in life," and may , in fact, "be problematic only in relation to age."[24] That sexual contact during the early years of adolescent development might be different from the sexual contact of older teens, that it might be more casual or spontaneous, less consciously initiated and associated with less intimate relationships, is not hard to understand. Those differences, and the developmental stages at which young people must be reached, have serious implications for the design of preventive interventions.

## INTERVENTION AND PROGRAM DESIGN

For purposes of discussion, programs to prevent adolescent pregnancy have been divided into three general classifications: those which seek to educate and instruct, those which offer reproductive health services, and those which seek to change the future options of young people in such a way as to affect their current behavior.

**Programs in the first area of intervention**, those that are largely educational, attempt to change levels of knowledge about the physiology of reproduction, the risks of pregnancy and sexually transmitted diseases (STDs), and, in some cases, the use and effectiveness of contraceptives. Many interventions also attempt to discuss values and attitudes, and to help young people understand the role of their sexual behavior in shaping their lives. Most of these programs are delivered in the context of a school curriculum, variously described and including a wide range of different components in units of very different length and depth. They are taught by faculty with different backgrounds, disciplines, and training, whose personal perspectives may combine with the specified curriculum to produce courses of quite different character. The involvement of well-trained guidance and health professionals in the delivery of the material and an atmosphere of open discussion and explicit interest in the students' concerns can make these courses valuable. There is evidence that a program specially conceived to postpone sexual onset, focused on improving young students' ability to resist peer and social pressures, and taught by health educators assisted by older students, was able to influence students to delay coital activity.[25]

However, as they are currently delivered in most school districts, there is no evidence that educational programs alone make an impact on the rate of adolescent sexual involvement or conception. Because they do change the level of information, they are an essential ingredient in a comprehensive program, but at the ages of highest risk, young people need a considerable investment in the counseling component that helps them to internalize and act upon their abstract knowledge. When education is combined with individual and small-group counseling and medical access in a supportive and proximate setting, there is evidence that behavioral change can be affected. A school-linked program that placed social workers in schools during the morning, but placed the afternoon clinic outside and close by the schools, showed dramatic effects including a postponement in first intercourse among those not yet sexually active, more frequent and more prompt clinic attendance, more effective contraceptive usage, and a reduction in both abortion and childbearing rates among those who were sexually active.[26]

**The second area of intervention** is the more traditional field of reproductive health services, offering contraception, treatment and detection of sexually transmitted diseases, and pregnancy testing in a medical setting. The delivery of optimal family planning services is basic to any pregnancy prevention initiative but, unfortunately, it is the service that has encountered the most opposition. Evidence from the program cited above[26] demonstrates that it is not the provision of contraceptive services that promotes sexual activity; the program can actually delay sexual activity. There is no evidence suggesting that such programs do, in fact, accelerate coital activity. This is not surprising because, with a mean delay of approximately a year between sexual onset and first clinic attendance,[27] the availability of contraception can hardly be seen as encouraging coital onset.

In order to increase the effectiveness of medical intervention as a means of preventing adolescent childbearing, a series of optimal services is required.

First, contraceptive effectiveness must be improved through: 1) more prompt access and 2) better education and continuation rates. It has been shown that the risk of pregnancy to young teens is not only early in their chronologic age but early in their sexual exposure; the median interval between first intercourse and first premarital conception is only six months, and less for those who initiate coitus at fifteen years of age or younger.[28] Therefore, outreach is essential. A good counseling program in connection with school-based education can accomplish that purpose, but other creative community programs are essential for out-of-school youth. Once in a clinic, the educational and guidance components are just as important as the medical services, and are particularly necessary in view of the poor continuation rates evidenced even by the self-selected young people who attend contraceptive facilities. The difficulties that a young teenager experiences in negotiating a strange health system and finding a source of care is matched by the challenge of maintaining a regimen, often without the help of an adult. Sporadic coital activity and frequent periods of abstinence may compound the problem.

There has been considerable attention to school-based services recently as a source of care in the area of pregnancy reduction; in fact, it was this promise that put many of them in place. Unfortunately, most are unable to offer the contraceptive assistance the young students require and therefore have not achieved that goal. However, one advantage of school-based clinical programs is the possibility they offer for follow-up. If school-linked facilities can offer contraceptive services there is evidence they can reduce adolescent pregnancy rates;[26,29] without such explicit services, there is no evidence that they can make a measurable change in fertility behavior.

In the older teen years, services similar to those that cater to adults are sufficient, but at all ages there is a need for improved contraceptive education. American women, including adult married women, are poor contraceptors compared to women in other developed countries.[3] This is due partly to a widespread misunderstanding of the relative risks of pregnancy and contraception. Even on a college campus, clinics would do well to make balanced sexuality education, contraceptive education, and STD education a part of their outreach programs.

Second, early pregnancy testing must be offered in order to: 1) give young patients viable options in choosing their outcomes while early pregnancy termination can still be performed; 2) permit those who choose to carry to term to enter prenatal facilities promptly; and 3) identify negative-test patients in time to offer them the counseling and contraceptive services that may reduce their high rate of subsequent conception.[30] Many sites that offer pregnancy tests provide counseling on pregnancy options and those that serve teens often offer contraception following a negative test. However, in-depth counseling for those whose tests are negative is rare; counselors often assume that patients will be relieved at the outcome of the test and be ready to adopt protective measures. Some sites permit "drop-off" pregnancy tests and give results by telephone. In view of the high documented risk to young women subsequent to a negative test, a policy of one-on-one consultation might well be extended to those who are not, as well as those who are, pregnant.

Third, optimal abortion services are required that give young women the same supportive care as prenatal services. Preferably, they should be free or at low cost, and accompanied by adequate counseling and follow-up contraception. In view of the medical and psychological safety of the procedure,[17,18] clinics serving teens are remiss if they do not present this option, especially since it has been well documented that over 80 percent of conceptions in this age group are unintended.[2] Because of the level of denial and procrastination typical of the young adolescent, it is frequently too late for first-trimester abortion when the pregnant teen first presents. This is one reason that open discussion and programs that explicitly address the reproductive health of adolescents are so important: they may provide continuity of care and be available as confidential testing sites when and if the need arises.

Fourth, prenatal services must be designed with an understanding of the social and economic risks of pregnant teens, not their medical risks alone. A case-management model that provides each young woman with the nutritional guidance, social support, and medical supervision she requires, appears to serve the needs of this age group best.[20] Because so much of the service required by young teens is not medical in nature, the staffing patterns of these facilities should include guidance professionals (e.g., social workers, counselors). However dedicated a medical staff, the clinicians rarely have the time that these young women require, may not have the necessary counseling skills, and are more expensive to the clinic.[31] Parenting education can begin as a part of the comprehensive prenatal program, but continuing support to the young mother while she brings her child in for well-baby care can be invaluable.

**The third major area of intervention** has been described as improving "life options"; much less specific in their parameters than either medical or educational services, these programs are premised on the notion that enlarged opportunities for the future may affect the choices young people make in their high-risk years. Some models include educational support and job training, some rely on mentors and role models to open new vistas, some offer counseling, parenting education, day care, or job placement to young mothers and sometimes to young males, as well. While none of these designs has shown that they can effect a long-term reduction in pregnancy rates (or repeat pregnancy rates), they address recognized problems among the disadvantaged and are generally accepted for the good they can do whatever their ultimate effects may be on fertility.[2]

## ROLE OF THE CLINICIAN

Although categoric services such as the educational and reproductive health services described above are vital, those persons who are more generally responsible for the education and health care of young people can provide an important service if an understanding of their needs in these sensitive areas permeates their professional contacts. Thus, it is important that clinicians in regular contact with young people from puberty on make it clear that they are willing to answer questions about reproductive health, indeed that they consider these issues an essential part of health care. For many pediatric clinicians that may not come easily. Their training may not have included pelvic examinations, the prescription of contraceptives, or discussions of sexually transmitted diseases. In the present climate, it seems safe to assume that all young people, male and female, have questions about pubertal development, sexual contact, and the risk of pregnancy and disease. It can also be assumed that an adolescent who does not see a clinician as a confidential advisor will not raise these issues except in times of crisis. Therefore it is incumbent upon the health professional to open these areas of discussion and to respond in supportive and nonjudgmental ways to the concerns of young patients. Similarly, it is incumbent on comprehensive health facilities to make it explicit that reproductive health is a part of their service and that requests in this area will remain confidential.

In reporting on their reasons for choosing the contraceptive facilities in which they were interviewed, young women made it clear that a "caring" staff was critical to the quality of service they sought.[27] Confidentiality was another standard, as were proximity and low cost. Continuity of care can also reduce the dangerous delays between coital onset and professional contraceptive services. Thus, there are specific qualities of service delivery that can make an impact on clinic attendance and contraceptive use. Although the availability of optimal services cannot be expected to affect the essential causes for the increase in adolescent conceptions and births in the U.S. today, it appears clear that without such services current trends toward single, premarital parenthood will probably not be reversed.

## REFERENCES

1. Zelnik M, Kantner JF: Sexual activity, contraceptive use, and pregnancy among metropolitan-area teenagers: 1971-1979. Fam Plann Perspect 12:230-237, 1980

2. Hayes CD (ed): Risking The Future. Vol I. National Research Council, National Academy of Sciences. Washington, DC, National Academy Press, 1987

3. Jones EF et al: Teenage Pregnancy in Industrialized Countries. Yale University Press, Alan Guttmacher Institute, 1986

4. Tanner JM: Growth at Adolescence. London, Blackwell, 1962

5. Zabin LS, Smith EA, Hirsch MB et al: Ages of physical maturation and first intercourse in black teenage males and females. Demography 23:595-605, 1986

6. Forrest JD, Hermalin A, Henshaw S: The impact of family planning clinic programs on adolescent pregnancy. Fam Plann Perspect 13:109-116, 1981

7. Upchurch DM, McCarthy J: The timing of a first birth and high school completion. Am Sociol Rev 55:224234, 1990

8. Moore KA, Waite LJ: Early childbearing and educational attainment. Fam Plann Perspect 9:220-225, 1977

9. Moore K, Burt M: Private Crisis, Public Cost: Policy Perspectives on Teenage Childbearing. Washington, DC, Urban Institute Press, 1982

10. Hofferth S: Social and economic consequences of teenage childbearing, Risking the Future. Vol I. Edited by CD Hayes. National Research Council, National Academy of Sciences. Washington, DC, National Academy Press, 1987, pp 123-144

11. McCarthy J, Menken J: Marriage, remarriage, marital disruption and age at first birth. Fam Plann Perspect 11:21-30, 1989

12. Moore KA: Teenage childbirth and welfare dependence. Fam Plann Perspect 10:233-235,1978

13. Mott FL: The pace of repeated childbearing among young American mothers. Fam Plann Perspect 18:5-12, 1986

14. Furstenberg FF, Brooks-Gunn J, Morgan SP: Adolescent Mothers in Later Life. Cambridge, Cambridge University Press, 1987

15. Strobino DM: The health and medical consequences of adolescent sexuality and pregnancy: A review of the literature. Risking the Future. Volume II. Edited by SL Hofferth and CD Hayes. Washington, DC, National Academy Press, 1987

16. Hardy JB, Welcher DW, Stanley J et al: Long-range outcome of adolescent pregnancy. Clin Obstet Gynecol 21:1215-1232, 1978

17. Cates W Jr, Schultz KF, Grimes DA: The risks associated with teenage abortion. N Engl J Med 309:621-624, 1983

18. Zabin LS, Hirsch MB, Emerson MR: When urban adolescents choose abortion: Effects on education, psychological status and subsequent pregnancy. Fam Plann Perspect 21:248-255, 1989

19. Elster AB, McAnarney ER, Lamb ME: Parental behavior of adolescent mothers. Pediatrics 71:494-503, 1983

20. Hardy J, Zabin LS: Adolescent Pregnancy in an Urban Environment. Baltimore, MD, Williams and Wilkins and Washington, DC, The Urban Institute, 1991

21. Piaget J: Intellectual evolution from adolescence to adulthood. Hum Dev 15:1-12, 1972

22. Elkind D: Egocentrism in adolescence. Child Dev 38:1025-1034, 1967

23. Erikson E: Identity: Youth and Crisis. New York, W.W. Norton and Company, 1968

24. Jessor R, Jessor SL: Problem Behavior and Psychosocial Development: A Longitudinal Study of Youth. New York, Academic Press, 1977

25. Howard M, McCabe JB: Helping teenagers postpone sexual involvement. Fam Plann Perspect 22:21-26, 1990

26. Zabin LS, Hirsch MB, Smith EA et al: Evaluation of a pregnancy prevention program for urban teenagers. Fam Plann Perspect 3:119-126, 1986

27. Zabin LS, Clark SD: Why they delay: A study of teenage family planning clinic patients. Fam Plann Perspect 13:205-217, 1981

28. Zabin LS, Kantner JF, Zelnik M: The risk of adolescent pregnancy in the first months of intercourse. Fam Plann Perspect 11:215-222, 1979

29. Edwards L, Steinman M, Arnold K et al: Adolescent pregnancy prevention services in high school clinics. Fam Plann Perspect 12:6-14, 1980

30. Zabin LS, Hirsch MB, Boscia JA: Differential characteristics of adolescent pregnancy test patients: Abortion, childbearing and negative test groups. J Adolesc Health Care 11:107-113, 1990

31. Zabin LS, Hirsch MB, Street R et al: The Baltimore pregnancy prevention program for urban teenagers: How did it work? Fam Plann Perspect 20(4):182-187, 1988

# 12

# Drug Abuse

ZILI AMSEL, ScD AND CARL G. LEUKEFELD, DSW

During the past two decades, schools and colleges have paid more attention to drug abuse with a major goal of identifying effective interventions. Unfortunately, research has been able to tell us more about what does not work than about what works in preventing drug abuse.[1-4] However, with growing information regarding the epidemiology of drug abuse and factors that influence health-related behaviors, a great deal of knowledge has accrued and promising approaches are now available.[5,6]

## NATURE AND SIGNIFICANCE OF THE PROBLEM

Observations from long-term studies of adolescents through junior and senior high school, and in many cases, through adulthood, indicate that patterns of substance use vary through the developmental cycle. It seems clear that the onset of certain illegal drug use, such as marijuana, begins during adolescence and is uncommon in later stages.[7] However, for those illegal drugs such as cocaine or non-prescription drugs, which are used initially during later adolescence, new use continues into early adulthood.[8,9]

Research has demonstrated the negative consequences of drug use not only during adolescence but also into adulthood. Health and school problems have been implicated with drug use as well as further involvement in deviancy and problems related to interpersonal relationships including family formation and parenting.[9,10] Current studies are examining the degree to which children of heroin and cocaine abusers are themselves substance abusers and impaired developmentally. Now we are confronted with a new problem associated with drug abuse – HIV infection and AIDS. Combatting the ravages of AIDS requires action. It is

146

apparent that with drug abuse these prevention activities must begin in childhood and continue through adolescence.

National estimates of adolescent drug abuse come primarily from The High School Senior Survey, Monitoring the Future, conducted by the Institute for Social Research, University of Michigan, and from the National Household Survey. Since 1975, The High School Senior Survey has collected data from approximately 16,000 seniors in a sample of about 130 public and private high schools across the country. The most recent survey[11] indicated that in 1989, 51 percent of respondents had used an illicit drug at least once in their lives, with 31 percent having tried an illicit drug other than marijuana. Overall, decreases in illicit drug use have been observed, although increased use of cocaine was noted in 1985 and 1986. This latter trend has reversed since 1987.

Information from the High School Senior Survey is available not only for lifetime drug use but also on drug use in the twelve-month period (exclusive of the prior month) and the 30-day period prior to the survey. The following provides an overview of drug use in this population.

## MARIJUANA

In 1989, marijuana was the most used illicit drug with 44 percent of responding high school seniors reporting use. The lifetime prevalence of marijuana use peaked in 1979 and 1980 at 60 percent. It should also be noted that the annual prevalence peaked in 1979 at almost 51 percent and the 30-day prevalence peaked in 1978 at 37 percent. These rates began to decrease in subsequent years to the 1989 rates of 44 percent, 30 percent, and 17 percent, respectively.

## ILLICIT DRUG USE OTHER THAN MARIJUANA

In 1989, the second most popular category of abused drugs was stimulants (19 percent), followed by inhalants (18 percent), cocaine (10 percent), hallucinogens (10 percent), opiates other than heroin (8 percent), sedatives (7 percent), and crack cocaine (5 percent). Increases in lifetime illicit drug use other than marijuana were noted between 1976 and 1982 when the percentages rose from 35 percent to 45 percent. This figure stabilized in the years 1983 and 1984 and then began to decrease to 36 percent. Annual and 30-day prevalence figures reflect similar trends. However, daily use of these drugs remained under 1 percent for specific drug categories. In 1986, 40 percent to 56 percent of those reporting use of a drug other than marijuana reported first use prior to the 10th grade.

## COCAINE

The use of cocaine by high school seniors began to increase in the late 1970s. Nine percent of seniors who completed the questionnaire in 1975 reported they had ever tried cocaine. However, this percentage gradually increased over subsequent years to 16 percent in the early 1980s and to 17 percent in 1985-86.[12] This decreased in 1989 to 10 percent. Crack, a more potent smokeable derivative of cocaine, was not included in the survey until 1986. However, there is evidence from prior surveys, that respondents began reporting the practice of smoking cocaine in 1983, at almost 3 percent. In 1986 when asked specifically about the use of crack, 4 percent of the respondents admitted they had tried it at least once. In 1989 this increased to 5 percent.

Since the High School Senior Survey includes only students who did not drop out of school prior to their senior year and only those attending school during the period in which the survey was administered, it has been criticized for underestimating drug-using behaviors. Estimates suggest that about one-third of 18 year olds are generally absentees or drop-outs.[13,14,15] Studies indicate higher drug use rates than found among these subgroups on the High School Senior Survey. For instance, there was higher drug use in a sample of absentees than in attendees, particularly for marijuana (56 percent and 38 percent) and barbiturates (28 percent and 16 percent).[14]

The Household Survey presents another view of drug abuse and includes respondents aged 12 and older for those in and out of school. The Survey was conducted biannually until 1979 when it became triennial. The most recent data are available for 1988 and show lifetime, annual, and past month use rates for age groups 12-17, 18-25, 26-34, and 35 and older. Drug-use data for the age group 12-17 for the 1972 to the 1988 surveys indicate that 24 percent of respondents reported marijuana and hashish use. Other drugs with high lifetime prevalence of use in 1988 were inhalants, 9 percent; non-prescription analgesics, 4 percent; non-prescription stimulants, 4 percent; cocaine, 3 percent; and non-prescription tranquilizers, 2 percent. Use of drugs in the year and month prior to the survey showed lower rates, with marijuana and hashish use at 13 percent and 16 percent, respectively; and inhalants, 4 percent and 2 percent, respectively. Use of cocaine and non-prescription analgesics, stimulants and tranquilizers ranged about 3 percent and 4 percent, and 1 percent and 2 percent, respectively, for the two time periods.

Although lower, trends for reported use over time since 1975 indicate similar peaks and declines in marijuana, cocaine, cigarettes, and alcohol as were noted for high school seniors. Therefore, comparing drug-use trends in these two surveys indicates similar curves suggesting that, in general, drug-use patterns may be cohort phenomena.

## COSTS

Drug abuse in our society is pervasive and costly. Cost data from 1980 indicate that drug abuse costs society an estimated $47 billion.[16] These costs are distributed in billions as: $25.7 in reduced workforce productivity, $18.3 in crime-related costs, $1.2 in drug abuse treatment, $1.2 in drug overdose deaths, and $.6 in health support services and lost employment. Experts believe that these amounts are underestimates of total costs to society, particularly since these figures do not include the added burden of AIDS and the current impact and consequences of crack cocaine.

## PREVENTIVE EFFORTS – OUTCOME

Defining prevention is a first step in exploring prevention efforts. Three perspectives underlie drug abuse prevention programs.[17] First, the public health model, which incorporates the concepts of primary, secondary, and tertiary prevention.[18] Primary prevention is directed toward preventing the onset of disease. Primary prevention activities include decreasing the incidence, new starts, or onset of disease. Many drug abuse prevention activities can be placed in this category of primary prevention. A common criticism of this definition of prevention is the overlap between categories as well as the fact that all prevention, treatment, and rehabilitation services could be categorized within this definition as prevention.

A second prevention perspective, called the communicable disease model, focuses on the host, agent, and environment.[19] The agent is the cause of the disease, and from the communicable disease model perspective, is the infection. The host relates to the human susceptibility or resistance to disease and can be influenced by multiple heredity and lifestyle factors.

A third perspective is the risk factor model, which is directed toward identifying factors related to psychological, social, as well as biological factors associated with the emergence of a health problem.[20] Risk factors have been used extensively to depict increased risks for drug abuse using correlation research and other research findings. These three ways of thinking provide some clarity about prevention, and they are useful for understanding different intervention approaches.

To a large degree questions related to the effectiveness of drug abuse prevention interventions center on research design, methodology, and on the differences as well as the inconsistencies between study findings. A prime example is the choice of outcome measures, i.e., no drug use as contrasted with occasional drug use. The choice of outcome measures obviously impacts significantly on a study's findings and consequently a program's effectiveness. There are additional methodologic issues, important for the prevention practitioner as well as the researcher to consider, which are related to the generalizability and strength of the intervention.[21]

In the early 1970s, it was believed that information could change drug-taking behavior in the United States. However, it was soon recognized that providing drug information alone was not effective. Therefore, in 1973, a moratorium was declared by the federal government on drug abuse information. However, with the advancement of knowledge regarding the neurotoxicity of drugs and influences on human behavior and behavior change, this position has changed drastically and information campaigns are now used extensively. For example, a most recent public service campaign is titled "Cocaine. The Big Lie." It was developed to counter increasing cocaine use among older teenagers and young adults, identified through surveys. It focuses on the addictive qualities of cocaine, its potential for producing severe health consequences, and the need to seek treatment; and incorporates key principles emerging from the field of health education research. Additional phases will focus on crack, the smokeable form of cocaine, and teenagers who are becoming addicted to crack.[22]

A number of school-based strategies have been tested in the U.S. to examine their effectiveness in preventing adolescent drug experimentation. Almost all of these strategies focus on preventing cigarette smoking, considered a "gateway" substance to the use of marijuana and other illicit drugs. By preventing the onset of tobacco use or delaying its use, researchers believe progression to illicit substance use will be prevented. These programs, based on social learning and problem behavior theory, have consistently reported positive effects in reducing (or delaying) onset of smoking.[23,24] In general, the interventions include using students who serve as peer role models to demonstrate social pressure-resistance skills by refusing drugs, rehearsing behaviors, feedback from fellow students on skill mastery, and developing knowledge about the short-term psychological and social consequences of cigarette use. The more successful programs also incorporate developing group norms that promote the disapproval of drug use. The results from a number of studies suggest that strategies are most effective when multiple program components are used, booster sessions are employed to reinforce behavior change, and interventions are targeted to specific age groups. Preliminary results also indicate that these prevention approaches reduce marijuana use as well as alcohol use among adolescents.[24,25]

## IMPLICATIONS FOR PLANNING AND POLICY

Drug abuse is a chronic and relapsing disorder once addiction is established. The implications for both school health and college health policy seem obvious. Major emphasis should be planned on continuing primary prevention approaches in the classroom as well as in living situations. Providing a drug-free environment will go a long way toward reducing the overall abuse of drugs in school and college settings. However, before drug prevention and intervention approaches can be initiated by student health services, school and college officials must recognize that drug abuse is an issue that deserves specific and continuous attention and support.

## REFERENCES

1. Berberian RM, Gross C, Lovejoy J et al: The effectiveness of drug education programs: A critical review. Health Educ Monogr 4: 377-398, 1976

2. Bracht GN, Follingstad D, Brakarsh D et al: Drug education: A review of goals, approaches, and effectiveness, and a paradigm for evaluation. Q J Stud Alcohol 11: 1279-1292, 1973

3. Goodstadt MS: Myths and methodology in drug education: A critical review of research evidence, Research on Methods and Programs of Drug Education. Edited by MS Goodstadt. Toronto, Canada, Addiction Research Foundation, 1974

4. Schapps E, Bartolt RD, Moskowitz J et al: A review of 127 drug abuse prevention program evaluations. J Drug Issues 11: 17-43, Winter, 1981

5. Donohew L, Bukoski WJ, Sypher W (eds): Persuasive Communications and Drug Abuse Prevention. Hillsdale, NJ, Erlbaum Press, 1991

6. Glynn TJ, Leukefeld CG, Ludford JP (eds): Preventing Adolescent Drug Abuse: Intervention Strategies. Washington, DC, U.S. Government Printing Office, 1983

7. O'Malley PM, Bachman JG, Johnson LD: Period, age, and cohort effects on substance use among American youth: 1976-1982. Am J Public Health 74: 682-688, 1984

8. Kandel D, Single E, Kessler RC: The epidemiology of drug use among New York State high school students: Distribution, trends, and change in rates of use. Am J Public Health 66(1):43-53, 1976

9. Newcomb MD: Consequences of teenage drug use: The transition from adolescence to young adulthood. Drugs and Society 1: 25-60, 1987

10. Kandel D, Davies M, Karus D, Yamaguchi K: The consequences in young adulthood of adolescent drug involvement. Arch Gen Psychiatry 43:746-754, 1986

11. NIDA Press Release: The 1989 National High School Senior Survey, Feb, 1990

12. Johnston LD, O'Malley PM, Bachman JG: National trends in drug use and related factors among American high school students and young adults, 1975-1986. DHHS Publication No. (ADM)87-1535, 1987

13. Clayton RR, Voss HL: Technical Review on Drug Abuse and Drop-Outs. Report for the National Institute on Drug Abuse. Rockville, MD, 1982

14. Kandel D: Reaching the hard-to-reach: Illicit drug use among high school absentees. Addict Dis 1: 465-480, 1975

15. Kandel D, Ravies VH, Logan JA: Sex differences in the characteristics of members lost to a longitudinal panel: A speculative research note. Public Opin Q 47:568-576, 1983

16. Harwood HJ, Napolitano DM, Kristinsen PL et al: Economic Costs to Society of Alcohol and Drugs and Mental Health: 1980. (RTI/2734/00-01FR). Research Triangle Park, NC, Research Triangle Institute, 1984

17. Bukoski WJ: A definition of drug abuse prevention research, Persuasive Communication and Drug Abuse Prevention. Edited by L Donohew, WJ Bukoski, M Sypher. Hillsdale, NJ, Erlbaum Press, 1991, pp 3-19

18. Last JM (ed): Scope and Methods of Prevention, Public Health and Preventive Medicine. New York, Appleton Century Croft, 1980, pp 3-18

19. Wilner D, Walkley R, O'Neil E (eds): Introduction to Public Health. New York, MacMillan Publishing Co, 1978

20. Arnold C, Kuller L, Greenlick, M (eds): Advances in Disease Prevention, Vol 1. New York, Springer Publishing Company, 1981

21. Leukefeld CG: Drug abuse prevention: Research needs, Prevention Research Findings: 1988. Prevention Monograph 3. Rockville, MD, Office of Substance Abuse Prevention, 1990, pp 46-52

22. National Institute on Drug Abuse: NIDA Capsules. Rockville, MD, 1988

23. Botvin GJ: Prevention of adolescent substance abuse through the development of personal and social competence, Preventing Adolescent Drug Abuse: Intervention Strategies. Edited by TJ Glynn, CG Leukefeld, PL Ludford. National Institute on Drug Abuse Research Monograph 47. Washington, DC, U.S. Government Printing Office, 1983, pp 115-140

24. Pentz MA, Dwyer JH, MacKinnon DP et al: A multi-community trial for primary prevention of adolescent drug abuse: Effects on drug abuse prevalence. JAMA 261 (22) 3259-3266, 1990

25. Pentz MA: Personal Communication, September 20, 1988

# Preventing Alcohol Abuse:
# A Move Toward a National Agenda

ELAINE M. JOHNSON, PhD

Problems associated with alcohol abuse and alcoholism continue to be one of this nation's leading public health concerns. Although illegal drugs, such as cocaine, receive the greatest amount of media attention, alcohol use among adolescents and alcohol abuse and alcoholism among adults account for the greatest adverse health and social consequences in our society. Alcohol use and abuse are associated with a wide variety of diseases, behavioral disorders, psychological malady, familial dysfunction, and economic hardships.

Paradoxically, the public health, social, and economic problem associated with the use and abuse of alcohol and alcoholism is the fact that such manifestations are the result of legal drug use. A person's drinking behavior arises out of the complexity of some not-so-completely understood processes and interactions that evidence possible genetic vulnerability, environmental predispositions, and societal influences.

This chapter will discuss some of the health and social consequences of alcohol-related problems of the 1990s in relationship to public health prevention efforts. To address this issue adequately, it is essential to examine some of the major planning and policy implications that can facilitate the accomplishment of the national health objectives as they pertain to alcohol problems.

## TRENDS AND NATIONAL SURVEYS

The National Institute on Alcohol Abuse and Alcoholism (NIAAA) reports that the per capita consumption of alcohol has had a steady decline since 1980. Yet, alcohol is still the most abused drug in America. Alcohol abuse and dependence continue to affect about 10 percent of adult Americans. A minimum of 3 out of 100 deaths in the United States can be attributed to alcohol-related causes.[1]

While the national drinking age was 21 in 1989, drivers under the age of 21 accounted for 15 percent of the alcohol-related automobile crashes. Additionally, as can be seen in Table 1, automobile crashes occurring among those in the 21-to-24 and 25-to-34 age groups were more likely to be alcohol-related than those in other age categories.

While the number of high school seniors who tried alcohol remained relatively stable from 1975 through 1987, there were some recognizable changes in the pattern of their use. The percentage of seniors who drank alcohol on a daily basis declined significantly.[2] (Figure 1, next page.) There was also a slight decline in the number of seniors who were occasional heavy drinkers. (Figure 2, next page.)

The 1990 High School Senior Survey conducted by the University of Michigan[3] found a decrease in the daily use of alcohol among high school seniors. However, the study revealed only modest declines in binge drinking among high school seniors. About one-third of the seniors reported having five or more drinks in a row on at least one occasion in a two-week period of time. Forty-one percent of the males in this study reported having five-plus drinks in a row in a two-week period. Four percent of the class of 1989 indicated they drank alcohol daily. The 30-day prevalence of alcohol use among this group revealed that 60 percent of high school

### Table 1
### Crash-involved Drivers by Age Group and Alcohol Involvement

| Age Group | No Number | No Percent | Yes Number | Yes Percent | Total Number | Total Percent |
|---|---|---|---|---|---|---|
| 15 and under | 34,000 | 97% | 1,000 | 3% | 35,000 | 100% |
| 16 to 20 | 2,050,000 | 97% | 61,000 | 3% | 2,112,000 | 100% |
| 21 to 24 | 1,438,000 | 95% | 73,000 | 5% | 1,510,000 | 100% |
| 25 to 34 | 2,967,000 | 97% | 144,000 | 5% | 3,111,000 | 100% |
| 35 to 44 | 1,967,000 | 97% | 67,000 | 3% | 2,055,000 | 100% |
| 45 to 54 | 1,060,000 | 97% | 32,000 | 3% | 1,092,000 | 100% |
| 55 to 64 | 766,000 | 98% | 17,000 | 2% | 784,000 | 100% |
| 65 and over | 779,000 | 99% | 9,000 | 1% | 788,000 | 100% |
| Total | 11,081,000 | 96% | 405,000 | 4% | 11,488,000 | 100% |

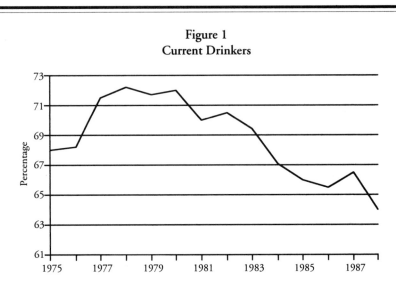

**Figure 1**
**Current Drinkers**

Percentage of high school seniors who are current drinkers (used alcohol in the past 30 days).
Source: Data from Johnston et al, 1989 (reference 2)

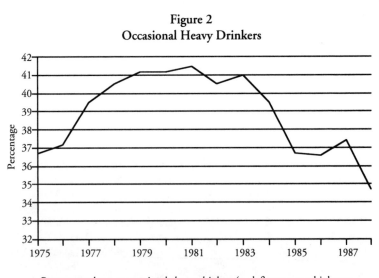

**Figure 2**
**Occasional Heavy Drinkers**

Percentage who were occasionaly heavy drinkers (took five or more drinks at a sitting during the past 2 weeks). 1975–1988
Source: Data from Johnston et al, 1989 (reference 2)

seniors used alcohol at least once during that 30-day period. Similar drinking patterns relative to the decline of use were also found among those 18 to 21 years who participated in the 1988 NIDA Household Survey.

Retrospective data on age of initiation from the annual high school senior surveys show that approximately 10 percent of seniors started alcohol use in the 6th grade, while more than 50 percent had used alcohol by the 9th grade.[4]

Studies investigating stability and changes in drinking patterns over time have reported conflicting results.[5,6] Nonetheless, data show that at age 31, a reasonable amount of alcohol abuse was evident among those who were abstainers as well as abusers at age 18.[5] Although there continues to be a consistent drop in the level of alcohol use among young people, there is still need for concern, especially regarding binge drinking. This is especially true since the use of alcohol is prohibited for people under the age of 21.

## COST TO SOCIETY

A 1990 national study by the Alcohol, Drug Abuse, and Mental Health Administration (ADAMHA) estimated that the total cost of public health problems attributed to alcohol abuse was $85.8 billion;[7] the economic cost of alcohol use and abuse to society in 1990 was $136 billion.[8] By 1995, the cost is expected to rise to $150 billion. This includes costs due to "loss of productivity," "excess mortality," "health care," and "property loss and crime."[9]

According to Assistant Secretary for Health Mason[10] of the U.S. Department of Health and Human Services (DHHS), these projections clearly demonstrate that alcohol use and abuse and alcoholism are having a tremendous impact on our nation and its resources. The ADAMHA study reported very substantial costs, which represent imposing health and social problems,[11] yet these figures do not represent the complete economic impact of the problem. Gaps in the data suggest that there is no way to determine the true magnitude of the problem, especially since alcohol abuse and alcoholism are disorders that often are underreported.

Frequently in the health arena, professionals refrain from formally noting alcohol abuse or alcoholism as the underlying cause of a patient's medical problem in order to reduce the possible stigma and embarrassment this may create for the patient. Nonetheless, there are a host of medical consequences that are associated with the use and abuse of alcohol. In medical care utilization studies, alcohol is believed to be a background factor in 20 percent to 40 percent of all inpatient hospital admissions and up to one-half of all visits to emergency rooms.[12]

Alcohol has been associated with four of the major causes of unintentional death in the U. S. – motor vehicle crashes, falls, drownings, and fires.[1] Even though there has been a decline in the rate of crash fatalities resulting from intoxication, still approximately one-half of all such crashes are alcohol-related. In 1988, then-Surgeon General Koop stated at the national Drunk Driving Workshop:

> "...an average of two or three of our fellow citizens are killed on our streets and highways every hour, around the clock, because they and others had their judgment and reflexes impaired by alcohol and other drugs. By this time tomorrow, some 65 Americans will have died on the highways in alcohol-related accidents."[13]

Almost identical statistics were mirrored in 1991 by Surgeon General Novello; she further concluded that:

> "...among those students currently in college, between 240,000 and 360,000 eventually will lose their lives due to drinking. This number equals the entire undergraduate student body of the 'Big 10' universities."[14]

Single episodes of drinking and persistent alcohol abuse and alcoholism contribute to adverse social and health consequences, the result of which affects not only the individual, but his or her family, significant others, community, and workplace.

As a final caveat, the major categories of costs associated with alcohol abuse and alcoholism include:[15]

1. treating the medical consequences of alcohol abuse and treating alcohol abuse and dependents themselves;
2. losses in productivity by workers who abuse alcohol;
3. loss to society because of premature deaths due to alcohol abuse;
4. cost of fetal alcohol syndrome, including cost of residential care, neonatal care, and treatment for abnormalities; and
5. cost involving the criminal justice system, social welfare administration, property losses from alcohol-related motor vehicle crashes and fires, and productivity of the victims of alcohol-related crime and individuals imprisoned as a consequence of alcohol-related crime.

The impact of these consequences is tremendous and the social, economic, and health costs are devastating.

## HEALTH CONSEQUENCES

Beverage alcohol (ethanol) is so common in our society that we seldom think of it as a drug.  Yet beer, wine, liquor, and the new wine cooler are all central nervous system depressants.[16] Numerous studies have shown that alcohol and its metabolites can serve as a toxic teratogen (an agent that produces defects in offsprings *in utero)* to the developing fetus.[17] A preponderance of case studies of children born to alcoholic mothers illustrate the effect of alcohol use on the developing fetus. The impact of maternal alcohol consumption on the fetus ranges from gross morphologic defects to a host of cognitive-behavioral aberrations.

Infants born with a constellation of abnormalities and major organ malfunctions are commonly classified as fetal alcohol syndrome (FAS) babies.[18] Throughout the gestational period, the maternal-placental-fetal system can have both direct and indirect actions resulting from the effects of alcohol use by the mother.[19] Infants of alcoholic mothers with less-defined medical disorders are referred to as "fetal alcohol effect" (FAE) infants. The treatment of infants with these two disorders is estimated to cost the health care system nearly one-third of a billion dollars per year.[20] Additionally, the variability in the nature and extent of abnormalities is related to several factors, including dose, chronicity of alcohol use, gestational stage, and duration of exposure and sensitivity of fetal tissue.[21] Adverse consequences of maternal alcohol consumption are not limited to infants born in these two categories. For example, research has shown that fetal exposure to alcohol is one of the leading causes of mental retardation.[1]

Alcohol consumption affects virtually every organ system of the human body. The medical consequences of beverage alcohol use vary from person to person, and from racial group to racial group. Some people are more predisposed because of differing levels of susceptibility and genetic make-up. Some of the major medical problems resulting from, or associated with, alcohol use and abuse are: 1) alcohol-induced liver disorders; 2) inflammation of the esophagus and peptic ulcers; 3) chronic pancreatitis; 4) increase in hypertension and ischemic heart disease; 5) cerebrovascular disorders; 6) cancer of the liver, esophagus, nasopharynx, and larynx; and 7) brain damage, blackouts, seizures, hallucinations, and peripheral neuropathy. It has been documented also that alcohol use and abuse contribute to numerous less-direct effects on the immune, reproductive, and endocrine systems.

# PREVENTION EFFORTS

A model of breadth, depth and lucidity, the NAS (National Academy of Science) report has helped recast U.S. alcohol policy into prevention terms.[8] The prevention of alcohol problems and the effective treatment of afflicted individuals have enormous potential for reducing illness and death and for improving the quality of life for millions of Americans.[22] In public health terms, prevention is usually defined at three levels – primary, secondary, and tertiary. Specifically, **primary prevention** presumes that the individual has never tried alcohol; **secondary prevention** seeks to stop the progression toward alcohol dependency and suggests that the potential user does not regularly use drugs; and **tertiary prevention** seeks to rehabilitate those who have become alcohol dependent. The public health perspective seems especially useful for encompassing workable solutions that recognize the stage of use and offer a greater range of responses to alcohol problems.

The definition of prevention as noted above is further broadened within the public health model to include agent, host, and environment. These elements are interactive and illuminate the complexity of problems associated with the use and abuse of alcoholic beverages. This model of prevention is particularly useful when developing strategies to address problems related to alcohol abuse and alcoholism. Using this framework, attention can be directed toward fostering strategies that address both individual and environmental needs and concerns. This conceptual framework allows program planners to organize and implement extensive alcohol prevention efforts, which attenuate specific individual and environmental factors within the context of the milieu of alcohol abuse and alcoholism. Since this model perceives the disorder as an interaction of the host (individual), environment, and agent (alcoholic beverage), it allows for a comprehensive approach to prevention. According to research conducted by NIAAA, the most promising strategies are those that combine a variety of approaches and can focus activities across all levels of prevention.

Targeting at-risk groups, especially young people, for education, prevention, and intervention activities in order to deter the misuse and abuse of alcohol is essential. Policy-makers and program implementors must recognize the need for a comprehensive and cooperative response to ameliorate alcohol abuse and alcoholism in the U.S. Two essential elements are necessary to accomplish the critical objective of preventing alcohol abuse and alcoholism: 1) programs must be focused and,

2) sufficient resources must be available to accomplish specific goals and objectives.

Several critical questions must be answered prior to the launching of a major prevention effort. Specifically, it is important to identify: 1) the scope and nature of the problem; 2) the target audience; 3) the diversity of the problem; and 4) any currently existing plans to address the problem. The 1986 Commission on the Prevention of Drug and Alcohol Abuse concluded that:

> "In principle, one can view the development of sound prevention programs as going through three steps, each informed by sound applied research: 1) policy formation and program design, 2) accountability evaluations, and 3) program assessment evaluations."[23]

Since alcohol abuse and alcoholism problems are ubiquitous and multifaceted, approaches to ameliorate the resulting dilemma must transcend racial, ethnic, and socioeconomic dimensions. A successful alcohol abuse and alcoholism prevention plan must be built upon a foundation that integrates assistance and support from the major significant segment of the target audience's *modus operandi*. The conceptual model must allow for multifaceted approaches and strategies. Further, there must be a clear and consistent communication of the behavior that is to be modified. For youth, this means communicating clearly that "any use of alcohol" is in fact abuse since alcohol use for people under the age of 21 is prohibited by law.

Since the formulation of the 1990 Health Objectives for the Nation,[24] considerable energy has been invested in reducing the incidence and prevalence of alcohol abuse and alcoholism among the nation's citizenry. The U.S. DHHS has assumed a proactive posture toward developing and supporting programs that deal with eradication of alcohol abuse and alcoholism in this country. For example, in 1991, the ADAMHA of DHHS is expected to spend an estimated $924.5 million (including block grant funds) on research, treatment, and prevention of alcohol abuse and alcoholism. The NIAAA has established the science base for many of the prevention initiatives related to taxation, labeling, and alcohol advertising. The Office for Substance Abuse Prevention (OSAP) is playing a major role in fostering prevention activities and programs that are designed to reduce the incidence of alcohol problems among children, youth, young adults, and women of child-bearing age. The efforts of OSAP along with other DHHS components are a part of a comprehensive national endeavor to reduce the incidence and prevalence of alcohol abuse and alcoholism in the U.S.

# POLICY PLANNING

The elements that have coalesced toward the formulation of a national alcohol policy are often in conflict and incorporate a mirage of legal and regulatory measures, industry efforts, and public health initiatives. Research and traffic crashes document that single episode drinking, alcohol abusers, and alcohol dependence are variables that must be considered since they can produce adverse social consequences. Public policy refers to those aggregate-level, legal, or regulatory measures that affect: 1) the level of consumption; 2) drinking practices; or 3) the environment in which drinking occurs. All of these factors directly influence the production, promotion, and distribution of alcoholic beverages.[25] Additionally:

> "...perhaps the most neglected, and possibly the most effective, policy tool available to the public for the prevention of youthful drinking problems is the appropriate use of excise taxes. ...alcohol is price-elastic and that reductions (in) per capita consumption will cause a reduction of alcohol-related problems, including cirrhosis of the liver, alcoholism, heavy drinking, and drunk driving."[25]

A modest increase in excise taxes will have as great or greater an effect on adolescent drinking as will an increase in the drinking age.[26] This is an area that has major implications for future alcohol policy. The higher the price increase the greater the per capita consumption decrease.[27]

Alcohol policy must be diversified in order to prevent alcohol use among youth, and alcohol abuse among the general public. When formulating local, state, or national alcohol policy, a broad spectrum of issues must be addressed:

1.  accessibility of alcoholic beverages to people under the age of 21, and issues for those of-age, e.g., concurrent sales, "2-for-1," "Happy Hour," promotion;

2.  consistency and coordination of local, state, and federal alcohol control, use, and pricing;

3.  appropriate utilization of scientific evidence that detail causal relationships between alcohol use and pernicious medical and economic consequences;

4.  utilization of law enforcement and legal deterrence regarding the prevention of alcohol-related problems;

5.  implications of social sanctions, parental use, and marketing practices relative to alcohol use among high school and college-age students; and

6.  relevancy of efforts toward the prevention, treatment, and rehabilitation of alcohol-related problems and dependencies.

Alcohol policy must be designed with a collaborating balance that allows for both an individual and community focus. A pivotal point for such policy should be its public health nucleus, not its morality judgment. Moreover, alcohol policy should provide the optimal parity for ensuring the success of prevention efforts. Currently, efforts are underway to promote a public health paradigm that reflects a coherent and comprehensive continuum of care that bridges all segments of society regardless of the varying drinking patterns of alcohol users.

## CONCLUSION

In order to improve the quality of health of American citizens and to reduce preventable death and disabilities resulting from alcohol abuse and alcoholism, the carefully orchestrated 1990 national health agenda has been advanced to the Year 2000. Since the initial framing of this agenda in 1979, it has been concluded that if alcohol were never carelessly used in our society, about 100,000 fewer people would die from unnecessary illness and injury (annually).[24] Healthy People 2000: National Health Promotion and Disease Prevention Objectives, the nation's health agenda, identifies specific objectives that both public and private constituencies can promote to reduce premature deaths, accidents, crime, and lost productivity. Section 4, Part II, of Healthy People 2000 focuses on ameliorating alcohol abuse and alcoholism, and it outlines specific objectives that deal with health status, risk reduction, and service and protection. Special attention is also given to remediating problems and issues related to personnel, surveillance and data, and research needs.[24]

During this decade, a concerted effort will be underway to ensure the continued decline of alcohol abuse among the nation's youth and young adults, and other at-risk groups. In March of 1991, a major initiative targeting college students was launched by the Office of the Surgeon General and Office for Substance Abuse Prevention as a part of the Healthy People 2000 agenda. This campaign promoted the objective that seeks to curtail the use of alcohol among youth and young adults under the age of 21 by 2000.

As public awareness increases, knowledge advances, and concerns heighten, we can expect to see more definitive endeavors relative to the prevention of alcohol abuse and alcoholism. All segments of society must assume an active role in promoting the accomplishment of the Healthy People 2000 alcohol abuse and alcoholism prevention objectives. Public education regarding the harmful effects of alcohol abuse and legislative and regulatory actions are necessary components for bringing about measurable change in the nation's health status by the year 2000. Our nation's colleges and universities should be at the apex of these efforts since they serve as the training ground for the future leadership of this country.

So often what occurs on a college campus serves as the precursor to the future directions of American society. Therefore, this population must answer the call, assisting on-going efforts, to consciously promote effective programs that eradicate alcohol abuse and alcoholism regardless of age, social class, ethnicity, political affiliations, or economic status. Hopefully by Year 2000, the product of a national effort will be characterized by a significant reduction in preventable death, disabilities, and diseases resulting from the use and abuse of alcohol among all segments of our society.

The U.S. Department of Health and Human Services is committed to attaining the Healthy People 2000 objectives. As our nation embarks upon the 21st century, the challenge to all Americans is to foster a society free of the negative health, social, and economic consequences of alcohol use and abuse.

## REFERENCES

1. U.S. DHHS, ADAMHA/NIAAA: Seventh Special Report to the U.S. Congress on Alcohol and Health. Washington, DC, U.S. Government Printing Office, Document No.: (ADM)90-1656, xxi and 6, 1990

2. Johnston LD, O'Malley PM, Bachman JG: Drug Use, Drinking, and Smoking: National Survey Results from High School Students, College Students, and Young Adults, 1975-1987. Rockville, MD, DHHS/ ADAMHA/ NIDA, (ADM)89-1638, 1989

3. NIDA: Class of 1990 National High School Senior Survey on Drug Abuse, Statement by the United State Department of Education Secretary. Rockville, MD, DHHS, 1991

4. Werner MJ: Adolescent Substance Abuse - Risk Factors and Prevention Strategies. Maternal and Child Health Technical Information Bulletin, Maternal and Child Health Bureau/HRSA, 1991

5. Temple MT, Filmore KM: The variability of drinking patterns and problems among young men, age 16-31: A longitudinal study. Int J Addict 20, 1595-1620, 1986

6. Windle M: Are those adolescent-to-early-adulthood drinking patterns so discontinuous? A response to Temple and Fillmore. Int J Addict 23(9), 907-912, 1988

7. Rice DP, Kelman LS, Dunmeyer S: The Economic Costs Of Alcohol And Drug Abuse And Mental Illness. San Francisco, CA, Institute for Health and Aging, UCSF, 1990

8. Walsh DC: The shifting boundaries of alcohol policy. Health Affairs, 9(2), 47-62, 1990

9. Bowen OR: Raising public awareness about the extent of alcohol-related problems: An overview. Public Health Rep 103, 559-563, 1988

10. Mason JO: Alcohol Abuse: Economic Cost to Society, Press Briefing, June 1990

11. Goodwin FK: Economic Cost to Society of Alcohol Abuse, Drug Abuse, and Mental Illness. Press Release, 1990

12. Burke TR: The economic impact of alcohol abuse and alcoholism. Public Health Rep 103, 564-568, 1988

13. Koop CE: Surgeon General's Workshop on Drunk Driving, Proceedings. Washington, DC, DHHS, 1988

14. Novello AC: Put on the Brakes. Spring Break Press Conference Statement, Washington, DC, 1991

15. Gordis E: Estimating The Economic Cost of Alcohol Abuse. Alcohol Alert (pamphlet). Rockville, MD, DHHS/PHS/ADAMHA/NIAAA Document No. 11 PH 293, 1991

16. Cook PS, Petersen RC, Moore DT: Alcohol, Tobacco, and Other Drugs May Harm the Unborn. Rockville, MD, DHHS/ADAMHA/Office for Substance Abuse Prevention, 1990

17. Jones KL, Smith DW: Recognition of the fetal alcohol syndrome in early infancy. Lancet, ii, 999-1001, 1973

18. Clarren SK, Sampson PD, Larsen J et al: Facial effects of fetal alcohol exposure: Assessment by photographs and morphometric analysis. Am J Med Genet, 26, 651-666, 1987

19. Rosett HL, Weiner L: Identification and Prevention of Fetal Alcohol Syndrome. Brookline, MA, Fetal Alcohol Education Program, 1985

20. Abel EL, Sokol RJ: Incidence of fetal alcohol syndrome and economic impact of FAS-related anomalies. Drug Alcohol Depend, 19, 51-70, 1987

21. Weiner L, Morse BA: Alcohol, pregnancy and fetal development, Women: Alcohol and Other Drugs. Edited by RC Engs. Washington, DC, Alcohol and Drug Problems Association, 1990, pp 61-68

22. U.S. DHHS, ADAMHA: Fiscal Year Justification of Appropriation Estimates for Committee on Appropriations. Washington, DC, U.S. Government Printing Office, Document No. (ADM)252-073, 1990

23. Commission on the Prevention of Drug and Alcohol Abuse: Final Report. San Francisco, California Department of Justice, 1986

24. U.S. Public Health Service: Healthy People 2000: National Health Promotion and Disease Prevention Objectives. Washington, DC, DHHS/PHS/Centers for Disease Control, 1990

25. Mosher JF: Public policies affecting the prevention of alcohol-related problems: Options for California, Prevention Action Plan for Alcohol-Related Problems. Edited by AM Mecca. California Health Research Foundation, 1985, p 9

26. Mecca AM (ed): Prevention Action Plan for Alcohol-Related Problems. San Francisco, California Health Research Foundation, 1985, p 10

27. Makela K, Osterberg E: Notes on Analyzing Economic Cost of Alcohol Use. Drinking and Drug Practices Surveyor, 15, 7-10, 1979

## Recommended Readings

Clarren SK, Smith DW: The fetal alcohol syndrome: A review of the world literature. N Engl J Med, 298, 1063-1067, 1987

Cook P: Alcohol taxes as a public health measure. Br J Addict, 77, 245-250, 1982

Engs RC, Hanson DJ: University students, drinking patterns and problems: Examining the effects of raising the purchase age. Public Health Rep 103(6), 667-673, 1988

Grant BF, Harford TC, Grigson MB: Stability of alcohol consumption among youth: A national longitudinal survey. J Stud Alcohol, 49, 253-260, 1988

Johnston LD, O'Malley PM, Bachman JG: Illicit Drug Use, Drinking, and Smoking: National Survey Results from High School Students, College Students, and Young Adults, 1975-1987. Rockville, MD, DHHS/NIDA, Document No. (ADM)89-1602, 1988

Johnston LD, O'Malley PM, Bachman JG: National Trends in Drug Use and Related Factors Among American High School Students and Young Adults, 1975-1986. Rockville, MD, DHHS/ADAMHA/NIDA, 1987

Moore MJ, Gerstein DR (eds): Alcohol and Public Policy: Beyond the Shadow of Prohibition. Washington, DC, National Academy Press, 1981

Mosher JF, Jernigan DH: New Directions in Alcohol Policy. Annu Rev Public Health 10, 245-279, 1989

National Household Survey on Drug Abuse: Main Findings. Rockville, MD, DHHS/National Institute on Drug Abuse, Document No.(ADM)88-1586, 1985

NIDA and NIAAA: Highlights from the 1987 National Drug and Alcoholism Treatment Unit Survey (NDATUS). Rockville, MD, DHHS, 1989

Roman PM: Women and Alcohol Use: A Review of the Research Literature. Rockville, MD, U.S. DHHS, 1988

Rosett HL: A clinical perspective of the fetal alcohol syndrome. Alcoholism, 4, 119-122, 1980

Sokol RJ: Alcohol and abnormal outcomes of pregnancy. Can Med Assoc J, 125, 143-8, 1980

Sokol RJ, Miller SI, Reed G: Alcohol abuse during pregnancy: An epidemiologic study. Alcoholism, 4, 135-145, 1980

U.S. DHHS, ADAMHA/NIAAA: Sixth Special Report to the U.S. Congress on Alcohol and Health. Washington, DC, U.S. Government Printing Office, Document No. (ADM) 87-1519, 1987

U.S. Department of Transportation: National Highway Traffic Safety Administration. General Estimates System. Washington, DC, U.S. Government Printing Office, Document No. HS807-665, 1989

# 14

# Tobacco

## Carol N. D'Onofrio, DrPH

Children and youth hold the key to preventing tobacco use – the single most important avoidable cause of death, disease, and disability in the United States.[1,2,3] Although tobacco use adversely affects people of all ages, the addiction that leads to life-threatening illness begins largely during childhood and adolescence. Over 90 percent of adults who smoke cigarettes start smoking before age 19,[4] and two-thirds of adult males who use smokeless tobacco (chewing tobacco and snuff) initiate use before they are 21 years old.[2] Progress in controlling the nation's major preventable health problem therefore depends on preventing and reducing tobacco use during the school-age years.

To underscore the magnitude of the problem, this chapter briefly reviews the health consequences of cigarette smoking and smokeless tobacco use, as well as the relationship of these practices to other high-risk behaviors. The onset of tobacco use and its prevalence during childhood, adolescence, and young adulthood are then discussed, followed by an overview of current approaches to prevention. A concluding commentary highlights planning and policy issues in student health relevant to achieving national health objectives for tobacco-use control.

## HEALTH CONSEQUENCES
## OF TOBACCO USE ADDICTION

Tobacco use is the most widespread form of drug dependence in the U.S.[5] The processes that determine addiction to tobacco are similar to those that determine addiction to other psychoactive substances such as heroin and cocaine.[6]

The tobacco plant naturally produces nicotine, a powerfully addictive drug. When tobacco is smoked or chewed, nicotine is rapidly absorbed into the bloodstream through the lungs or oral mucosa and delivered to the central nervous system. Pharmacologic processes interact with behavioral conditioning in complex ways so that numerous daily circumstances, activities, and emotions become cues for tobacco use. Prolonged ingestion of nicotine leads to tolerance, a tendency toward increased consumption, and physical dependence.[6,7] Use continues, despite a desire to quit, and in many cases, despite clear harm to the individual.[2] Cessation is often accompanied by withdrawal symptoms, and relapse is common. Nicotine addiction can become established quickly in children,[2] as evidenced by the difficulty that youth who smoke and chew tobacco often have in quitting.[6,8,9,10]

## CIGARETTE SMOKING

One-fourth or more of all regular smokers die of smoking-related diseases. Thus if adult smoking rates remain at the current level of about 29 percent, 20 million of the 70 million children now living in the U.S. will smoke cigarettes as adults and at least 5 million of them will die as a consequence. As former Surgeon General Koop observed: "This figure should alarm anyone who is concerned with the future health of today's children."[2]

More than one of every six U.S. deaths, or an estimated 390,000 deaths annually, is directly attributable to cigarette smoking.[2] Smoking causes more premature deaths than caused by AIDS, cocaine, heroin, alcohol, fire, automobile accidents, homicide, and suicide combined.[11] The cigarette toll includes an estimated 87 percent of lung cancer deaths, 30 percent of all cancer deaths, 21 percent of deaths from coronary heart disease, 18 percent of deaths from stroke, and 82 percent of deaths from chronic obstructive pulmonary disease.[2,12] Smoking also causes over 145 million days of excess bed disability and over 80 million excess days of work lost each year.[13] The annual cost of smoking-related health care and lost productivity in the U.S. has been estimated at about $65 billion, or $2.17 per pack of cigarettes sold.[14]

Tobacco smoke contains over 4,000 known compounds, including many that are pharmacologically active, toxic, mutagenic, or carcinogenic.[2] The fact that the constituents of cigarette smoke have diverse biological effects helps to explain why smoking has multiple adverse health consequences. Although the tobacco industry has developed filtered, low-tar, and other cigarette forms purported to reduce the health hazards of smoking, no cigarette or level of smoking can be considered safe.[15] The start of even modest cigarette smoking during the school-age years reduces lung function, increases respiratory symptoms, and results in pathologic changes.[16,17] Conversely, smoking cessation has major and immediate health benefits for people of all ages and for those with and without smoking-related disease.[18]

## MATERNAL SMOKING DURING PREGNANCY

Maternal smoking during pregnancy retards fetal growth and is associated with an increased incidence of spontaneous abortion, stillbirth, premature delivery, low birth weight, sudden infant death syndrome, and infant mortality.[2,19] In the U.S., cigarette smoking during pregnancy accounts for 20 to 30 percent of low birthweight babies,[20] up to 14 percent of preterm deliveries, and about 10 percent of all infant deaths.[2,21] The risk of these outcomes increases with the number of cigarettes smoked by pregnant women. Smoking cessation prior to or early in pregnancy can partly reverse the reduction in infant birth weight associated with maternal smoking.[2]

Estimates based on scarce statistics indicate that between one-fourth and one-third of women in the U.S. smoke during pregnancy.[12] A comparison of data collected from married women in 1967 and 1980 revealed a decline in smoking rates during pregnancy for some groups, but rates among married teenagers remained fairly constant at 39 percent for whites and 27 percent for blacks.[22] The prevalence of smoking among unmarried pregnant adolescents is unknown, but likely to be higher.

## ENVIRONMENT TOBACCO SMOKE

Exposure to environmental tobacco smoke (ETS) is a cause of disease, including lung cancer, in healthy non-smokers.[23,24] Estimates indicate that more non-smokers will die as a result of exposure to ETS than from exposure to any other air pollutant.[25]

Infants who are nursed by smoking mothers and who are exposed to ETS in their home absorb tobacco constituents, even when smoke is blown away from the baby, room ventilation is increased, or smoking occurs in another room.[26] Children of parents who smoke are more likely than the children of non-smokers to develop bronchitis, pneumonia, and other lower respiratory tract infections and to be hospitalized for these conditions, especially during the first year of life. Otitis media, the most common childhood illness requiring medical treatment, is considerably more common among children whose parents smoke. Parental smoking may also compromise lung function in young children and the developing lungs of the growing child.[12,23,24,25]

Since many children whose parents smoke become smokers themselves,[27] the long-term effects of exposure to ETS during childhood have been difficult to study.[23] However, a recent investigation found that approximately 17 percent of lung cancers among adult non-smokers can be attributed to high levels of exposure to ETS during childhood and adolescence.[28] Parental smoking may also contribute to the rise of chronic airflow obstruction in later life.[23,24]

A 1986 survey found a cigarette smoker living in 39 percent of households with one or more children aged six or younger. The proportion of children living with smokers therefore is almost certainly higher.[12]

## Smokeless Tobacco

Snuff "dipping" and tobacco chewing increase the risk for cancers of the oral cavity. Short-term effects include gingival recession and oral leukoplakias (precancerous white patches), as well as sores, blisters, and ulcers on the gums, lips, and tongue. Other effects on both soft and hard tissues of the mouth are suspected, but have not been confirmed.[29] Swallowing the excess saliva produced by smokeless tobacco use can produce nausea and other symptoms.[30,31] Because smokeless tobacco use can lead to nicotine dependence, scientists also are concerned that its use may result in increased cigarette smoking.[32]

# Tobacco use and Other High-Risk Behaviors

Tobacco use by youth is widely recognized as the "gateway" to other high-risk behaviors. Both cigarette smoking and smokeless tobacco use are highly correlated with use of alcohol, marijuana, and other drugs.[4,9,33-40] Although young people often experiment with alcohol before they try tobacco, tobacco use is more likely to lead to dependence. Moreover, increasing levels of tobacco use are associated with increased use of other psychoactive substances, and development of tobacco dependence appears to precede development of dependence on alcohol and illicit drugs.[4,9,33,34,40,41,42]

Adolescent females who smoke and drink are likely to begin intercourse at an earlier age and to be less effective users of contraception than girls who abstain from tobacco and alcohol use.[43,44,45] Tobacco use by youth is also linked with low school achievement, rule-breaking, and general delinquency.[2,46] Smoking and chewing in combination with other behaviors often multiply the risk of health, as well as social, problems. For example, use of tobacco with alcohol substantially increases the risk of developing oral and pharyngeal cancers.[47] Girls who smoke and use oral contraceptives greatly increase their risk of cardiovascular disease.[2,16]

## TOBACCO USE BY CHILDREN AND YOUTH

American children and youth under age 18 annually consume nearly 19 billion cigarettes (947 million packs), plus 26 million containers of smokeless tobacco.[48] Over 4 million American teenagers regularly smoke,[49] and half a million males between 12 and 17 years of age use smokeless tobacco at least weekly.[29] Every day of the year, more than 3,000 additional young people in the U.S. try their first cigarette,[50] and an unknown number try snuff "dipping" and tobacco chewing. These youth are replacements for the 1,000 older Americans who die daily from smoking-related disease and for the 500 Americans per day who quit smoking.[51,52] The younger the individuals are when they start to smoke, the more likely they are to become heavy smokers in later years and to have difficulty in quitting.[53,54] Unfortunately, by all methods of calculation, the average age of smoking initiation is dropping.[2,55,56]

The onset of smoking is viewed as a process evolving from preparation and anticipation, to initiation, experimentation, and then maintenance of regular smoking.[57,58] Less is known about the etiology of smokeless tobacco use, but the process of onset appears similar.[59] Different determinants seem to be influential at each stage of onset,[2,5,7,58,60,61] and children, as well as cohorts,[62] progress through these stages at a variable pace. These concepts imply that the challenges of prevention change with the child's development, personal characteristics, and social environment.

### EARLY CHILDHOOD

Through early learning from their environment, children develop attitudes about tobacco use and their intentions to try it. Prevention may be most effective at this stage;[57] however, tobacco use by family members undermines preventive efforts. Parents and older siblings who smoke or chew teach children that tobacco use is socially acceptable, model the specific behaviors involved in use, and increase youngsters' access to tobacco products.[58] Some children report trying their first puff of a cigarette or taste of chewing tobacco at age five or six.[63] In such cases, tobacco frequently is supplied by a family member.

## LATE CHILDHOOD AND EARLY ADOLESCENCE

The proportion of children who have tried tobacco gradually increases through the upper elementary grades, and then jumps sharply with the transition to middle or junior high school.[58] Substantial increases occur each year thereafter. Two recent surveys found that among high school students who had ever smoked, about one-quarter had smoked their first cigarette by grade six, one-half by grade eight, three-fourths by grade nine, and 94 percent by grade eleven.[64,65] Whites start smoking at a younger age than blacks,[2] and males tend to begin smoking earlier than females,[2] but girls catch up with higher rates of initiation in grades seven to nine.[65] Trial of smokeless tobacco varies markedly by gender, age, and geographic region. For example, the proportion of sixth-grade boys who have tried smokeless products ranges from 6.7 percent in New York City to 68.2 percent in rural Montana.[32] Youth who try smokeless tobacco also tend to experiment with cigarettes.[36,37,39,59]

Children may try tobacco for many different reasons; however, having friends who smoke or chew is the single best predictor of initiation.[36,58,60] The great majority of teenagers first use tobacco socially with peers.[36,66,67] While most youngsters have an initial aversive reaction, those who experience few symptoms or feel dizziness may rapidly try tobacco again.[58,68] With continuing experimentation, social and physiologic reinforcement is experienced and conditioned.[58] By the 8th grade, 8 percent of both boys and girls report smoking a pack or more of cigarettes in the past month, and this proportion more than doubles by grade ten.[65] A number of light smokers make the transition to daily smoking by age 14.[9,69]

## OLDER ADOLESCENCE

About two-thirds of the seniors graduating in 1989 reported ever smoking, 29 percent smoked in the past 30 days, 19 percent were daily smokers, and 11 percent smoked a half-pack or more per day.[9,70] Since school drop-outs may smoke at a rate as high as 75 percent,[71,72] data from seniors underestimate smoking prevalence in those 17 to 19 years old.

Smoking among high school seniors declined by approximately one-third from the mid-1970s to the early 1980s, but very little change has occurred subsequently.[2,9,55,56,62,70] Since 1977, the rate of daily smoking among senior girls has consistently exceeded that of senior boys by about four percentage points.[9] This difference may be offset by increased male use of smokeless tobacco, which has been heavily marketed to young men in recent years.[36,73] Between 1970 and 1986, males 17 to 19 years of age increased their use of snuff fifteenfold and that of chewing tobacco more than fourfold to become the age group with the highest rate of smokeless tobacco use in the U.S.[2] In 1985, over 8 percent of males 17 to 19 years of age reported current use of smokeless tobacco.[2] Regular use of smokeless tobacco by girls is rare, except among American Indians.[30,32,74-77]

Reflecting the inverse relationship between smoking and educational level in the adult population,[78] the prevalence of daily smoking among seniors who plan to attend college is less than half that of seniors who are not college bound (14% vs 30%).[2] However, whereas black adults are more likely to smoke than whites (34% vs 29%), black high school seniors are much less likely to report daily smoking than their white classmates (8% vs 20%).[2] Black and Asian adolescent males are also less likely to use smokeless tobacco than are whites and Hispanics, while American Indian males report higher rates of use than youth in other ethnic groups. Nonetheless, ethnic patterns of smokeless tobacco use may vary by region.[30,32,75]

Little is known about adolescent cessation of tobacco use, but several studies indicate that from 18 to 25 percent of youth who smoke stop within one year.[79,80,81] Data from Germany suggest that teenagers may go through several cycles of experimentation, regular smoking, and cessation before becoming either confirmed smokers or quitters.[82]

## Young Adults

The transition to adulthood is marked symbolically by the 18th birthday, at which age young people in most states can legally purchase tobacco for the first time.[2] Other changes in work, school, and living arrangements alter social status and roles, initiating processes of self-redefinition. Recognizing opportunity during this vulnerable period, the tobacco industry has identified those in the 18 to 24 year age group as a prime marketing target.

Data collected from ever-smokers 20 to 24 years of age indicate that about 33 percent of these males and 37 percent of the females start smoking between ages 18 and 20.[2] A longitudinal study also revealed that initiation of cigarette smoking increases sharply through the late teenage years.[4] Follow-up surveys to the annual survey of high school seniors have found more modest increases in smoking initiation after high school, but respondents who were active smokers while in high school reported smoking more intensively after graduation.[62,83]

Provisional data for 1987 indicate that 31 percent of males and 28 percent of females 20 to 24 years of age smoked. Smoking was reported by 44 percent of males and 38 percent of females who had less than 12 years of education, compared to 16 percent of males and 15 percent of females who attended college.[2] Whites smoked at a higher rate than blacks (31% vs 26%).[2] Older data indicate that smoking is less prevalent among young Mexican-Americans, particularly females.[84] There are no reliable estimates of smoking prevalence among other ethnic groups.[2] In 1987, nine percent of males 18 to 25 years of age regularly used smokeless tobacco.[30]

Smoking rates among college students vary with the type of institution attended. In a 1989 survey of full-time college freshmen, "frequent smoking" within the past year was reported by 12 percent of men in two-year colleges, 7 percent of those enrolled in four-year institutions, and slightly under 6 percent of those attending universities. Comparable figures for freshmen women were 16.6 percent, 9.2 percent, and 7.5 percent, respectively.[85] After a 22-year decline in the proportion of college freshmen who reported frequent smoking, rates rose in 1988. In this same year, a record high percentage of freshmen said they frequently felt depressed, while a declining proportion rated their emotional health above average.[86] These data are consistent with research associating tobacco use with stress.[6,87]

Several studies show that a large proportion of young adults who smoke have made one or more attempts to quit, but smoking cessation in this age group is limited.[2,27,88,89]

## PREVENTIVE EFFORTS

Approaches to tobacco-use prevention have evolved through 25 years of progress.[2] When simply teaching young people about the health hazards of smoking proved to be ineffective,[90,91] behavioral theories were applied to develop more sophisticated educational programs.[92,93,94] Despite unique features, these programs all focus on middle and junior high school students, provide multiple sessions, require teacher training, and emphasize: 1) the short-term physiologic and social consequences of tobacco use, 2) social influences promoting use, 3) social norms discouraging use, and 4) development of specific skills to deter use. Field trials funded by the National Cancer Institute and other evaluations have shown that both stand-alone tobacco education programs containing such essential elements and comprehensive health education offered in at least two grades have positive, albeit modest, effects in delaying the onset of tobacco use.[95,96,97] Schools and others can now obtain many of these tested programs.[98]

With increasing recognition that the social environment influences tobacco use by youth, some school-based programs have attempted to involve peers, parents, community groups, and mass media in prevention.[2] Community agencies and coalitions have also sought to involve schools in coordinated approaches to tobacco control. Efforts in both directions are fostering the development of comprehensive community-based programs that integrate education and policy initiatives. Contemporary approaches to prevention thus include the adoption and enforcement of policies that restrict tobacco use on school grounds and in other public places, restrict tobacco sales and the distribution of free samples to minors, control children's access to cigarette vending machines, raise tobacco taxes, and increase controls over tobacco marketing.[2] Another important thrust is analysis and activism to expose the tactics of the industrial giants who spend over $3.2 billion annually advertising and promoting cigarettes in the U.S.[99-103]

## ACHIEVING NATIONAL HEALTH OBJECTIVES

National health objectives for the year 2000 set challenging targets for tobacco-use control. These include reducing smoking initiation among youth and smoking prevalence among adults to no more than 15 percent, reducing smokeless tobacco use to a prevalence of no more than 4 percent among men 18 to 24 years of age, reducing to no more than 25 percent the proportion of children age six and younger who are exposed to cigarette smoke at home, increasing to 50 percent the proportion of smokers age 20 and older who make serious attempts to quit each year, and increasing smoking cessation among pregnant women to 60 percent.[12]

Health programs for students of all ages are strategic focal points for the organization, leadership, and advocacy necessary to achieve these objectives. Minimum tasks are to assure that tobacco is included in anti-drug programs, that schools are tobacco-free environments, that students in grades six through eight participate in an effective tobacco education program, and that programs and services for pregnant teenagers promote smoking cessation.[12,50,98,104]

New programs need to be developed and evaluated for preventing tobacco use among younger children[105] and for both preventing use and encouraging cessation among high school and college students. Different models and more targeted programs are needed to reach high-risk youth, including especially school absentees and drop-outs, those with one or more parents who use tobacco, low-achiever groups, and students from special populations.[50,61]

Effective measures must be found to protect children from exposure to environmental tobacco smoke, particularly at home. Promising approaches include case-finding and parent education, assisting children in exerting their rights to clean air,[105] and giving voice to the distress of those forced to breathe smoke from other people's cigarettes.[106] More broadly, tobacco education programs should recognize students as resources, as well as targets for prevention. Meaningful opportunities for students to participate in school and community tobacco control programs therefore should be created and the development of youth leadership should be fostered in the movement toward a tobacco-free society.

## REFERENCES

1. U.S. Department of Health, Education, and Welfare: Healthy People: The Surgeon General's Report on Health Promotion and Disease Prevention. DHEW (PHS) publication no. 79-55071. Washington, DC, U.S. Government Printing Office, 1979

2. U.S. Department of Health and Human Services: Reducing the Health Consequences of Smoking: 25 Years of Progress. A Report of the Surgeon General. DHHS publication no. (CDC) 89-8411. Washington, DC, U.S. Government Printing Office, 1989

3. U.S. Department of Health and Human Services: The Health Consequences of Smoking: Cancer. A Report of the Surgeon General. DHHS publication no. (PHS) 82-50179. Washington, DC, U.S. Government Printing Office, 1982

4. Kandel DB, Logan JA: Patterns of drug use from adolescence to young adulthood: I. Periods of risk for initiation, stabilization and decline in drug use from adolescence to early adulthood. Am J Public Health 74(7):660-66, 1984

5. Pollin W: Why People Smoke Cigarettes. PHS publication no 83-50185. Rockville, MD, National Institute on Drug Abuse, 1983

6. U.S. Department of Health and Human Services: The Health Consequences of Smoking: Nicotine Addiction. A Report of the Surgeon General. DHHS publication no. (CDC) 88-8406. Washington, DC, U.S. Government Printing Office, 1988

7. Kozlowski LT, Wilkinson DA, Skinner W et al: Comparing cigarette dependence with alcohol and other drug dependence: Greater or equal 'difficulty quitting' and 'urges to use,' but less pleasure from cigarettes. JAMA 261:896-901, 1989

8. Office of the Inspector General: Youth Use of Smokeless Tobacco: More than a Pinch of Trouble. Washington, DC, U.S. Department of Health and Human Services, 1986

9. Johnston LD, O'Malley PM, Bachman JG: National Trends in Drug Use and Related Factors among American High School Students and Young Adults, 1975-1986. DHHS publication no. (ADM) 87-1535. Washington, DC, U.S. Government Printing Office, 1987

10. McNeill A, West R, Jarvis M et al: Cigarette withdrawal symptoms in adolescent smokers. Pediatrics 74:479481, 1987

11. Warner KE: Health and economic implications of a tobacco-free society. JAMA 258(15):2080-2086, 1987

12. U.S. Department of Health and Human Services: Healthy People 2000. National Health Promotion and Disease Prevention Objectives. Conference Edition, 1990

13. U.S. Department of Health, Education, and Welfare: Smoking and Health: A Report of the Surgeon General. DHEW publication no. (PHS) 79-50066. Washington, DC, U.S. Government Printing Office, 1979

14. U.S. Congress, Office of Technology Assessment: Smoking-Related Deaths and Financial Costs. Washington, DC, U.S. Congress, 1985

15. U.S. Department of Health and Human Services: The Health Consequences of Smoking. The Changing Cigarette: A Report of the Surgeon General. DHHS publication no. (PHS) 81-50156. Washington, DC, U.S. Government Printing Office, 1981

16. Freedman DS, Srinivasan SR, Shear CL et al: Cigarette smoking initiation and longitudinal changes in serum lipids and lipoproteins in early adulthood: The Bogalusa Heart Study. Am J Epidemiol 124(2):207-219, 1986

17. American Thoracic Society: Health effects of smoking on children. Am Rev Respir Dis 132(5):1137-1138, 1985

18. U.S. Department of Health and Human Services: The Health Benefits of Smoking Cessation: A Report of the Surgeon General. Washington, DC, U.S. Government Printing Office, 1990

19. Holsclaw SD, Topkham AL: The effects of smoking on fetal, neonatal and childhood development. Pediatr Ann 7:105, 1978

20. Kleinman JC, Madans JH: The effects of maternal smoking, physical stature, and educational attainment on the incidence of low birthweight. Am J Epidemiol 121(6):843-55, 1985

21. Kleinman JC, Pierre MB, Madans JH et al.: The effects of maternal smoking on infant and fetal mortality. Am J Epidemiol 127:274-288, 1988

22. Kleinman JC, Kopstein A: Smoking during pregnancy 1967-1980. Am J Public Health 77:832-825, 1987

23. U.S. Department of Health and Human Services: The Health Consequences of Involuntary Smoking: A Report of the Surgeon General. DHHS publication no. (CDC) 87-8398. Washington, DC, U.S. Government Printing Office, 1986

24. National Research Council: Environmental Tobacco Smoke. Measuring Exposures and Assessing Health Effects. Washington, DC, National Academy Press, 1986

25. Eriksen MP, LeMaistre CA, Newell, GR: Health hazards of passive smoking. Annu Rev Public Health 9:47-70, 1988

26. Greenberg RA, Bauman KE, Glover LH et al: Ecology of passive smoking by young infants. J Pediatr 114:774-780, 1989

27. Green DE: Teenage Smoking: Immediate and Long-term Patterns. U.S. Department of Health, Education, and Welfare, National Institute of Education, 1979

28. Janerich DT, Thompson WD, Varela LR et al: Lung cancer and exposure to tobacco smoke in the household. N Engl J Med 323:632-636, 1990

29. U.S. Department of Health and Human Services: The Health Consequences of Using Smokeless Tobacco: A Report of the Advisory Committee to the Surgeon General. NIH publication no. 86-2874. Bethesda, MD, 1986

30. Boyd GM, Glover ED: Smokeless tobacco use by youth in the U.S. J Sch Health S9(5):189-194, 1989

31. Christen AG, McDaniel RK, Doran JE: Snuff dipping and tobacco chewing in a group of Texas college athletes. Texas Dental J 97(2):6-10, 1979

32. Boyd G et al: Use of smokeless tobacco among children and adolescents in the United States. Prev Med 167:402-421, 1987

33. Boyle MH, Offord DR: Smoking, drinking, and use of illicit drugs among adolescents in Ontario: Prevalence, patterns of use, and sociodemographic correlates. Can Med Assoc J 135:1113-1121, 1986

34. Newcomb M, Bentler P: Frequency and sequence of drug use: A longitudinal study from early adolescence to young adulthood. J Drug Educ 16(2):101-120, 1986

35. U.S. Department of Health and Human Services: Drug Abuse and Drug Abuse Research. Triennial Report to Congress from the Secretary. Department of Health and Human Services. DHHS publication no (ADS) 87-1486. Washington, DC, U.S. Government Printing Office, 1987

36. Ary DV, Lichtenstein E, Severson HH: Smokeless tobacco use among male adolescents: Patterns, correlates, predictors, and the use of other drugs. Prev Med 16:385-401, 1987

37. Dent CW, Sussman S, Johnson CA et al: Adolescent smokeless tobacco incidence: Relations with other drugs and psychosocial variables. Prev Med 16:422-431, 1987

38. Welte JW, Barnes GM: Youthful smoking patterns and relationships to alcohol and other drug use. J Adolesc 10:327-340, 1987

39. Murray DM, Roche LM, Goldman AI et al: Smokeless tobacco use among ninth graders in a North-Central metropolitan population: Cross-sectional and prospective associations with age, gender, race, family structure, and other drug use. Prev Med 17:449-460, 1988

40. Henningfield JE, Clayton R, Pollin W: Involvement of tobacco in alcoholism and illicit drug use. Br J Addict 85:279-292, 1990

41. Yamaguchi K, Kandel DB: Patterns of drug use from adolescence to young adulthood: II. Sequences of progression. Am J Public Health 74:668-672, 1984

42. Brunswick AF: Young black males and substance use, Young, Black, and Male in America: An Endangered Species. Edited by JT Gibbs. Dover MA, Auburn House, 1988, pp 166-187

43. Zabin LS: The association between smoking and sexual behavior among teens in U.S. contraceptive clinics. Am J Public Health 74:261-263, 1984

44. Zabin LS, Hardy JB, Smith EA et al: Substance use and its relation to sexual activity among inner-city adolescents. J Adolesc Health Care 7:320-331, 1986

45. Gibbs JT: Psychosocial correlates of sexual attitudes and behaviors in urban early adolescent females: Implications for intervention. J Soc Work and Hum Sexuality 5:81- 97, 1986

46. Jessor R, Jessor S: Problem Behavior and Psychosocial Development: A Longitudinal Study of Youth. New York, Academic Press, 1977

47. McCoy GD, Wynder EL: Etiological and preventive implications in alcohol carcinogenesis. Cancer Res 39:2844-50, 1979

48. DeFranza JR, Tye JB: Who profits from tobacco sales to children. JAMA 263(20):2784-2787, 1990

49. The Insider's Newsletter on Smoking Cessation 2(5):2, 1990

50. Glynn TJ: Essential Elements of School-Based Smoking Prevention Programs. J Sch Health 59(5):181-188, May, 1989

51. Warner KE: Selling Smoke: Cigarette Advertising and Public Health. Washington, DC, American Public Health Association, 1986

52. Altman D, Slater M, Albright C et al: How an unhealthy product is sold: Cigarette advertising in magazines, 1960-1985. J Advertising 17:26-32, 1987

53. U.S. Department of Health and Human Services: Smoking and Health: A National Status Report. Publication no. (CDC) 87-8396. U.S. Department of Health and Human Services, Office on Smoking and Health, Rockville, MD, 1987

54. McGinnis JM: Tobacco and health: Trends in smoking and smokeless tobacco consumption in the United States. Annu Rev Public Health 8:441-467, 1987

55. Johnston LD, O'Malley PM, Bachman JG: Psychotherapeutic, licit, and illicit use of drugs among adolescents: An epidemiologic perspective. J Adolesc Health Care 8:36-51, 1987

56. Johnston LD, O'Malley PM, Bachman JG: Use of Licit and Illicit Drugs by American High School Students: 1975-84. Rockville, MD, National Institute of Drug Abuse, 1985

57. Levanthal H, Cleary PD: The smoking problem: A review of the research and theory in behavioral risk modification. Psych Bull 88(2)370-405, 1980

58. Flay BR, d'Avernas JR, Best JA et al: Cigarette smoking: Why young people do it and ways of preventing it, Pediatric and Adolescent Behavioral Medicine. Edited by P Firestone and P McGrath. New York, Springer-Verlag, 1983, pp 132-183

59. Peterson AV, Marek PM, Mann SL: Initiation and use of smokeless tobacco in relation to smoking. NCI Monogr 8:63-69, 1989

60. Krohn MD, Skinner WF, Massey JL et al: Adolescent cigarette use, Advances in Adolescent Mental Health. Volume 1, Part B. Edited by RA Feldman and AR Stiffman. Greenwich, CT, JAI Press, 1986, pp 147-194

61. Cleary PD, Hitchcock JL, Semmer N et al: Adolescent smoking: Research and health policy. Milbank Q 66(1):137-171, 1988

62. O'Malley PM, Bachman JG, Johnston LD: Period, age, and cohort effects on substance use among young Americans: A decade of change, 1976-86. Am J Public Health 78(10):1315-1321, 1988

63. Young M, Williamson D: Correlates of use and expected use of smokeless tobacco among kindergarten children. Psychol Rep 56:63-66, 1985

64. Bachman JG, Johnston LD, O'Malley PM: Monitoring the Future: Questionnaire Responses from the Nation's High School Seniors. 1986. Ann Arbor, MI, Institute for Social Research, University of Michigan, 1987

65. American School Health Association, Association for the Advancement of Health Education, Society for Public Health Education, Inc.: The National Adolescent Student Health Survey. Oakland, CA, Third Party Publishing, 1989

66. Biglan A, McConnell S, Severson HH et al: A situational analysis of adolescent smoking. J Behav Med 7:109-114, 1984

67. Friedman LS, Lichtenstein E, Biglan A: Smoking onset among teens: An empirical analysis of initial situations. Addict Beh 10:1-13, 1985

68. Hirschman RS, Leventhal H, Glynn K: The development of smoking behavior: Conceptualization and supportive cross-sectional survey data. J Appl Soc Psychol 14(3):184-206, 1984

69. Baugh JG, Hunter SMacD, Webber LS et al: Developmental trends of first cigarette smoking experience of children: The Bogalusa Heart Study. Am J Public Health 72: 1 161-4, 1982

70. The University of Michigan Press release: Drug use continues to decline, according to U-M survey: Cocaine down for third straight year. News and Information Services, February 9, 1990

71. Pirie PL, Murray DM, Luepker RV: Smoking prevalence in a cohort of adolescents including absentees, dropouts, and transfers. Am J Public Health 78(2):176-179, 1988

72. Yates GL, MacKenzie R, Pennbridge J et al. A risk profile comparison of runaway and non-runaway youth. Am J Public Health 78(7):820-821, 1988

73. Connolly GN, Winn DM, Hecht SS et al: The re-emergence of smokeless tobacco. N Engl J Med 314(16):1020-1027, 1986

74. Hall RL, Dexter D: Smokeless tobacco use and attitudes toward smokeless tobacco among Native Americans and other adolescents in the Northwest. Am J Public Health 78(12):1586-1588, 1988

75. Orlandi MA, Boyd GM: Smokeless tobacco use among adolescents: A theoretical overview. NCI Monogr 8: 5-12, 1989

76. Schinke SP, Schilling RF, Gilchrist LD et al: Native youth and smokeless tobacco: Prevalence rates, gender differences, and descriptive characteristics. NCI Monogr 8:39-42, 1989

77. Centers for Disease Control: Prevalence of oral lesions and smokeless tobacco use in Northern Plains Indians. MMWR 37:608-611, 1988

78. Pierce JP, Fiore MC, Novotny TE et al: Trends in cigarette smoking in the United States: Educational differences are increasing. JAMA 26(1):56-60, 1989

79. Chassin L, Presson CC, Sherman SJ: Cognitive and social influence factors in adolescent smoking cessation. Addict Beh 9:383-390, 1984

80. Hansen WB, Collins LM, Johnson CA et al: Self-initiated smoking cessation among high school students. Addict Beh 10(3):265-271, 1985

81. O'Rourke T, Nolte AE, Smith AJ: Improving anti-smoking education: Profiling the ex-smoker. J Drug Educ 15(1):7-22, 1985

82. Semmer NK, Cleary PD, Dwyer JH et al: Psychosocial predictors of adolescent smoking in two German cities: The Berlin-Bremen study. MMWR 36(45):35-105, 1986

83. O'Malley PM, Bachman JG, Johnston LD: Period, age, and cohort effects on substance use among American youth. 1976-1982. Am J Public Health 74:682-688, 1984

84. Rogers RG, Crank J: Ethnic differences in smoking patterns: Findings from NHIS. Public Health Rep 103(4):387-393, 1988

85. American Council on Education and University of California at Los Angeles. Annual Survey of College Freshmen: Weighted National Norms, Fall 1989. Los Angeles, Higher Education Research Institute, UCLA, 1989

86. Associated Press: College freshmen smoking more, changing attitudes, survey finds. January 9, 1989

87. Wills TA: Stress, coping, and substance use in early adolescence, Coping and Substance Abuse. Edited by S Shiffman and TA Wills. New York, Academic Press, 1985, pp 67-94

88. Fisher EB, Gritz ER, Johnson CA: Cessation of smoking. The Health Consequences of Smoking: Cancer. A Report of the Surgeon General. U.S. Public Health Service. DHHS pub. no. (PHS) 82-50179. Washington, DC, 1982, pp 189-304

89. Raveis VH, DB Kandel: Changes in drug behavior from the middle to the late twenties: Initiation, persistence, and cessation of use. Am J Public Health 77(5):607-611, 1987

90. Thompson EL: Smoking education programs, 1960-1976. Am J Public Health 68:250-257, 1978

91. Flay BR: Mass media linkages with school-based programs for drug abuse prevention. J Sch Health 56(9):402-406, 1986

92. Evans RI, Raines BE: Control and prevention of smoking in adolescents: A psychosocial perspective, Promoting Adolescent Health: A Dialog on Research and Practice. Edited by TJ Coates, AC Petersen, C Perry. New York, Academic Press, 1982, pp 101-136

93. Flay BR: Social psychological approaches to smoking prevention: Review and recommendations, Advances in Health Education and Promotion. Vol 2. Edited by WB Ward. Greenwich, CT, JAI Press, 1987, pp 121-180

94. Bell CS, Battjes R (eds): Prevention Research: Deterring Drug Abuse among Children and Adolescents. NIDA Research Monograph 63. DHHS pub no (ADM) 85-1334. U.S. DHHS, PHS, ADAMHA, NIDA, 1985

95. Glynn TJ: Essential elements of school-based smoking prevention programs. J Sch Health 59:181-188, 1989

96. Connell DB, Turner RR, Mason EF: Summary of findings of the School Health Education Evaluation. Health promotion effectiveness, implementation, and costs. J Sch Health 55(8):316-321, 1985

97. Brody JE: Personal Health. The New York Times, May 4, 1989, p B9

98. Glynn TJ: School Programs to Prevent Smoking: The National Cancer Institute Guide to Strategies that Succeed. NIH pub no 90-500. Bethesda, MD, National Cancer Institute, 1990

99. Warner KE: Selling Smoke: Cigarette Advertising and Public Health. Washington, DC, American Public Health Association, 1986

100. Davis RM: Current trends in cigarette advertising and marketing. N Engl J Med 316:725-732, 1987

101. Blum A: Counter-Advertising to Minority Groups. DOC News and Views, Spring 1987, p 1

102. Maxwell B, Jacobson M: Marketing disease to Hispanics: The selling of alcohol, tobacco, and junk foods. Washington, DC, Center for Science in the Public Interest, 1989

103. Centers for Disease Control: Cigarette advertising — United States, 1988. MMWR April 26, 1990

104. D'Onofrio CN: Making the case for cancer prevention in the schools. J Sch Health 59(5):225-230, 1989

105. D'Onofrio CN: Tobacco Talk: Suggestions for Teachers, Parents, and Other Care-Givers of Children to Age 10. Santa Cruz, CA, Network Publications/ETR Associates, 1991

106. Mitchell L: Growing Up in Smoke. London, Pluto Press, 1990

# 15

# Children and Youth with Special Health Care Needs

Deborah Klein Walker, EdD

The wide range of needs of children and youth with chronic health conditions and their families is beginning to be acknowledged by providers and advocates in both the health and education sectors of society. Because of parent advocacy and policy studies conducted during the past decade, education and public health mandates and practices at all levels of government have slowly evolved.

The responsibilities of schools for providing services to handicapped children changed drastically in the 1970s due to the passage of the landmark civil rights legislation, Public Law 94-142, the Education for All Handicapped Children Act of 1975. Although the implementation varies tremendously by school system and state, overall, schools have responded to the needs of children with special problems.[1] Within the health care system, which has no equivalent civil rights legislation, services to these children and their families vary, dependent largely on the family's residence and socioeconomic status and the state's commitments through the Medicaid and Title V programs. Recent changes in Title V of the Social Security Act as mandated in the Omnibus Reconciliation Act of 1989, have redirected the delivery of health services to children and youth with special health care needs in each state.

This chapter will provide a profile of children and youth with special health care needs, a description of their school-based needs, an overview of the laws and programs in the educational sector and health sectors that impact on the delivery of school-based services to meet the identified needs, and a concluding section with recommendations and implications for future services.

## CHARACTERISTICS OF THE POPULATION

Children and youth with "special health care needs" is the term used today to refer to those who have a chronic illness or disabling condition that requires specialized health and related services. This generic term is preferred over those used in the past – handicaps, physical disabilities, crippling conditions, chronic illnesses, and developmental disabilities – since it focuses on the needs and functional status of the children rather than a specific diagnosis or condition.

Children with special health conditions represent about 10 to 15 percent of the population of children and youth from birth to 20 years of age. These estimates emerge consistently from secondary analyses of population-based and clinical studies of prevalence.[2] Of this group about 10 percent (or 1 to 2 percent of the total population) are considered to have a severe chronic illness, defined as one that interferes significantly with normal functioning and development.[3] In contrast to the adult population in which chronic health conditions are relatively few in number but relatively prevalent in society, the special health conditions of childhood and youth are varied in number and relatively rare. Examples of special health conditions of children and youth include arthritic diseases, juvenile-onset diabetes, muscular dystrophy, cystic fibrosis, spina bifida, sickle cell anemia, AIDS, congenital heart disease, chronic kidney disease, hemophilia, leukemia, cleft palate, and asthma. Over the past few decades there has been a marked decline in mortality and morbidity from infectious diseases along with an increased survival of children with severe chronic illnesses such as cystic fibrosis and leukemia. Although children with HIV infection and children dependent on medical supports such as tracheostomies, respirators, and oxygen have received considerable attention in the public arena recently, their numbers are small, representing less than a fraction of 1 percent of the population.

Numerous studies and reports during the 1980s have pointed out that children with special health care needs and their families share a common set of issues and concerns. Ongoing health conditions are costly to treat; require daily care by family members; are rare and unpredictable; require multiple providers and treatments; and often involve pain, discomfort, and embarrassment from the condition itself, or its treatment or both.[3] Findings from studies of parents' reported needs and concerns further support a non-categorical approach to services for this group of children and youth.[4]

## SCHOOL-BASED NEEDS

Since educational settings play a crucial role in the life of all children, they must be flexible and adapt to the needs of children with special health concerns so that they can benefit maximally from the schooling experiences with their peers. Whatever the diagnosis or severity of the condition, children and youth with special health care needs are at high risk for developing school problems in both the learning and psychosocial domains. Studies using clinical samples and population-based survey data have confirmed that children and youth with chronic health conditions have a significantly higher risk of displaying behavioral problems, independent of socioeconomic status.[5] Many children are low achievers in school because of these secondary psychosocial problems rather than cognitive or physical impairments. In addition, frequent absences from group activities with peers can create major image and attitudinal problems that lead to behavioral and learning problems. Another potential source of school problems is the negative attitude about a child's motivation on the part of teachers or peers. Unfortunately, these problems often arise out of ignorance or lack of understanding of a particular chronic condition, or of the effect of the condition or a treatment on a child's functioning.[6,7]

In light of these potential problems that children with special health care needs face in school settings, the child's peers, teachers, and other school personnel need to be aware of the child's condition and its impact on the child's performance. In order to best design and implement the educational program and health services in the school setting to meet the child's needs, a set of questions about the child's functioning (Table 1, next page) must be answered by the child's physician or other health care providers.[8]

Depending upon the answers to the questions, a school program including the delivery of appropriate school health services should be designed by a team consisting of the child's parents, school personnel, medical providers in the community, and the child or youth (when appropriate). Almost every child or adolescent with a special health concern will need special considerations made by the school setting at some point in his or her school career. The set of special services potentially needed is quite broad and includes the following: support therapies (including physical, occupational, speech and language), modified physical education, schedule modifications, transportation, building accessibility, toileting or lifting assistance, school health services (including administration of medications, implementation of medical procedures, emergency preparations, and care coordination), counseling services (for school, career, and personal issues), and sensitivity training and support (for peers and school staff).[7]

The responsibility for the care of children with special health care needs in school settings is shared by many divisions within the school bureaucracy, e.g., regular education, special education, school health, pupil personnel services. There is great variability across the country by state and within each state by local school system regarding how the needs of these children are handled on a daily basis and how the state and federal special education laws and the state and local health codes and regulations are implemented. How the education and health systems' responses to the needs of these children shape the delivery of school-based services to this population will be outlined in the next sections.

---

### Table 1
### Questions Educators Frequently Ask Physicians About Handicapped Children for Program Planning and Daily Management Procedures

1. Does the child's present condition require any specific physical restrictions?
2. Can the child participate in physical education and on any sports team without restrictions?
3. Is there a need to shorten or modify the school day?
4. Is the child presently taking medication? How will it affect the child's behavior?
5. Are there special emergency precautions that should be learned by school staff?
6. Does the child need special protective equipment?
7. Does the child use any special equipment?
8. Should the child have preferential seating?
9. Does the child need physical, occupational, or speech therapy?
10. Should the child receive special counseling?
11. Does the child require a modified diet?
12. Does the child need assistance with toileting?
13. What is the prognosis of the child for the future?
14. What is the child's understanding of the problem and his/her present condition? Are further explanations necessary?

## EDUCATIONAL OPTIONS

The educational placement and related services received by a child should be based on information about the child's developmental level, academic learning potential, and daily functioning competencies. Many children with special health concerns will be eligible for special classroom placements and related services under the state and federal special education law. Public Law 94-142 covers services for a wide range of handicaps, including mental retardation, deafness and hard of hearing, speech impairments, visual impairments, serious emotional disturbances, orthopedic impairments, other health impairments, and learning disabilities.[7] In October, 1990, the term "handicapped" was eliminated and the law renamed the "Individuals with Disabilities Education Act of 1990" (IDEA).

The law requires that children and youth be identified, evaluated in a multidisciplinary process using culturally appropriate instruments, and placed in the "least restrictive environment" or with nonhandicapped peers to the maximum extent possible. An individualized educational plan (IEP) must be developed for each child upon entrance into special education and updated annually. Developed out of a strong civil rights activist movement, the federal law mandates strong due-process requirements for protecting the rights of the children and their families in acquiring and maintaining services.[7]

The educational placements used for children with special needs vary along a continuum of integration with nonimpaired peers from least to most restrictive: regular class, special resource class or special class in a regular school, homebound tutoring or hospital program, special day school, and residential school. The law states that related services must be provided to children if they are necessary for the child to benefit from special education instruction. The set of "related services" defined under the federal statute for possible inclusion in a child's individualized education plan are comprehensive and similar to the list of school-based needs for children with special health care needs:

> transportation and such developmental corrective and other supportive services as are required to assist a handicapped child to benefit from special education... speech pathology and audiology, psychological services, physical and occupational therapy, recreation, early identification and assessment of disabilities in children, counseling services, and medical services for diagnostic and evaluation purposes...school health services, social work services in schools and parent counseling and training (PL 94-142 Federal Regulations)

Since its passage, several amendments to PL 94-142 have encouraged states to significantly expand services to children in the preschool years. The most comprehensive mandates were passed in 1986 in PL 99-457.[9] This amendment gives incentives to states to serve preschool children, ages three to six, as well as to set up a new discretionary program for infants and toddlers (Part H of PL 94-142). Part H provides some federal dollars to states to create a service system for at-risk infants and toddlers (birth through age 2) and their families. Although states have discretion in determining the definition of which at-risk children are served and how key requirements of the systems will be met, all states at the end of the five-year planning cycle in the early 1990s must have entitlement to services from birth if they are to continue to get federal dollars for early childhood services. The major components of an early intervention system required by states include public awareness, screening and identification, diagnosis and multidisciplinary evaluations, child- and family-focused intervention programs, case management and interagency coordination, procedural safeguards, individual family service plans (IFSP), data collection and reporting systems, comprehensive personnel development programs, and a central directory of services.[10] Finally, Part H requires that health and education systems join with other human service agencies in a state through an Interagency Coordinating Council to plan and implement services; this type of collaboration can be a model for service delivery for other age groups as well.

## SCHOOL HEALTH SERVICES

Many needs of children and youth with special health conditions should be met by the school health program, regardless of whether or not the child is in special education or some other special program. However, unlike special education, there is no federal statute or set of health codes that mandate health services in schools. In addition, there is no guaranteed right to health care similar to the entitlement of children to education. Therefore, the delivery of health services in schools varies tremendously by local educational authority and depends on a number of factors, including local and state resources, state guidelines and codes, personnel training, historical precedent, and bureaucratic structures.[11]

Ideally, all schools should have a full-time, well-trained school nurse who would serve as the coordinator for children with special health care needs within the school and between the school and the child's health care providers in the community. Specifically, the nurse should act as the manager of the child's health care within the school, which includes communicating within the school with teachers and other school staff (e.g., principal, secretary, classroom and special subject teachers); communicating about the child's care with the child's physician(s) and other human service providers in the community; counseling the child, family, and staff about health issues; advocating for the child's health needs and rights; and educating the school and community about children with chronic conditions.[12]

A major responsibility of the school health program is the development and implementation of policies concerning the administration of medications and various health procedures that occur during the school day. A 1985 survey of state policies or guidelines for the administration of these procedures in schools found that the majority of states had some guidelines for the administration of medications while only a few had them for health procedures such as catheterization, seizure management, respiratory care, tube feeding, and colostomy/ileostomy care.[13]

Another important issue in schools who have children with special health care needs is the training of school personnel who might be present when a child has a medical emergency. Planning contingencies for emergencies with appropriate training and follow-up is extremely important because the school nurse or physician is usually not present when an emergency occurs.[7,8]

Today, the delivery of school health services may be under the direct auspices of the local board of education, the local health department, or a combination of both. Furthermore, even if the school health services are directed by the educational authorities, those staff responsible for school health at the district level are usually in a different bureaucratic hierarchy from that of special education and, in many cases, from that of other pupil personnel services (e.g., counseling, social work, psychological services).

Although the majority of school health programs are based on an information and referral model centered around the school nurse, a growing number of school systems have expanded their programs to include the delivery of primary health care services. This model has been especially useful during the past decade in urban areas where the primary care services in the community are not adequately meeting the children's needs. As might be expected, children with chronic conditions, such as asthma, are major users of these school-based health services. In either model of the delivery of school health services, a comprehensive school program integrating health education activities and environmental protection is best. In addition, a team approach, which involves the principal, school nurse, social worker, guidance counselor, teacher, and other school personnel, has been shown to be effective in addressing school health issues.

In the future, public health departments may take a more active role in the development and implementation of health services in schools, for children with special health care needs, in response to the mandates of Title V of the Social Security Act as amended in the Omnibus Reconciliation Act of 1989. This federal law explicitly requires one-third of the Title V (Maternal and Child Health) block grant dollars to be used in developing community-based, family-centered, coordinated systems of care for children with special health care needs.[14] Since schools are a major place where children and youth spend time during the day, they must be considered as a major site for the delivery of care in the community-based systems. Currently states use these dollars to provide direct clinical care services or case management to these children and their families, to provide training and technical assistance to schools regarding health procedures and policies, and to support school-based health centers.

## CURRENT PRACTICES AND IMPLICATIONS

In practice there is great variability across the country in how the education and health laws and guidelines are implemented, leaving many children who have special health care needs without adequate services in the schools. One major factor in determining how services are provided in schools relates to the interpretation of the child's eligibility for special education. Those children who need special instruction because of a learning problem are clearly eligible for special education and hence to related services. Those who do not need special classroom instruction on an ongoing basis but do need special health and other related services (e.g., a child with juvenile rheumatoid arthritis who needs physical therapy, a child with asthma who has frequent absences because of hospitalizations, a child with diabetes who needs a special lunch, a child with a shunt who needs a modified physical education program) are handled in one of three ways by school systems today: they are enrolled in special education and have related services including special health services included in the IEP; they are given the equivalent of special education services because of Section 504 of the 1972 Rehabilitation Act, which provides for equal access to the handicapped in facilities receiving federal dollars; they do not receive special education services but do receive school health and other special services available in the regular school setting.[7]

Although the third option can be an adequate response to meet the child's needs without the benefit of special education entitlements, it is frequently not enough today with schools confronting major budget constraints. The dilemma today is that many school nurse positions have been cut from school district budgets in financially tight times; this has drastically altered the type and quality of school health services available in many schools. Furthermore, access to special education is not usually adequate either, because many school systems limit the type and amount of related services offered to the child and his or her family. Ironically, however, the services available through the special education mandates are often the only therapies and counseling services many families can access since public and private insurance coverage is not comprehensive enough to meet the needs of children with special health care needs. Consequently, many children and youth with special health care needs are not being adequately monitored by trained school health personnel and are at great risk of not reaching their fullest potential in school.

In conclusion, the key policy issues that need to be addressed concerning the delivery of school health services to children and youth with special health conditions center around five key issues: conflicting and inadequate financing structures, inconsistent legal mandates in education and health, bureaucratic and organizational barriers at all levels of government, inadequacies in personnel recruitment and training, and minimal public commitment.

The following are a few recommendations that need to be addressed at the local and state level to improve the delivery of health services in schools for children with special health care needs:

1.  Clarify who is eligible for special education and public health services.
2.  Improve communication and relationships among all school and community personnel.
3.  Develop and implement explicit local and state school health codes to deal with identification and tracking, care coordination, administration of medication and health procedures, and emergencies.
4.  Clarify physician's and other health providers' roles with respect to the school setting.
5.  Provide training and personal support to school and other personnel.
6.  Develop state and federal legislation to insure provision of adequate health services.
7.  Educate school and community personnel about the needs of children with chronic health conditions.

# REFERENCES

1. Singer JD, Butler JA: The Education for All Handicapped Children Act: Schools as agents of social reform. Harvard Educational Review 57:125, 1987

2. Gortmaker SL, Sappenfield W: Chronic childhood disorders: Prevalence and impact. Pediatr Clin North Am 31:3, 1984

3. Hobbs N, Perrin JM, Ireys HT: Chronically Ill Children and Their Families. San Francisco, Jossey-Bass, 1985

4. Walker DK, Epstein SG, Taylor AB et al: Perceived needs of families with children who have chronic health conditions. Children's Health Care 18:196, 1989

5. Gortmaker SL, Walker DK, Weitzman M et al: Chronic conditions, socioeconomic risks, and behavioral problems in children and adolescents. Pediatrics 85:267, 1990

6. Weitzman M: School and peer relations. Pediatr Clin North Am 31:59, 1984

7. Walker DK: Public education: New commitments and consequences, New Directions in Caring for Children with Chronic Illness. New York, Springer, 1989, pp. 41-60

8. Walker DK: Care of chronically ill children in school. Pediatr Clin North Am 31:221, 1984

9. Garwood SG, Sheehan R: Designing a comprehensive early intervention system: The challenge of Public Law 99-457. Austin, TX, Pro-ed, 1989

10. Meisels SJ: Meeting the mandate of Public Law 99-457: Early childhood intervention in the Nineties. Am J Orthopsychiatry 59:451, 1989

11. Walker DK, Butler J, Bender A: Impact on child health delivery of trends in U.S. public education, Children in a Changing Health Care System. Edited by MJ Schlesinger and L Eisenberg. Baltimore, Johns Hopkins University, 1990, pp. 265-296

12. Wold SJ (ed): School Nursing: A Framework for Action. St. Louis, Mosby, 1981

13. Wood S, Walker DK, Gardner J: School health practices for children with complex medical needs: A national survey of guidelines. J Sch Health 56:215, 1986

14. Brewer EJ, McPherson M, Magrab PR: Family-centered, community-based coordinated care for children with special health care needs. Pediatrics 83:1055, 1989

# 16

# Dental Health

KENNETH C. TROUTMAN, DDS, MPH

## DENTAL HEALTH STATUS AND NEEDS

Dental diseases are a major health problem for children, adolescents, and young adults. In 1987, children under 18 years had 3.6 million days of restricted activity, 1.1 million bed days, and 470,000 lost school days associated with dental conditions.[1]

## DENTAL CARIES

Dental caries (tooth decay) rank among the most prevalent diseases in our society. It starts soon after primary teeth erupt in early childhood and can continue throughout adulthood. In 1987, the cost of dental care in the United States was more than $32.8 billion, a significant amount of which was spent to repair decayed teeth.[2] Yet, much dental caries goes untreated because less than half of the population receives dental care in any given year.

Only a few years ago, most people believed that tooth decay was inevitable and had to be endured. Today, we know that this disease can be prevented. Scientists have established that the process of tooth decay requires essentially four factors: 1) a susceptible tooth, 2) certain bacteria, 3) certain foods in the diet, and 4) the presence of these first three factors in the mouth for a sufficient amount of time to cause enamel decalcification. The disease does not occur if any one of these factors is missing.[3] (See Figure 1, next page.)

Between 1979-80 and 1986-87, there was a continuing decline in the prevalence of dental caries in primary and permanent teeth for all ages of school children. This rate of decline approximated the rate that was observed during the 1970s.[4,5,6] During the 1980s, the average overall decayed-filled-surface rate for primary teeth (dfs) in those children between 5 and 17 years decreased from 5.31 to 3.91. Similarly, the decayed-missing-filled-surface (DMFS) rate for permanent teeth in those children and youth between 5 and 17 years decreased from 4.77 to 3.07. In addition, during this period, at each age between 5 and 17 years, the percent of children who were caries-free increased. Overall, the percent of all school-age children who were caries-free increased from 36.6 percent to 49.9 percent. [7-10] (See Table 1, next page.)

In addition, while the decay (D) and missing (M) components of the DMFS decreased, the filled (F) component increased, thus indicating increased dental care. In all age categories, female children had higher rates

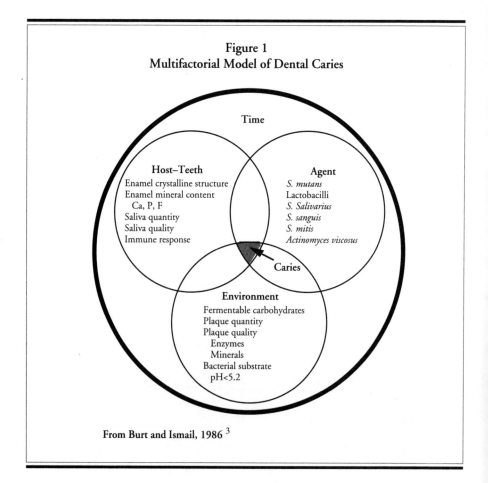

**Figure 1**
**Multifactorial Model of Dental Caries**

Time

**Host–Teeth**
Enamel crystalline structure
Enamel mineral content
Ca, P, F
Saliva quantity
Saliva quality
Immune response

**Agent**
S. mutans
Lactobacilli
S. Salivarius
S. sanguis
S. mitis
Actinomyces viscosus

Caries

**Environment**
Fermentable carbohydrates
Plaque quantity
Plaque quality
Enzymes
Minerals
Bacterial substrate
pH<5.2

From Burt and Ismail, 1986 [3]

of dental caries than their male counterparts, and white children had lower DMFS scores than nonwhite.

Various explanations for the causes of the rapid decline of oral diseases have been proposed in the literature.[11,12] It has been suggested that improved oral health status is possibly due to a combination of a number of influences including better living conditions, increased education of the public, improved access to health care, increased understanding of disease processes, and especially the development of methods to prevent and control dental caries, such as water fluoridation, topical fluorides, fluoride toothpastes, and dental sealants.[9,11,12,13]

Although recent decline in dental caries must be looked upon as a public health success, we must not become complacent. There still exists a large block of children who are **not** caries-free and who continue to require diligent preventive and treatment programs. This group must not be overlooked. As few as 26 percent of the children have 58.9 percent of the decayed, filled, and missing teeth.[14,15] We must continue our efforts to identify these children in order to begin early preventive measures. Fifty percent of all children still experience dental caries in their permanent teeth, and unfortunately, children's dental caries rates increase with age.[16] Studies indicate that specific population groups are at greater risk and that

### Table 1
### Mean DMFS for U.S. Children Aged 5-17

| Age | NHANES 1971-74[7] Mean DMFS | NDCPS 1979-80[8,9] Mean DMFS | NIDR,1986-87[10] Mean DMFS |
|---|---|---|---|
| 5 | 0.15 | 0.11 | 0.07 |
| 6 | 0.41 | 0.20 | 0.13 |
| 7 | 0.69 | 0.58 | 0.41 |
| 8 | 0.86 | 0.25 | 0.71 |
| 9 | 3.59 | 1.90 | 1.14 |
| 10 | 4.14 | 2.60 | 1.69 |
| 11 | 4.58 | 3.00 | 2.33 |
| 12 | 6.36 | 4.18 | 2.66 |
| 13 | 8.67 | 5.41 | 3.76 |
| 14 | 9.60 | 6.53 | 4.68 |
| 15 | 11.67 | 8.07 | 5.71 |
| 16 | 15.12 | 9.58 | 6.68 |
| 17 | 16.90 | 11.04 | 8.04 |
| All Ages | 7.06 | 4.77 | 3.07 |

the variations in dental caries rates are associated with age, geographic location, ethnicity, socioeconomic status, and availability of oral preventive measures.

## GINGIVAL AND PERIODONTAL DISEASE

It has been reported that 92 percent of all school children in the U.S. have mild or moderate gingival inflammation; therefore, these children would benefit from improved oral hygiene procedures at home and regular visits to the dental office to reinforce oral hygiene instruction.[17] Severe gingival conditions that warranted special attention by a dentist or periodontist were reported for 3 percent of children (1.4 million).[18] In the U.S., periodontal diseases (gum diseases) that require care affect more than 50 percent of adolescents.[15,19] It has been suggested that a majority of school children would benefit from gingival treatment and improved oral hygiene.

## MALOCCLUSION

With intervention during early childhood, malocclusion is usually an oral condition that can be corrected; improved function and appearance will enhance oral health. Premature loss of primary teeth is associated with risks of subsequent malocclusion and crowding in the permanent dentition. Orthodontic problems are especially significant for adolescents. The 1973 National Health Survey reported 75 percent of children, ages 6 to 11 years, and 89 percent of youth, ages 12 to 17 years, had some degree of occlusal disharmony; 8.7 percent of children and 13 percent of youth had a severe handicapping malocclusion for which treatment was highly desirable; while 5.5 percent of children and 16 percent of youth had a severe handicapping malocclusion that required mandatory treatment. Only about 5 million (11.7 percent) school-age children (5 to 17 years) were receiving or had completed orthodontic treatment.[18]

The increasing success of fluorides and other methods for the prevention of caries should yield significant progress in reducing the prevalence of malocclusion in children. However, there remains a considerable need for prevention and treatment of developing malocclusions in our nation's children.

# PREVENTIVE MEASURES

Although we know that dental diseases are preventable, most preventive efforts are not directed toward preventing the diseases from occurring but toward preventing their recurrence. Primary prevention and early intervention are of the utmost importance in controlling dental diseases. The conscientious application of a relatively few routine procedures can control most dental diseases. It is an indictment on our society that dental diseases are allowed to rampage through all socioeconomic levels. In the years to come, it is hoped that through the cooperative efforts of all health disciplines, the dental problems that affect most people can be eliminated. If health services for children are to be interdisciplinary and comprehensive, then oral health must be a part of such programs; and physicians, nurses, and teachers must become aware of the role that oral health plays in the general health of children.

## DIET

Regardless of a person's age, diet may be a risk factor for the incidence of dental caries. The role diet plays is not as clear as once thought. Although the frequency of sugar consumption still plays a part in the prevalence of dental caries, the role that feeding practices have on dental caries is more evident in baby bottle-nursing tooth decay, the major oral health problem among children under three years of age. Allowing a child to feed for extended periods, sleeping with a bottle containing liquid conducive to the formation of dental caries (milk, juice, or sweetened water), or by demand breast feeding throughout the night can cause this condition. Baby bottle-nursing tooth decay is often found in lower socio-economic, Native American, and Hispanic populations; however, it is an increasing problem among young children of middle- and upper-class parents.[20]

Research has concentrated so much on various aspects of sugars that questions naturally arise about other foods that may have etiologic roles in the caries process. There is certainly more to the problem than the ability of a food substance to produce acid in the oral environment. Table 2 (next page) illustrates the many factors involved.[21] Each of these factors can influence the development and severity of caries, and their different interactions can yield various degrees of susceptibility to caries following the ingestion of a food that is particularly active in promoting caries.

## FLUORIDE AND DENTAL CARIES

The most important factors in the decrease in dental caries are the availability of fluoridated water supplies and dentifrices (toothpastes), and a series of other topical fluoride regimes. By 1985, over 52 percent of the U.S. population was receiving optimally fluoridated water.[22,23] Nearly 90 percent of all dentifrices sold during 1981-85 contained fluoride. A large number of children participated in school-based fluoride mouth-rinse programs, and fluoride-containing mouth rinse was available for home use. In addition, fluoride in the form of dietary supplements has been prescribed for some children (tablets and drops) for home use.[22] Specifically, more than 91 percent of children under age 17 used fluoridated toothpaste and varying percentages of children used fluoride mouth rinses, dietary fluoride supplements, or had dental sealants placed. However, children below the poverty line and nonwhite children received less dietary fluoride supplementation than their respective counterparts above the poverty line and white children.

## Community Water Fluoridation

The delivery of fluoridated water is by far the most cost-effective method to assure the continuous systemic and topical exposure of teeth to fluoride from development through eruption. It also maximizes patient compliance. Fluoride occurs naturally in nearly all water and foods. It is an essential nutrient for proper growth and development. Fluoridation is the adjustment of the fluoride content of a community's water supply to an

---

**Table 2**
**Factors that Determine Caries Experience**

1. Bacteria (oral flora)
2. Structure and composition of enamel and dentin
3. Morphology and alignment of teeth
4. Nutritional status and infectious episodes during tooth development
5. Fluoride status (available fluoride concentration in oral fluids, plaque, and external layers of enamel)
6. Oral hygiene habits
7. Saliva flow rate and composition
8. Food consumed
   a. composition
   b. texture
   c. pH
9. Dietary patterns
   a. amount
   b. combinations
   c. frequency of intake
   d. eating order

Modified from: Navia 1981[21]

optimal concentration for the prevention of tooth decay. The optimal range is 0.7 to 1.2 ppm (parts per million) fluoride depending upon the climate. (It is assumed that more water is drunk in warm than in cold regions.[24,25]) This procedure provides systemic benefits to teeth that are developing in the jaws as well as topical benefits to erupted teeth.

Fluoridation is inexpensive and benefits the entire community regardless of age, economic or educational level, individual motivation, or the availability of dental manpower. No direct action is required of an individual, yet fluoridation can reduce tooth decay by as much as 50 percent to 65 percent among children who consume optimally fluoridated water from birth.[25,26] With the almost universal use of fluoridated toothpaste today, however, the differential may currently be only about 18 percent.[11] Moreover, through its topical effect, the improvement in dental health continues for life if consumption of fluoridated water continues. For all these reasons water fluoridation is the foundation upon which all local, state, or national programs to prevent dental decay should be based. Approximately 60 percent of the population of the U.S. enjoys the benefits of either optimally adjusted or naturally fluoridated water. Nevertheless, about 73 million other people in this country do not benefit from fluoridation because their water systems are not fluoridated, and about 37 million cannot benefit because they live in areas that lack central water systems.[27] It is clear that to improve oral health, additional methods of delivering fluorides, particularly to children, are required.

## School Water Fluoridation

An effective way to provide the benefits of fluoride to children living in geographic areas that lack central water supplies is to fluoridate school water supplies. This method reduces dental decay by about 40 percent.[28] It is particularly suitable for many rural schools that consolidate kindergarten through grade 12 in the same or adjacent buildings. Approximately 4,000 rural schools have independent water supplies suitable for fluoridation. Of those, over 450 have now fluoridated their water supplies.[28] A disadvantage of school fluoridation is that its use is limited to school hours only and to areas in which home water supplies of all students have low levels of naturally occurring fluoride. Because the availability of fluoride is limited to school hours, school drinking water is fluoridated to a level of 4.5 parts per million instead of the usual community water level of 1.0 ppm.[28]

## Professional Application of Topical Fluorides

Fluoride can also be applied topically to teeth by a dentist or a dental assistant. A fluoride solution may be painted on the teeth or fluoride gel applied in a mouth tray. To be effective for caries-prone children, the procedure should be done at least semi-annually. Although professionally applied fluorides may reduce tooth decay by 30 percent to 40 percent, in comparison to other methods they are expensive, due to the cost of required dental manpower.

## Supervised Self-applied Fluorides

The use of self-applied fluorides is not new. Toothpastes with fluoride have long been available to help reduce tooth decay, and their use is recommended for everyone. Regular, supervised use of a fluoride tooth-paste can reduce children's tooth decay by at least 15 percent to 30 percent.[24] Another procedure recommended by some dentists is the daily use of a fluoride mouth rinse. This method provides topical benefits. For individuals who are highly caries-prone, dentists sometimes prescribe a higher concentration of fluoride in the form of a gel, which is applied in a plastic tray that resembles a mouth guard.

## Supervised Self-applied Fluoride Programs in School Settings

For the past two decades, considerable research has focused on the use of fluoride mouth rinses in schools. Because most children are prone to tooth decay and most regularly attend grade school, preschool, or day-care facilities, school settings are logical places for administering self-applied fluorides. Studies show that once-a-week fluoride mouth rinsing can reduce new tooth decay 20 percent to 50 percent and the daily use of a fluoride tablet in school can reduce it 30 percent to 40 percent.[29] These results are based on the use of the respective agent only on school days.[30] Today, an estimated 12 million children in this country are using a fluoride mouth rinse once a week or a fluoride tablet once a day in schools, preschools and day-care centers.[29] Such school programs reach nearly all children in a community whether or not the children see a dentist regularly.

## Recommended Supplemental Fluoride Therapy

For many years, dentists and physicians have prescribed drops and tablets of supplemental fluoride for children residing in areas with inad-equate levels of fluoride in the drinking water. This method of application provides systemic as well as topical benefits that approximate those derived from fluoridation, providing the supplements are taken as recommended.

Although some parents and their children successfully practice this procedure, many families fail to utilize the supplements as directed or discontinue them at too early an age for sustained protection.

To assure the greatest protection for primary as well as permanent teeth, fluoride supplementation should begin as soon as possible after birth and be continued on a daily basis thereafter until about 16 years of age.[30,31] Early initiation of treatment with fluoride supplements produces the best caries-protective results. When preschoolers receive dietary fluoride supplements, their tooth decay rate is lowered 50 percent to 70 percent. When a fluoride supplement program is started at 6 years of age, the decay is reduced 20 percent to 45 percent.[32]

For fluoride supplements to provide optimal anti-caries protection, prescriptions must be tailored to the specific needs of the individual patient. This requires:

1.  establishing the fluoride content of the patient's water supply;
2.  determining the proper dosage for the patient's age;
3.  selecting the appropriate type of supplement; and
4.  teaching the patient and parents how to use the supplement properly.

## Selecting Appropriate Fluoride Supplements

Fluoride supplements are available as drops, solutions, lozenges, and tablets in addition to or combined with vitamins. Selection is based primarily on the personal preference of the patient and the practitioner, who must consider the child's age, ability to chew and swallow tablets, and the relative cost of the preparations. Several vehicles for delivering sodium fluoride may be used for systemic supplementation. Solutions that dispense 0.125 mg of fluoride per drop are convenient formulations for infants because the dose can be adjusted easily. Tablets that contain 0.25 or 0.5 mg of fluoride ion can usually replace the solution for children at about three years of age: if the child prefers, has all primary teeth erupted, and can properly chew and swallow a chewable tablet. The patient's age, ability to chew and swallow, and degree of development and cooperation are the main factors to consider when determining which type of supplement to prescribe.

Other important factors to take into account include:

1.  the daily topical use of fluoride by the child, i.e., fluoride dentifrice, and oral fluoride rinses;
2.  special dietary habits of the individual, i.e., foods with high fluoride content;
3.  actual caries prevalence (in older children); and
4.  oral hygiene status (in older children).

The child's age and the fluoride concentration in drinking water are the two most important factors to consider when prescribing a fluoride supplement. When the fluoride content of the home or school water supply is unknown, samples must be analyzed. Because of daily variations in some public water supplies, the collection and testing of water samples on two or three separate days produces the most accurate measurements. Table 3 represents the supplemental dietary dose schedule recommended by the American Academy of Pediatrics, The American Academy of Pediatric Dentistry, and the American Dental Association.[30,31,33]

In fluoride-deficient areas, the use of fluoride tablets is the best way to provide both systemic and topical benefits to teeth. Weekly mouth rinsing with fluoride solutions has been shown to add protection against decay in children who also receive systemic fluoride. Therefore, programs that combine weekly fluoride rinsing with daily fluoride tablets or with the ingestion of optimally fluoridated water are ideal.

## SEALANTS

A preventive procedure that would lower caries prevalence considerably, if it were more frequently employed, is the application of sealants.

Table 3
Recommended Fluoride Dose Levels for Specific Ages

Dietary Fluoride Supplementation Dose Schedule*
in Milligrams of Fluoride Per Day**

| Age (years) | Fluoride Content of Water | | |
|---|---|---|---|
| | < 0.3 ppm | 0.3 to 0.7 ppm | >0.7 ppm |
| Birth to 2*** | 0.25 mg F | 0 mg F | 0 mg F |
| 2-3 | 0.50 mg F | 0.25 mg F | 0 mg F |
| 3-13 (16)*** | 1.00 mg F | 0.50 mg F | 0 mg F |

* Recommended by the American Dental Association and the American Academy of Pediatric Dentistry and the American Academy of Pediatrics.[30,31,33]

** 2.2 mg of sodium fluoride provides 1.0 mg fluoride ion.

***American Academy of Pediatrics recommends initiation at 2 weeks of age and continuing until age 16 years.[31]

Results of the National Preventive Dentistry Demonstration Program (NPDDP)[34] showed sealants to be the single most effective available procedure for the reduction of the current caries incidence.[32,34] Even when substantial caries decline has occurred, precisely those surfaces still most susceptible to significant caries attack – pit and fissure surfaces of molars – can be protected almost completely from decay. The highest proportion of tooth decay in 17 year olds is found on the occlusal (biting) surfaces. As much as 80 percent of the dental caries observed is on tooth surfaces with pits and fissures.[17] Publicity given to the benefits and improved technology of sealants should aid their promotion and increase their use.

## ORAL HEALTH EDUCATION AND PROMOTION

A major issue in the progress of oral health is the need to adopt preventive oral health measures, to minimize the gap in information between scientifically based knowledge and the selection and application of oral health measures by health professionals, the public, government agencies, institutions, and communities.[35-39] Only when these groups become aware of and committed to the significance and positive impact of preventive oral health methods will they request, adopt, and utilize proven oral health measures, for themselves, their institutions, and their communities.

Established professional and community networks are not utilized effectively to communicate, motivate, and apply proven oral health measures. Professionals associated with health care facilities, health profession schools, and public health programs have not collectively initiated adoption of effective oral health education measures.[40] No comprehensive system is available to identify oral health resources and develop programmatic approaches that may transfer information to individuals, groups, and communities interested in oral health measures. Although several reports stress the importance of access to such resources in the adoption of oral health measures, these resources are not readily available.[40,41]

A variety of initiatives in patient, community, and professional education have been utilized to transfer oral health information to professionals and the public. Many diverse groups and individuals have developed and promoted these interventions.[42,43] However, assessment of the long-term effectiveness of some of these initiatives indicates limitations.[44] Presently, no coordinated strategy provides a resource to communities for oral health information. Prevention requires vigilance and commitment in both public and professional education, and at present there is a deficiency in such education. The increased use of oral hygienists in elementary and high school programs would contribute significantly to the promotion of oral health.

# DENTAL HEALTH SERVICES

Despite the much improved dental care Americans receive, a high degree of need still exists. Estimates from the 1979-80 National Dental Caries Prevalence Survey (NDCPS)[9] indicate that even given the decline in caries, some 21 million restorations were required in primary teeth and 32 million surfaces needed restoration in the permanent teeth of children ages 5 to 17.[9,45] High caries levels have been endured for so long that by comparison the current caries decline in permanent teeth appears attractive, but there is a danger in becoming complacent about a disease whose prevalence and economic impact remains significant in comparison to other diseases. Recent surveys, however, indicate increased dentist visits for preventive services and the increasing use of fluoride toothpaste.[46,47]

## Cost of Dental Services

Current (1988) annual expenditures for dental care in the U.S. amount to about $29.4 billion.[48] Preventive dental services account for about 8 percent of dental expenditures; basic dental restorations (silver amalgam fillings) account for 50 percent; and reconstructive, aesthetic, and prosthetic dental services account for about 43 percent. Included in reconstructive services is 3 percent for orthodontic treatment.[45]

## Payment for Dental Services

Traditionally, dental services have been paid for on a fee-for-service basis by direct out-of-pocket consumer payments. This method is still by far the predominant method of payment for dental services. This direct payment for dental services may help explain some of the dynamics of the dental care market. People seem to think they are paying high amounts for dental care because they pay directly out of their pocket. As a result, among "poor children," 85 out of every 100 decayed teeth go unfilled.[49] Out of the $29.4 billion spent for dental care in 1988, $16.3 billion or 55.4 percent of the total expenditure was paid by patients out-of-pocket. Public health programs paid for $700 million, or 2.4 percent.[48] Private dental insurance paid only about $4.6 billion, 15.5 percent of the total expenditures for dental care.[48] Dental insurance plans have been very slow to follow medical care coverage, most likely due in part to the need to afford the average citizen some protection for hospital and medical costs before focusing on dental costs. Only about 65 million people have some dental care coverage today.[49,50] Almost 60 percent of U.S. children between 2 and 17 years of age have no dental health insurance.[51,52]

## Publicly Financed Dental Care

The availability of financial resources to support oral health programs varies dramatically among states and among local health departments. Public health mechanisms for the provision of effective oral health programs for school-age children, adolescents, and young adults, though available in some areas, still are not sufficiently widespread to meet the needs of this population. The adequacy of financial resources and the program goals committed to these tasks need to be assessed to effectively improve the oral health of this population. During the 1980s, there was a 15 percent decrease in total dollar Medicaid dental expenditures, a 23 percent decrease in dollars per dental recipient, and a 400,000 decrease in the number of child recipients.[1,50] Oral health components need to become an integral part of all state and local health departments as well as specific federal agencies.

# ORAL HEALTH OBJECTIVES FOR THE NATION

The eradication of dental caries in children must be one of our goals for the next decade. The great strides that have been made in the last two decades indicate that this is a realistic goal. The obligation of our health care professions must be to apply the knowledge of oral disease prevention that exists today to as much of our nation's population as possible.

Recent national caries surveys have indicated that as much as 80 percent of the carious teeth in American children can be found in only 20 percent of the nation's children.[53] A major objective of the American Academy of Pediatric Dentistry for the year 2000 is to improve access to dental/oral health care for those now deprived of needed services.[53] Most health professionals and health care planners recognize that large segments of the population do not have access to dental care for a variety of reasons. These segments include children with special health care needs (chronically ill, homebound, developmentally and mentally disabled, emotionally impaired), some minority groups, and the financially disadvantaged. A significant portion of the 20 percent of the nation's population who exhibit 80 percent of the caries falls into these groups. Special attention must be paid to these groups so that they too can be brought into the mainstream of effective dental/oral health care. Therefore, there must be the objective of the education of the population at large, as well as health care professionals, public health and other government officials, that dental/oral health care is necessary, desirable, and a sound investment for all people.

Significant scientific dental health information that has come to light in the past decade should be reflected in the nation's health objectives.[53]

This information may be summarized as follows:

1.  Adjusting local water supplies to optimal therapeutic fluoride levels significantly reduces caries prevalence.
2.  In geographic areas where public water supplies are not adjusted to optimal therapeutic fluoride levels, supplementation for children from birth through the teenage years significantly reduces caries prevalence.
3.  Fluoride dentifrices used daily in appropriate amounts, and other forms of topically applied fluoride, significantly reduce caries prevalence.
4.  The majority of the caries present in our nation's children today occur in the pits and fissures of occlusal (chewing) surfaces of teeth.
5.  Pit and fissure sealants are highly effective in preventing occlusal caries.
6.  The combination of systemic fluoride supplements, fluoride dentifrices, and other forms of topically applied fluoride and sealants has been predicted to have the capacity to eliminate more than 90 percent of caries in children.
7.  Increased emphasis on the identification of the 20 percent of the population that represents 80 percent of the dental caries in our nation's children is necessary to institute early prevention procedures to eradicate dental caries in these children.
8.  Dietary modification recommendations alone do not appear to be effective in significantly reducing caries prevalence, particularly in comparison to the situation where systemic fluoride supplementation, topical fluoride application, and fluoridated dentifrice are used.
9.  Increased emphasis on prevention, early diagnosis, and treatment of developing malocclusions in children can be expected to decrease the national prevalence of malocclusion.
10. Increased emphasis on prevention, early diagnosis, and treatment of developing malocclusions in children can be expected to decrease the national prevalence of periodontal disease.
11. Early identification and intervention and regular pediatric dental/oral health care can be expected to further reduce the prevalence of caries, periodontal disease, and malocclusion in the nation's children.
12. The need for access to pediatric dental/oral health care is particularly acute among the disadvantaged segments of the nation's population.

Although these goals may be ambitious, they are attainable. However, their attainment will require the cooperative efforts of all health care providers, teachers and parents.

# REFERENCES

1. Kouig KG: Advances in clinical research on dental caries, Pediatric Dentistry – Scientific Foundations and Clinical Practice. Edited by RE Stewart et al. St. Louis, The CV Mosby Co., 1980, pp 598-609

2. Health Care Financing Administration: Office of the Actuary. Data from National Cost Estimates, October, 1988. Washington, DC, DHHS News Press Release, November 18, 1988

3. Burt BA, Ismail A: Diet nutrition and food cariogenicity. J Dent Res 65 (Special Issue):1475-1484, 1986

4. Harvey C, Kelly JE: Decayed, Missing and Filled Teeth among Persons 1-74 Years, United States 1971-74. Hyattsville, MD, National Center or Health Statistics (DHHS pub. no.(PHS) 81-1673. Vital and health statistics; series 11; no 223.), 1981

5. National Institute of Dental Research: The Prevalence of Dental Caries in United States Children. Bethesda, MD (NIH pub. no. 82-2245) National Institutes of Health, 1981

6. Brunelle JA: Personal communication, National Institute of Dental Research, January 1989

7. Harvey CR, Kelly JE: U.S. Public Health Service National Center for Health Statistics. Decayed, Missing and Filled Teeth among Youths 1-17 Years United States 1971-74. DHHS Publication No. (PHS) 81-1678-Ser. 11-No. 223. Washington DC, Government Printing Office, 1981

8. Brunelle JA, Carlos JP: Changes in the prevalence of dental caries in U.S. school children 1961-1980. J Dent Res 61(Spec. Issue.):1346-51, 1982

9. U.S. Department of Health and Human Services: The Prevalence of Dental Caries in United States Children, The National Dental Caries Prevalence Survey. NIH Publication NO. 83-2246, 1982

10. Nowjack-Raymer R, Gift HC: Contributing factors to maternal and child oral health. Public Health Service Workshop on Oral Health of Mothers and Children - Background issue papers. Edited by JEM Steffensen and JP Brown. Washington DC, National Center for Education in Maternal and Child Health, 1989, pp 35-52

11. Brunelle JA, Carlos JA: Recent trends in dental caries in U.S. children and the effect of water fluoridation. National Institute of Dental Research, 1989

12. Weintraub JA, Burt BA: Oral health status in the United States: Tooth loss and edentulism. J Dent Educ 49:368-78, 1985

13. Burt BA: The future of the caries decline. J Public Health Dent 45:261-69, 1985

14. National Center for Health Services Research and Health Care Technology Assessment: Dental insurance improves access to care but raises costs. NCHSR Research Activities 112:3-4, 1988

15. Ismail A et al: Dental caries and periodontal disease among Mexican American children from five southwestern states 1982-1983. MMWR 37: 33-45, 1988

16. Robert Wood Johnson Foundation: Preventing Tooth Decay: From a Four-year National Study, Special Report number two. Princeton, NJ, The Foundation, 1983

17. Swango PA, Brunelle JA: Age and surface caries attack from the National Caries Prevalence Survey. J Dent Res 62: 270, 1983

18. National Institute of Dental Research: Dental needs of United States children, 1979-1980. Bethesda, MD, National Institute of Health (NIH pub. no. 83-2246), 1982

19. Gift HC, Corbin SB: Year 2000 Draft Oral Health Objectives for the Nation. Monograph, March 27, 1989

20. Ripa LW: Nursing caries: A comprehensive review. Pediatric Dent 10(4):286-282, 1988

21. Navia JM: Models for food cariogenicity testing: Report of a collaborative study using animal models, Foods, Nutrition and Dental Health, Vol. 3. Edited by JJ Hefferren. Park Forrest S, IL, Patho Pub Inc, 1981, pp 1-13

22. Brunelle JA, Carlos JA: Recent trends in dental caries in U.S. children and the effect of water fluoridation: National Institute of Dental Research, 1989 Conference, Cincinnati, OH, February 22, 1989; Abstract 3

23. Carlos JP: Validity of prenatal fluorides questioned: Efficacy of prenatal fluorides reaffirmed. Letter to the editor. J Dent Child 55:94-95, 1988

24. Wei SHY: Fluorides and dental health, Pediatric Dentistry - Scientific Foundations and Clinical Practice. Edited by RE Stewart et al. St. Louis, CV Mosby, 1982, pp 717-779

25. Brunelle JA, Carlos JP: Recent trends in dental caries in U.S. children and the effect of water fluoridation, National Institute of Dental Research, 1989

26. Marshell E: The fluoride debate: One more time. Science 24(7):276-277, 1990

27. McCann D: Fluoride and oral health – a story of achievement and challenges. JADA 118:529-540, 1989

28. Horowitz HA, Heifetz SB, Law FE: Effect of school water fluoridation on dental caries: Final results in Elk Lake, Pennsylvania after 12 years. JADA 105:832-38, 1972

29. U.S. Department of Health, Education, and Welfare: National Institute for Dental Research: Preventing Tooth Decay - A Guide for Implementing Self-Applied Fluoride in Schools, DHEW No. (NIH) 77-1196, 1977, pp 2-3

30. American Academy of Pediatric Dentistry: Oral Health Policy: Preventive Dentistry-Fluoridation, 1978 and Protocol for Fluoride Therapy, 1985

31. American Academy of Pediatrics Committee on Nutrition: Fluoride supplementation (RE6069). Pediatrics 77(5):758-761, 1986

32. Bohannan HM, Bader JD: Future impact of public health and preventive methods on the incidence of dental caries. J Canad Dent Asso. 50(3):229-33, 1984

33. American Dental Association: Prescribing fluoride supplements. Accepted Dental Therapeutics, 39th ed. Chicago, The American Dental Association 1982, pp 347-351

34. Bell RM et al: Treatment Effects in the National Prevention Dentistry Demonstration Program. Santa Monica, CA, Rand, 1984; R-3072-RWJ

35. O'Neill HW: Opinion study comparing attitudes about dental health. J Am Dent Assoc 109:910-915, 1984

36. Cohen LK, Bryant PS: Social Sciences and Dentistry – A Critical Bibliography, volume II. London, Quintessence Pub Co., 1984

37. Silversin J, Kornacki MJ: Acceptance of preventive measures by individuals institutions and communities. Int Dent J 34:170-176, 1984

38. Bart BA: The prevention connection linking dental health education and prevention. Int Dent J 32:188-195, 1983

39. National Institute of Dental Research: Challenges for the eighties, long-range research plan. Washington, DC, Department of Health and Human Services, 1983

40. Gift HC: The National Institutes of Health promotion models application to oral health. Presentation at Annual Meeting Association of State and Territorial Dental Directors and National Oral Health Conference, Cincinnati, OH, February 22, Abstract 4, 1989

41. Steffensen JEM, Brown JP: Oral health information in federal health information clearinghouses and resource centers. Program and Abstracts American Public Health Association Annual Meeting, Boston, MA, November 1988

42. Centers for Disease Control: Combined Health Information Database. Literature search related to Oral Health, October 31, 1988

43. Kuthy RA, Odom JG: Local health agencies dental programs and services. Columbus OH, American Oral Health Institute, 1987

44. Horowitz AM, Frazier PJ: Effective public education for achieving oral health. Family Community Health 3:91-101, 1980

45. National Institute of Dental Research: U.S. Department of Health and Human Services. NIDR Research News 173:2-3, 1982

46. AC Nielsen Company: Marketing information services, 1984

47. Douglass CW, Cole KO: Utilization of dental services in the United States. J Dent Educ 43(4):223-38, 1979

48. Washington Memorandum: American Dental Association, Washington, DC, May 11, 1990

49. Greene JC: Dental health needs of the nation. J Am Dent Asso., 84:1073 1075, May 1972

50. Social Security Administration: Social Security Bulletin: Annual Statistical Supplement, 1988, Washington DC, Govt. Printing Office, 1988 pp. 299-301

51. Jack SS, Bloon B: Use of dental services and dental health: United States, 1986. DHHS Pub No (PHS) 88-153. Series 10, No 165 Washington, DC, Govt. Printing Office, 1988

52. Feldstein PJ, Roehrig CS, Hall J: An Econometric Model of the Dental Sector. Boston, MA, Policy Analysis, Inc., June 1977

53. American Academy of Pediatric Dentistry: Dental Health Objective for the Year 2000, 1989

# 17

# Physical Activity

JAMES F. SALLIS, PHD AND NELL FAUCETTE, EDD

The importance of physical activity to the current and future health of students has only recently been recognized. In past decades, physical activity and physical education were seen as either unrelated or adjuncts to student health programs. Because of the large number of well-designed studies indicating that regular physical activity in adulthood reduces morbidity and mortality to a substantial degree, the promotion of physical activity is increasingly being viewed as one of the central goals of student health.

## BENEFITS

The documented health benefits of physical activity for adults and children are extensive. In the past 20 years several large, long-term studies of adults have shown that physical inactivity is a major risk factor for cardiovascular disease (CVD) and premature mortality.[1,2] Epidemiologic data suggest that adults can cut their risk of CVD by 50 percent or more by being active regularly.[3] Because CVD accounts for about half of all deaths in the U.S., the promotion of healthful physical activity is a high public health priority.

Regular physical activity can benefit children as well. Numerous studies indicate that children who are more fit and more active tend to be leaner and have lower blood pressure levels.[4] Physical activity has been shown to effectively promote long-term weight loss both in obese children[5] and adolescents.[6] Physical activity has also been associated with higher levels of beneficial HDL-cholesterol in children.[7] Associations between physical activity and risk factors are similar for adults and children.[8] Since risk factor levels in childhood predict risk levels in young adulthood,[9] decreasing risk factors in children is an important health consideration.

In addition to benefits related to the prevention of CVD, physical activity appears to promote improved mental health in adults[10] and enhance self-esteem in children.[11] Physical activity has been shown to improve the mood of individuals experiencing mild anxiety or depression.[12] Physical activity enhances the uptake of calcium in the bones, and this may act to reduce fractures in later life.[13] Some scientists believe that muscular strength and flexibility can help prevent back pain and other injuries in adulthood.[14]

These numerous health benefits have led the U.S. Public Health Service to recommend regular physical activity for all children and adults. These recommendations were included in the Year 1990 Health Objectives for the Nation, and additional physical activity objectives were added to the Year 2000 plan.

# RISKS

The benefits of physical activity are extremely important; however, physical activity can have serious risks. The two major risks are cardiovascular complications and musculoskeletal injuries. In general, physical activity reduces the risk of CVD, but during the actual vigorous exercise session, the risk of sudden cardiac death is increased, especially in children with congenital heart defects or adults with advanced heart disease.[15]

Deaths of apparently healthy people during exercise or sports make headlines when they occur, but the basic fact remains that virtually everyone in the population could lower his CVD risk through regular physical activity. Individuals with known or suspected heart conditions should consult their physician before starting a vigorous exercise program.

Annually, millions of adults and children experience musculoskeletal injuries during physical activity.[16] Highly active individuals endure greater risks than those who participate in more moderate levels of activity.[17] Annual rates of injury among recreational exercisers range from 7 percent to 54 percent.[18] More severe injuries occur during contact sports and from overuse during extreme training or competition. Because various sports are sponsored by schools and colleges, school health programs should consider including injury prevention instruction for athletes.

Musculoskeletal injuries are of particular concern for children. Although there are few longitudinal studies that document long-term effects of overuse and injuries to epiphyseal growth centers, many believe injuries or overuse can retard or alter bone development.[19] As a result, youth sport programs restrict children's levels of continuous participation in order to reduce the possibility of overuse injuries.

In addition to these physical risks, individuals who overtrain can become obsessive about their behaviors. These participants can become anxious and depressed when deprived of extreme levels of activity.[20] Obsessive exercise is also one of the means used by anorexics to lose excessive amounts of weight.[21] Because anorexia is most prevalent among high school and college females, this is a concern for school health professionals.

Most of the risks are due to excessive exercise. Thus, benefits are maximized and risks are minimized at moderate amounts of physical activity. School health programs should help students develop habits of regular moderate activity.

## MEASUREMENT

Measurement of physical activity is problematic because type, intensity, duration, and frequency vary from hour to hour and day to day. Since no ideal measurement tool exists, the approach to assessment should be based on available resources and the types of information needed. Some instruments estimate overall caloric expenditure but do not provide information on type or intensity of activities. Others provide information on type and duration of activity, but not on intensity.

Of the numerous measures of physical activity that have been applied to children and youth,[22] the three most commonly used approaches are self-report, direct observation, and activity monitors. Parent reports can be used for crude rankings of activity levels of young children,[23] but they are of limited use because parents do not observe much of their children's activity.

The preferred type of self-report format is the diary because it does not rely on the child's memory skill. Children as young as the third grade can keep valid diaries.[24] The primary difficulty with diaries is that children need frequent prompting to complete them. Activity recalls have the disadvantage of relying on memory, but they have the advantage that the investigator has more control over the completion of the measure. For children younger than high school age, there is no self-administered activity report that has been shown to be valid.[25] High school or college students should be able to use any of the self-administered recall measures that have been shown to be valid for adults.[26] Interviewer-administered seven-day physical activity recalls have been found to be reasonably valid for children as young as 11 years.[27] While this 10 to 15 minute interview has marginal reliability and validity for fifth-grade students, it is highly reliable and valid with eighth- and eleventh-grade students.[28]

Direct observation measures have been developed primarily for young children, although the same measures could be applied to any age group. Observations are costly in staff time, but observers can be trained to collect highly reliable and valid data. Detailed information about physical activity and related variables, such as social interactions, can be gathered simultaneously. Several direct observation coding systems have been validated for use with young children.[29,30]

The most cost-efficient approach to assessing physical activity over extended time periods is probably monitoring with electronic or mechanical monitors. Pedometers are not reliable[22] and microcomputers are expensive,[31] but two types of monitors are being used increasingly to study physical activity in children and youth. Telemetric heart rate monitors have been used for some time,[32] and commercially available models store up to 16 hours of heart rate data that can be downloaded directly to a computer. Heart rate can be used to estimate time spent in activities of various intensities[28,32] or to estimate overall activity.[33] The Caltrac accelerometer (Hemokinetics, Inc., 2923 Osmundsen Road, Madison, WI, 53711-5139) is an inexpensive motion sensor that estimates cumulative activity. This monitor appears to be the most valid activity monitor available for both children and adults.[34,35] Objective monitors have limitations in that they break down, they do not reflect all types of activity, and they do not correlate well with one another.[35] However, they are appropriate for many purposes.

## LEVELS OF PARTICIPATION

Due to the limitation of measurement tools, it is not possible to determine accurately what percent of a given population is physically active. In addition, definitions of physical activity differ by study. For improving cardiovascular fitness, 20 minutes of vigorous exercise three times per week is generally recommended.[36] However, for health benefits, such as reducing CVD, it is clear that moderate levels of physical activity confer substantial benefits.[1,2]

Even though adults could cut their risk of CVD in half through regular physical activity,[3] fewer than 10 percent are vigorously active on a regular basis. At least 40 percent of American adults are extremely sedentary.[37,38] Studies generally show that physical activity declines during the teen years,[28,39] and the decline continues throughout adulthood.[38]

It is even more difficult to estimate the percentage of children and adolescents who are physically active, because a healthful level of physical activity has not been defined for children. Using data from adult studies, it was estimated that 90 percent or more of children are active at the minimal level required for health benefits.[40] However, at the present time, insufficient data are available to predicate the necessary levels of physical activity needed for health benefits to occur in children.

There has been some concern about the cardiorespiratory fitness levels of American children, but children are the most fit portion of the population.[41] Although there is insufficient evidence to determine that cardiovascular fitness levels have declined during the past decade,[42] it is clear that children's levels of obesity are increasing rapidly.[43] It is possible that the 54 percent increase in the prevalence of obesity in six- to eleven-year old children from 1963 to 1980 could be related to a decrease in their physical activity.

School health professionals should be concerned about physical activity rather than physical fitness, because it is only through activity that fitness can be improved. Though there are no universally accepted criteria for desired levels of physical activity by children, several studies have assessed the activity levels of children from preschool to high school age. Though preschool children are often assumed to be highly active, limited data from two studies indicated that students were inactive in unstructured free-play environments.[44,45] Others found that elementary age children observed during recess were seldom vigorously active.[46,47]

Three studies using heart rate monitoring over entire days produced similar results across different age groups. These estimates of time children spent in moderate-intensity activity varied from 15 to 45 minutes per day[28,32,39] in children aged 6 to 17. Even during youth, teenagers were found to be vigorously active about half the number of minutes per day as pre-teens. While these results indicated that most children are active and appear to be meeting American College of Sports Medicine (ACSM) recommendations for adult activity levels, even young children spent less than 2 percent of their day in physical activity. This indicates that there is much room for improvement, especially considering that levels of physical activity begin to decline at about age six and continue to decline throughout life.

## DETERMINANTS

Some children are clearly more active than others, but what influences how active children are? This is an important question because understanding the determinants of physical activity could lead to more effective interventions. Unfortunately, relatively few studies have examined this question for children or adolescents. It appears from several studies that boys are generally more active than girls,[28,48] and as noted above, adolescents are less active than children.[28,39]

It is not likely that being female and becoming older cause low levels of physical activity. The more reasonable explanation is that girls are not rewarded for physical activity as much as boys, and there are more barriers to being physically active as we age.

Boys receive a great deal of encouragement from their families and from society to play sports and to be physically active. Most fathers want their boys to become sports stars, but even in late 20th-century America, girls are encouraged to develop other skills.

Several studies have shown that families influence the physical activity of young children[29] and adolescents.[49] Family influence is often direct, as in encouragement to be more or less active.[29] Possibly an even more important influence on the child is the parent's own physical activity patterns. Active parents tend to have active children, regardless of the child's gender.[49] Therefore, one way to promote activity in youth is to promote activity in parents.

Children experience many of the same barriers to physical activity that adults complain about.[50] Adults say that they do not have time for exercise, but many children also have music classes, tutoring, chores, or other activities after school that make it difficult to find regular times for physical activity. There are many powerful competitors for children's time. Television networks make certain that children's programs are broadcast whenever children are likely to be home. There is a seemingly infinite variety of video games designed especially to keep children indoors and inactive. Increases in single-parent families and concerns about the safety of neighborhoods lead parents to tell children to stay inside. This decreases children's opportunities for activity. Adolescents frequently have even more extracurricular activities than children, and, as soon as they obtain their licenses, they typically prefer driving cars to pedaling bicycles.

While children are in school, most are exposed to regular physical education classes,[51] even if there are limited opportunities for physical activity during those classes.[47] Sports teams and dance classes are generally available to secondary school students. After graduation from high school or college, there are no structured physical activity programs for most adults. From the world of school, which structures at least some activity, adolescents and young adults are thrown into the world of work where it is every person for him- or herself. Relatively few worksites have health promotion programs that provide support for physical activity. This abrupt transition may explain why the largest drop in physical activity seems to occur during young adulthood.[38] The implication of age-related decreases in activity is that school physical education programs should place a high priority on preparing youth for lifetime physical activity.

## INTERVENTION

Within school curricula, physical education classes offer an ideal setting to implement interventions aimed at promoting higher levels of activity for students. Unfortunately, many schools have failed to provide students adequate time for such programs.[51,52] Observations of physical education (PE) classes indicate that students' activity levels are usually quite low. Observations of 30-minute classes found that the average child was vigorously active for only two minutes. In one observation of 226 PE classes taught by classroom teachers in several Southern California districts, time devoted to different types of activities was categorized.[53] Most of these classes consisted of game play in which only a few students were active while the remaining students waited for turns. What is more, only 5 percent of the classes had fitness activities as the major focus.

Although these statistics are discouraging, attempts to implement school-based health-related interventions have been quite successful. Cooper and colleagues[54] were the first to report the effects of a jogging program on the fitness level of high school students. Numerous other studies with elementary school students showed that PE programs emphasizing cardiovascular fitness activities can be beneficial to students' health. Increases in activity at school were documented by self-report,[55] direct observation,[56] and heart rate monitoring.[57] One study showed that physical education specialists spent twice as much class time (40%) as the control schools

(21%) in fitness activities.[56] At least four studies found that children participating in health-related PE improved cardiovascular fitness.[58-61] Additionally, decreases in skinfold thicknesses for students in the experimental groups were reported.[59,60]

When school-based interventions targeted physical activity without involving PE classes, results have been much less encouraging. One diet and physical activity program was designed to reduce CVD risk factors in fourth- and fifth-grade students. Behavioral self-management procedures were designed to help children identify and change health-related behaviors. The six-session physical activity component was intended to increase activity during daily recess. This program appeared to have no effect on levels of physical activity observed during recess; however, there were significant changes in dietary behavior.[62]

The five-year Know Your Body comprehensive health promotion program for fourth- through eighth-grade students focused on diet, physical activity, and cigarette smoking.[63] However, the intervention by classroom teachers did not include a physical education component. At the conclusion of the program, there were significant changes in total cholesterol, dietary intake, and health knowledge, but there were no effects on fitness levels.

In addition to interventions via PE conducted within the regular school day, after-school programs can offer opportunities for physical activity for children. For example, Future Fit, an after-school program designed for fourth- and fifth-grade students produced significant changes in students' knowledge, attitudes, and behaviors as noted by parents at home.[64]

When students move into a college environment, typically they are no longer required to complete physical education requirements or participate in extracurricular physical activities. If students do so, it is because they have made a personal commitment to activity or take pleasure in being participants in sports and games. With all the demands on students' time, levels of activity decrease greatly during this period even though physical education departments typically offer a variety of courses designed to promote physical fitness, and recreational sport departments provide ongoing opportunities for sport involvement. Specific strategies for promoting continued physical activity need to be developed for college-age students.

Family-based programs can be developed as part of the school health program. Such programs can be effective for children and early adolescents, but family involvement is no guarantee of success. For example, a structured health promotion program for families with children in the fifth and sixth grades that was successful in changing dietary habits was not successful in promoting physical activity.[65] This study highlights the difficulty of establishing a pattern of regular physical activity and suggests that intensive programs are needed to overcome the many barriers to being physically active.

Two very effective family-based programs targeted highly selected populations and used a clinical behavior modification approach. In the first, the least-fit elementary school children were identified.[66] Families were enrolled in a 12-week program during which they were taught to develop reinforcement programs to increase their children's activity. Behavioral consultants called the parents each week to assist them with the program. In this small study virtually all of the children increased both activity and fitness levels. A similar approach was used in working with obese children.[5] Therapists devised behavioral contracts between parents and children to change diet and physical activity. This reinforcement program produced weight losses that have been maintained up to five years.[67] Both of these programs show that training parents to systematically reinforce children with very low activity levels can be effective. Because these particular methods are not applicable to the general population, other approaches need to be developed. In addition, family-based programs are less relevant to the college population.

Various public health interventions to promote physical activity in children and youth, in addition to school and family programs, have been proposed but not evaluated. Millions of children participate in youth sports, but several major sports such as baseball and football neither provide much physical activity nor teach children skills that are relevant to lifetime activity. Some sports programs are beginning to focus on girls, but this trend needs to be accelerated. Changes in the emphasis of youth sports programs to make them more responsive to the health needs of children should be implemented. Similar changes to promote fitness-oriented activities could be made in city recreation programs that serve young people. School-sponsored and publicly funded recreation programs are particularly relevant to economically disadvantaged youth who do not have access to other resources. Programs are needed for large numbers of children during summers when they are not participating in school-related activities.

# COMMENTARY

The current and future health benefits of physical activity require that promotion of regular moderate to vigorous physical activity must be one of the primary targets of school and college health programs. For maximum public health benefit, programs should emphasize activities and skills that are relevant for lifetime physical activity.

There is some controversy as to whether children are currently active enough to obtain health benefits, but there is little disagreement that children and adolescents could benefit by becoming more active. Innovative and effective school health programs could help stop the age-related decline in physical activity by preparing students to continue being active after they leave structured school programs.

The greatest resource for promoting physical activity is physical education; school health and physical education professionals must work together to improve the health of students. School health programs should focus on those needs that are related to the promotion of healthful physical activity among the entire population of students:

1. Physical education programs should teach activities and injury-prevention methods simultaneously.

2. Physical education programs should provide high levels of physical activity for all students throughout the class.

3. Physical education programs should emphasize activities and activity planning skills that can be carried into adulthood. This means that a shift from an emphasis on team sports to an emphasis on individual activities should occur.

4. Athletic programs would serve public health better if they promoted extra-curricular physical activities for many students rather than team sports for the elite few.

5. Methods of involving families in the promotion of children's physical activity need to be developed and evaluated.

6. Programs are needed to promote physical activity during the summer and other school vacations.

7. A basic need is to provide access to all physical activity programs to groups that have traditionally had limited access, such as females, racial/ethnic minorities, and the economically disadvantaged. This applies to physical education, school athletics, youth sports leagues, and other public and private recreation agencies.

School health professionals should work with other agencies with an interest in youth sports and physical activity to develop a comprehensive approach to promoting healthful physical activity in all children.

## REFERENCES

1. Paffenbarger RS, Hyde RT, Wing AL et al: Physical activity, all-cause mortality, and longevity of college alumni. N Engl J Med 314:605-613, 1986

2. Leon AS, Connett J, Jacobs DR et al: Leisure-time physical activity levels and risk of coronary heart disease and death: The Multiple Risk Factor Intervention Trial. JAMA 258:2388-2395, 1987

3. Powell KE, Thompson PD, Caspersen CJ et al: Physical activity and the incidence of coronary heart disease. Annu Rev Public Health 8:253-287, 1987

4. Montoye HJ: Risk indicators for cardiovascular disease in relation to physical activity in youth, Children and Exercise XI. Edited by RA Binkhorst, HCG Kemper, WHM Saris. Champaign, IL, Human Kinetics:3-25, 1985

5. Epstein LH: Adherence to exercise in obese children. J Cardiac Rehabil 4:185-195, 1984

6. Becque MD, Katch VL, Rocchini AP et al: Coronary risk incidence of obese adolescents: Reduction by exercise plus diet intervention. Pediatrics 81:605-612, 1988

7. Thorland WG, Gilliam TB: Comparison of serum liquids between habitually high and low active preadolescents. Med Sci Sports Exerc 13:316-321, 1981

8. Sallis JS, Patterson T, Buono MJ et al: Relationship of cardiovascular fitness and physical activity to cardiovascular disease risk factors in children and adults. Am J Epidemiol 127:933-941, 1988

9. Cresanta JL, Burke GL, Downey AM et al: Prevention of atherosclerosis in childhood: Prevention in primary care. Pediatr Clin North Am 33:835-858, 1986

10. Taylor CB, Sallis JF, Needle R: The relationship between physical activity and exercise and mental health. Public Health Rep 100:195-202, 1985

11. Gruber JJ: Physical activity and self-esteem development in children: A meta-analysis, Effects of Physical Activity on Children. Edited by American Academy of Physical Education. Champaign, IL, Human Kinetics:30-48, 1986

12. Simons A, McGowan CR, Epstein LH et al: Exercise as a treatment for depression: An update. Clin Psychol Rev 5:553-568, 1985

13. Harris SS, Caspersen CJ, DeFriese GH et al: Physical activity counseling for healthy adults as a primary preventive intervention in the clinical setting: Report for the U.S. Preventive Services Task Force. JAMA 261:3590-3598, 1989

14. Jopling RJ: Health-related fitness as preventive medicine. Pediatr Rev 10:141-148,1988

15. Siscovick DS: Risks of exercising: Sudden cardiac death and injuries. Exercise, Fitness, and Health: A Consensus of Current Knowledge. Edited by C Bouchard, RJ Shephard, T Stephens, JR Sutton, BD McPherson. Champaign, IL, Human Kinetics:707-714, 1990

16. Kelsey JL: Acute musculoskeletal injuries, Epidemiology of Musculoskeletal Disorders. New York, Oxford University Press, 1982, pp192-206

17. Macera CA, Jackson KL, Hagenmaier GW et al: Age, physical activity, physical fitness, body composition, and incidence of orthopedic problems. Res Q Exerc Sport 60:225-233, 1989

18. Andersson G, Malmgren S, Ekstrand J: Occurrence of athletic injuries in voluntary participants in a 1-year extensive newspaper exercise campaign. Internat J Sports Med 7:222-225, 1986

19. Malina RM: Growth, exercise, fitness, and later outcomes. Exercise, Fitness, and Health: A Consensus of Current Knowledge. Edited by C Bouchard, RJ Shephard, T Stephens, JR Sutton, BD McPherson. Champaign, IL, Human Kinetics:637-654, 1990

20. Morgan WP: Negative addiction in runners. Phys Sportsmed 7:57-70, 1979

21. Epling WF, Pierce WD: Activity-based anorexia: A biobehavioral perspective. Internat J Eating Disords 7:475-585, 1988

22. Saris WHM: The assessment and evaluation of daily physical activity in children: A review. Acta Paed Scand (Suppl) 318:37-40, 1985

23. Murphy JK, Alpert BS, Christman JV et al: Physical fitness in children: A survey method based on parental report. Am J Public Health 78:708-710, 1988

24. Baranowski T, Dworkin R, Cieslik CJ et al: Reliability and validity of self-report of aerobic activity: Family Health Project. Res Q Exerc Sport 55:309-317, 1984

25. Sallis JF: Self-report measures of children's physical activity. J Sch Health 61(5): 215-219, 1991

26. Washburn RA, Montoye HJ: The assessment of physical activity by questionnaire. Am J Epidemiol 123:563-576, 1986

27. Wallace JP, McKenzie TL, Nader PR: Observed vs. recalled exercise behavior: A validation of a seven-day exercise recall for boys 11 to 13 years old. Res Q Exerc Sport 56:161-165, 1985

28. Sallis JF, Buono MJ, Roby JJ et al: 7-day recall and other physical activity self-reports in children and adolescents. Medicine and Science in Sports and Exercise, in press, 1991

29. Klesges RC, Coates TC, Moldenhauer-Klesges LM et al: The FATS: An observation system for assessing physical activity in children and associated parental behavior. Behav Assess 6:333-345, 1984

30. Puhl J, Greaves K, Hoyt M et al: Children's activity rating scale (CARS): Description and calibration. Res Q Exerc Sport 61:26-36, 1990

31. Taylor CB, Kraemer HC, Bragg DA et al: A new system for long-term recording and processing of heart rate and physical activity in outpatients. Computers Biomed Res 15:7-17, 1982

32. Gilliam TB, Freedson PS, Geenen DC et al: Physical activity patterns determined by heart-rate monitoring in six 7 year-old children. Med Sci Sports Exerc 13:65-67, 1981

33. Freedson PS: Field monitoring of physical activity in children. Pediatr Exerc Sci 1:8-18, 1989

34. Klesges RC, Klesges LM, Swenson AM et al: A validation of two motion sensors in the prediction of child and adult physical activity levels. Am J Epidemiol 122:400-410, 1985

35. Sallis JF, Buono MJ, Roby JJ et al: The Caltrac accelerometer as a physical activity monitor for school-age children. Med Sci Sports Exerc 22 (5): 698-703, 1990

36. American College of Sports Medicine: Guidelines for graded exercise testing and exercise prescription, 3d ed. Lea & Febiger, Philadelphia, 1986

37. Caspersen CJ, Christenson GM, Pollard RA: Status of the 1990 physical fitness and exercise objectives - evidence from NHIS 1985. Public Health Rep 101: 587-592, 1986

38. Stephens T, Jacobs DR, White CC: A descriptive epidemiology of leisure-time physical activity. Public Health Rep 100:147-158, 1985

39. Verschuur R, Kemper HCG: The pattern of daily physical activity. Med Sport Sci 20:169-186, 1985

40. Blair SN, Clark DG, Cureton KJ et al: Exercise and fitness in childhood: Implications for a lifetime of health, Perspectives in Exercise Science and Sports Medicine. Vol. 2. Youth, Exercise, and Sport. Edited by CV Gisolfi and DR Lamb. Indianapolis, Benchmark: 401-430, 1989

41. Simons-Morton B, O'Hara NM, Simons-Morton D et al: Children and fitness: A public health perspective. Res Q Exerc Sport 58:295-302, 1987

42. Pate RR, Shephard RJ: Characteristics of physical fitness in youth, Perspectives in Exercise Science and Sports Medicine. Vol. 2. Youth, Exercise, and Sport. Edited by CV Gisolfi and DR Lamb. Indianapolis, Benchmark: 1-46, 1989

43. Gortmaker SL, Dietz WH, Sobol AN et al: Increasing pediatric obesity in the U.S. Am J Dis Child 14:535-540, 1987

44. Kucera M: Spontaneous physical activity in preschool children, Children and Exercise XI. Edited by RA Binkhorst, HCG Kemper, WHM Saris. Champaign, IL, Human Kinetics:175-182, 1985

45. Sallis JF, Patterson TL, McKenzie TL et al: Family variables and physical activity in preschool children. J Dev Behav Pediatr 9:57-61,1988

46. Hovell MF, Bursick JH, Sharkey R et al: An evaluation of elementary students' voluntary physical activity during recess. Res Q Exerc Sport 49:460-474, 1978

47. Parcel GS, Simons-Morton BG, O'Hara NM et al: School promotion of healthful diet and exercise behavior: An integration of organizational change and social learning theory interventions. J Sch Health 57:150-156, 1987

48. Tell GS, Vellar OD: Physical fitness, physical activity, and cardiovascular disease risk factors in adolescents: The Oslo youth study. Prev Med 17:12-24, 1988

49. Sallis JF, Patterson TL, Buono MJ et al: Aggregation of physical activity habits in Mexican-American and Anglo families. J Behav Med 11:31041, 1988

50. Dishman RK, Sallis JF, Orenstein DR: The determinants of physical activity and exercise. Public Health Rep 100:158-172, 1985

51. Ross JG, Dotson CO, Gilbert GG et al: What are kids doing in school physical education? J Phys Educ Recreat Dance 56:73-76, 1985

52. Ross JG, Pate RR, Corbin CB et al: What is going on in the elementary physical education program? J Phys Educ Recreat Dance 58:78-84, 1987

53. Faucette N, McKenzie TL, Patterson P: Descriptive analysis of nonspecialist elementary physical education teachers' curricular choices and class organization. J Teaching Phys Educ 9(4): 284-93, 1990

54. Cooper KH, Purdy JG, Friedman A et al: An aerobic conditioning program for the Fort-Worth, Texas School District. Res Q Exerc Sport 46:345-350, 1975

55. Shepard RJ, Volle M, Lavalle H et al: Required physical activity and academic grades: A controlled study, Proceedings of the 10th Pediatric Work Physiology Symposium. Edited by J Ilmariene. Berlin, Springer-Verlag, 1984

56. Simons-Morton BG, Parcel GS, O'Hara NM: Implementing organizational changes to promote healthful diet and physical activity at school. Health Educ Q 15:115-130, 1988

57. MacConnie SE, Gilliam T, Greenen D et al: Daily physical activity patterns of prepubertal children involved in a vigorous exercise program. Internat J Sports Med 3:202-207, 1982

58. Duncan B, Boyce WT, Itami R et al: A controlled trial of a physical fitness program for fifth grade students. J Sch Health 53:467-471, 1983

59. Dwyer T, Coonan WE, Leitch DR et al: An investigation of the effects of daily physical activity on the health of primary school students in South Australia. Internat J Epidemiol 12:308-313, 1983

60. Maynard EJ, Coonan WE, Worsley A et al: The development of the lifestyle education program in Australia, Cardiovascular Risk Factors in Children: Epidemiology and Prevention. Edited by BS Hetzel and GS Berenson. Amsterdam, Elsevier, 1987, pp123-149

61. Siegel JA, Manfredi TG: Effects of a ten-month fitness program on children. Phys Sports Med 12:91-97, 1984

62. Coates TJ, Jeffery RW, Slinkard LA: Heart healthy eating and exercise: Introducing and maintaining changes in health behaviors. Am J Public Health 71:15-23, 1981

63. Walter HJ, Hofman A, Vaughan RD: Modification of risk factors for coronary heart disease: Five-year results of a school-based intervention trial. N Engl J Med 318:1093-1100, 1988

64. Connor MK, Smith LG, Fryer A et al: Future Fit: A cardiovascular health education and fitness project in an after-school setting. J Sch Health 56:329-333, 1986

65. Nader PR, Sallis JF, Patterson TL et al: A family approach to cardiovascular risk reduction: Results from the San Diego Family Health Project. Health Educ Q 16:229-244, 1989

66. Taggart AC, Taggart J, Siedentop D: Effects of a home-based activity program: A study with low-fitness elementary school children. Behav Modif 10:487-507, 1986

67. Epstein LH, Wing RR, Koeske R et al: Long-term effects of family-based treatment of childhood obesity. J Consult Clin Psychol 55:91-95, 1987

# 18

# The Evaluation of Health Education Programs for Youth: Methods and Challenges

FRANCES MARCUS LEWIS, RN, PHD

The future health of the nation rests soundly in the health behavior of its youth. This health behavior, which includes lifestyle practices, health-related skills, consumption practices, and attitudes and beliefs about health is influenced by modeling and programmatic instruction the youth experience from health professionals, and from schools, friends, family, and the media.[1,2]

The claims we make for health education programs are ultimately justified – or challenged – on the basis of information we obtain on their effectiveness. Such claims are best examined in evaluation studies. Through evaluation we can partly put to rest the question of the potential merit of a program. We can examine whether short- or long-term effects were achieved, as well as the processes through which the program caused the observed effects.[3,4] Cost-effectiveness data, as well, can be obtained in order to answer the question: What did we achieve for how much?[5] The purpose of the current chapter is to introduce evaluation designs and their application to intervention studies with youth. School health education programs serve as the prototype to understand ways in which to evaluate the effectiveness of health-related interventions.

## WHAT IS EVALUATION?

There are two types of evaluations: formative (or process) evaluations and outcome (or impact) evaluations. Formative evaluations deal with the short-term impact and acceptability of the program to the study partici-pants during the program's implementation.[3,6] Outcome or impact evalu-ation focuses on the effects of the program on the study participants.

Outcome evaluations address the shorter-term effects like changes in attitudes and beliefs; impact evaluations include the longer-range effects on mortality and morbidity.

Multiple categories of health-related outcomes can be impacted by interventions: attitudes and beliefs (long-lasting predispositions); motor skills; knowledge; perceptions; lifestyle management; behavioral adjustment (behavior reflecting normatively acceptable functioning in areas like school performance and peer and family interaction); self conception (self-appraisal); consumption behavior (things young people choose to purchase or ingest); morbidity; and mortality. Each of these categories can be reflected in the types of outcome or impact measures to be used in an evaluation study.

## CASTING THE RESEARCH QUESTION: THE BASIS FOR THE EVALUATION DESIGN

At the basis of every evaluation is a question about the program or intervention. We could be asking: Did this program work or make a difference? By that question we are asking if there were changes in the participants as a result of the intervention or program. We could also be asking: Did the program or intervention achieve effects over those achieved by another program?

Every evaluation question has an implicit or explicit point of comparison or standard against which you are judging the efficacy of the program.[3] To have relatively high confidence in the answers to these questions, a control or comparison group or a time-series design is needed.

Evaluation designs that use a control group are true experimental designs involving random assignment. The presence of a control group allows the evaluator to "control for" the influence of other variables (besides the program) that could cause the observed effects. Evaluation designs that use a comparison group are quasi-experimental designs. In quasi-experimental designs, a naturally occurring group, as similar as possible to the intervention group, is used as comparison. Time-series designs can also be used with confidence to examine the effects of a program. In a time-series design, program participants serve as their own controls and are observed prior to the program and over time after the program is completed.

Designs that do not use either a comparison or a control group are vulnerable to criticism. If there are observed differences, the evaluator will not be on firm ground to argue that the program, and not some competing cause, produced the observed changes. These alternative causes are called threats to validity. There are two types of threats: internal threats and external threats to validity. Understanding threats to validity assists in the choice of a particular evaluation design.

## THREATS TO INTERNAL VALIDITY

Eleven types of threat to internal validity are described here and are summarized in Box 1, below.

---

### Box 1

### Eleven Sources of Threat to the Internal Validity of Experimental Evaluations

1. **History:** Experiences or events of the participants that occur concurrent to the experimental treatment, program or intervention.

2. **Maturation:** Developmental changes in the participants (emotional, cognitive, or physical) that occur concurrent to the program, intervention or experimental intervention.

3. **Testing:** Reactivity in the participants due to being measured or tested prior to the actual intervention.

4. **Instrumentation:** Methods used to generate the evaluation data (including measurement process, form of instrument, or people administering the methods).

5. **Regression artifact:** Sampling of extreme scorers (either extremely high or extremely low) who tend to regress toward the mean.

6. **Differential attrition or mortality:** Different rates of drop-outs occur between the treatment and control groups.

7. **Selection effects:** Dissimilarity or non-equivalence between the experimental group and the control group.

8. **Diffusion or imitation of treatments:** Contamination occurs between the treatment and the control group.

9. **Compensatory equalization of treatments:** Resources are given to the control group that attempt to "make up" for the group's assignment to the control.

10. **Compensatory rivalry:** An accentuated performance occurs in those receiving the less desirable treatment.

11. **Resentful demoralization:** An exceptionally negative performance occurs in those receiving the less desirable treatment.

---

The **history** of the experimental participants may affect the outcomes. For example, children experiencing an intervention on healthy dietary practices in their school might also be participating in a wellness awareness program through their community center that increases their knowledge level about healthy food choices. If knowledge and attitudes about healthy food choices are the outcome variables, scores will be affected or confounded by participation in the community center program. We would be in a weak position to argue that the intervention caused the observed changes; instead it might be that the community center program actually caused the changes.

The **maturation** of the experimental participants may affect the outcomes. When people mature or develop over the course of the experimental intervention, we must expect that their maturation, not just our intervention or experimental treatment, caused the observed changes. It is common, for example, for children to become more internalized in their perceptions of control over their health as they grow older.[7] These changes are expected as a result of the maturation process, not just because of an intervention designed to increase their sense of personal responsibility for their own health.

The **testing** or measurement process itself can cause a reaction in the participants of an experiment. Participants react to being measured or monitored. This reactivity, not the experimental treatment, could cause the observed changes. For example, children measured on their own level of functioning and coping with chronic illness might be stimulated to improve their coping skills as a result of the measurement process itself. This effect could occur in addition to any effects caused by our experimental manipulation.

**Instrumentation** or errors introduced in the process of measurement itself, including observer or coder error, can cause effects besides those potentially produced by an experimental intervention. Observers, for example, may record changes when they really did not occur, particularly if the observer thinks that the child being measured is part of an experimental treatment group. The form of the instrument itself may also cause changes in the desired outcome, even if actual changes did not occur. For example, if response options in questionnaires ranged from 1 to 5 after the intervention but ranged only from 0 to 4 prior to the intervention, increases may reflect an instrumentation threat, not an actual change caused by the experimental treatment.

A **regression artifact** may cause the observed changes, not the experimental intervention. This threat to a study's internal validity is a result of including children in the study who have extremely low or extremely high scores on the outcome measures. These extreme-scoring students would be expected to obtain scores in the center or mean of the sample, that is, regress toward the mean, the next time they were measured even if the intervention had no effect. Children with extremely high scores on a measure of behavioral problems, for example, might be expected to have less severe scores at the second time of measurement even if the intervention did not work.

**Differential attrition,** or the different rates with which individuals drop out from the treatment or control groups, may account for differences in the outcome measures even if the intervention had no effect. If older children dropped out at a faster rate from the experimental treatment group than did older children in the control group, and the experimental group scored higher at outcome than did the comparison group, we would be in a weak position to claim that the observed effects were due to the program rather than to this differential dropout rate. It may be that the obtained results occurred because the remaining children in the treatment group were comprised of younger children compared to the controls.

**Selection** relates to the differences that exist between the types of subjects or respondents recruited into the experimental group as contrasted with those recruited into another group. Selection is a major potential threat to internal validity in quasi-experimental designs. It is also possible that selection interacts with maturation, history, and instrumentation to threaten the internal validity of the results.

Four additional threats to the internal validity of an experiment were recently identified: **diffusion or imitation of treatments, compensatory equalization of treatments, compensatory rivalry,** and **resentful demoralization.**[8] These last four threats have particular interest and importance for the investigator because they can never be ruled out solely through randomization.

**Diffusion or imitation** of treatments involves contamination between the treatment and the control group. This is a particularly relevant threat to the internal validity of an experiment conducted within a setting that allows participants in the treatment group to interact or exchange information with the control group.[9] Participants in one group may learn information that was intended only for the other group. **Compensatory equalization** of treatments involves some source – most typically administration – giving resources to the control group or otherwise compensating for resources or goods that were held back from them compared to the experimental group. **Compensatory rivalry** by participants receiving the less desirable treatment involves social competition in which the control group may be motivated to perform in ways that decrease the expected differences between the treatment and the control groups. Compensatory rivalry is sometimes called the "John Henry effect." **Resentful demoralization** of participants involves a retaliation or an accentuated negative performance in the participants who receive the less desirable treatment. Participants know they are receiving the less desirable treatment and purposefully shut down or perform poorly.

## THREATS TO EXTERNAL VALIDITY

Even if we successfully control for all the threats to internal validity, there are still other factors to consider that can threaten the generalizability of our results: these are the threats to external validity. Threats to external validity involve the treatment variable and some other variable.[10]

Increasingly, external validity or generalizability, not just internal validity, deserves our attention.[11,12,13] There are four important threats to external validity: interaction between selection and treatment, interaction between testing and treatment, reactive situational effects, and multiple treatment or combined effects.

It is always possible that the results you observe are due to the population from which the experimental and control groups were obtained. There is an **interaction effect between the subjects** selected into the study and the experimental manipulation. This is sometimes referred to as subject-treatment interaction. The uniqueness of the population interacts with the experimental treatment to produce the observed results, but these results would not necessarily occur if the program or intervention were implemented with another population.

There may also be an **interaction between the testing process and the treatment** that could threaten the external validity or generalizability of the results. This threat occurs when subjects have been measured or tested prior to the intervention and the results occur only if the test is given. This means that the obtained results are generalizable to other situations only when the pretest is administered. This threat to external validity is particularly important when the pretest sensitizes the participants, thus making them more influenced by the program or intervention that follows the pretest.

**Reactive situational effects** include multiple factors that are associated or linked with the experimental treatment itself but are not planned components of the intervention. These situational factors can threaten the external validity or generalizability of the results because they would not necessarily be present in other settings to which we wanted to generalize. Categories of situational effects include the physical setting of the experiment, the personality or otherwise unique features of those implementing the experiment, the subjects' awareness of their participation in an experiment, and the newness or novelty of the program. For example, a teaching-support program for adolescent weight reduction conducted in the home-like atmosphere of a newly designed student union building might cause effects that would otherwise not occur in a more typical classroom setting. In another example, a smoking prevention program for middle-school children might affect higher quit-smoking rates in a school with a smoke-free environment than in a school in which students and teachers are permitted to smoke.

**Multiple treatment effects** threaten the external validity of study results. When participants are involved in more than one experiment or program at the same time, it may be that the effects of the multiple programs in combination with each other, not just the program being singled out for assessment, produce the results. This means that we could not expect a single isolated program to have the same effects as the program in combination with others.

Despite the multiple threats to internal and external validity, there are solid design choices you can make to control for these threats. Some of these designs are easily implemented; others require more administrative control or fiscal resources. The choice of an evaluation design should be based on controlling the plausible or most likely threats to internal and external validity relevant to your setting. Three types of experimental designs that guard against most or all of the threats to internal validity are now reviewed: a pretest- post-test control group design, a post-test only control group design, and a Solomon four-group design.

## EXPERIMENTAL EVALUATION DESIGNS

Experimental designs are characterized by the **random assignment** of study subjects into either the treatment or the control group. By randomly assigning subjects, we increase the probability that both the treatment and the control groups will be similar at the start. Randomization controls for most of the threats to the internal validity of the experiment and increases the experiment's external validity by controlling for selection-treatment interaction. Using a conservative guideline, random assignment equates the experimental and control groups prior to intervention when there are approximately 100 or more subjects allocated into each group;[3] random-ization is particularly important when the expected results of the intervention are small.[14]

Random assignment or randomization, however, cannot be assumed to equate the treatment and control groups in the case of small samples assigned to each group. Rather, the comparability of the treatment and the control groups should be inspected in the pretest data.

## PRETEST- POST-TEST CONTROL GROUP DESIGN

The pretest- post-test control group design involves random assignment of subjects into a treatment or a control group. A pretest is administered at the beginning and a post-test at the end of the experimental intervention and at the same time to the subjects in the control group. Extensions of this design include multiple treatment groups and multiple post-tests.[15] When there are multiple treatment groups, the subjects are randomly assigned to one of them.

There are multiple advantages to the pretest- post-test control group design with random assignment. All the threats to internal validity are controlled for, namely those due to history, maturation, testing, instrumentation, regression artifact, differential attrition, and selection. The design also controls for the interaction of selection and maturation and other interactions that could affect the interpretation of the effect of the experimental treatment. Any differences between the treatment and the control groups cannot be attributed to one of these internal validity factors.

Note, however, that there is no control for reactive situational effects in the pretest- post-test control group design. A threat due to this means that something unique could happen within any treatment session to produce the observed results. Examples of such unique events could include the particularly sensitive or empathic introductory remarks offered by a physician lecturer that was not planned in the program, or the presence of a cocaine-addicted youth who introduces personal testimony that was not part of the programmed intervention. (See reference 10 for a discussion of this problem in terms of intra-session history.)

The pretest- post-test control group design also does not control for the interaction of testing or selection and the treatment manipulation. The obtained effects could not generalize to subjects who did not receive a pretest. It is always plausible that the pretest sensitized the subjects to the experimental treatment, thereby interacting with the treatment to produce the obtained results. It is also possible that selection interacted with the experimental variable to produce the obtained results. Thus, although selection was controlled for as a threat to the internal validity of the experiment, it is possible that observed differences are relevant only to the particular population from which the experimental and treatment groups were obtained. The more this particular threat to external validity occurs, the more difficult it is to recruit subjects into the experimental study. Those subjects who are indeed finally recruited into the study are probably unlike the larger population to which we want to generalize.

We can also extend our discussion to include interactions between the experimental treatment and other factors like instrumentation, maturation, and history. It is always possible that the observed differences are due to the measurements used in the study; it is the interaction of the experimental treatment with the particular measurement that produces the results, not the treatment manipulation. Alternatively, it is possible that the results are specific or unique to the sampled participants who were all of a particular age. Similarly, it is possible that the obtained results, while internally valid, may pertain only to the particular historical period in which the study was conducted. Any observed results in smoking cessation programs in the mid- to late 1980s, for example, could be due to the attention given to anti-smoking campaigns by federal policy; the National Cancer Institute; and the National Heart, Blood, and Lung Institute; not just to the effects of an intervention program at a particular site.

## POST-TEST ONLY CONTROL GROUP DESIGN

The post-test only control group design is another sound alternative to the pretest- post-test control group design if the evaluator is assured that both the treatment and the control groups are similar prior to the experimental manipulation. In this design, subjects are randomized into treatment and control group but do not receive the pretest prior to the intervention. Currently this design is underutilized but represents a sound alternative. This design controls for the same threats to internal validity as the pretest- post-test control group design. It also has the advantage of controlling for the potential interaction of testing with the experimental treatment because it omits the pretest as a source of potential threat to the external validity of the experiment. It is argued that the post-test only design is usually preferred to the pretest- post-test control group design except when randomization does not equalize the groups.[10]

## Solomon Four-Group Design

Although seldom used, the Solomon Four-Group Design is a true experimental design that explicitly considers external validity. The design allows the investigator to evaluate both the effects due to testing and the effects due to the interaction of testing and the experimental manipulation. Subjects in this design are randomly assigned to one of four groups. Groups 1 and 2 in the design are the same two groups as the pretest- post-test control group design: the randomly assigned treatment group and the randomly assigned control group. Group 3 receives the treatment and the post-test but not the pretest. Group 4 receives only the post-test. All pretests and post-tests are administered at the same time to all subjects.

The Solomon Four-Group Design has two more advantages. It allows the investigator to estimate the combined effects of maturation and history on the outcomes. This is done by comparing the post-test only results from Group 4 with the pretest results of Groups 1 and 2. The design also allows the investigator to interpret more competently past research in an area that utilized the pretest- post-test control group design. More specifically, the Solomon Four-Group Design lets the evaluator estimate the likelihood that past study results were affected by an interaction between testing and the treatment manipulation.[10]

# QUASI-EXPERIMENTAL EVALUATION DESIGNS

Sometimes the physical constraints, political reality, or resources of a situation do not allow the evaluator to assign subjects randomly to an experimental treatment or control group. Quasi-experimental designs are a great boon under these circumstances. Selected examples of these designs are now reviewed: time-series design, multiple time-series design, and non-equivalent control group design.

## Time-Series Design

The key feature of the time-series design is the presence of periodic measurements on the subjects at multiple times prior to and after the experimental manipulation.[16,17] Young school-age children, for example, can be evaluated at weekly intervals on their skill performance in carrying out bicycle safety. After week four, these same children participate in a new training program on bicycle safety. Evaluations of skill performance continue as before. The evaluator is interested in knowing whether the new bicycle training program improved the children's performance. A time-series design would be a viable evaluation design to consider.

The time-series design has some limitations because of the threats to internal and external validity it does not control. Its most serious limitation is that it does not control for effects due to history. It is always possible, for example, that a concurrent program other than the new bicycle training program caused the observed changes. For example, a state-wide bicycle safety campaign could have been mounted in the media that affected the observed changes. Alternatively, the parent-teacher association could have emphasized the importance of bicycle safety at its monthly parent meeting. If, however, the evaluator can systematically rule out plausible alternative causes, then the credibility of the results from this design are more protected. However, ruling out potential concurrent causes with this design is not always easy. The seasoned evaluator probably uses this design under only three conditions: when the cycle of periodic measurements and experimental manipulation can be repeated with multiple samples and in various settings; when there is no possibility of using a more controlled design; and when periodic measurements will occur anyway, this design capitalizes on them.

Under some circumstances the results obtained from the time-series design could be threatened by instrumentation. This is particularly likely if the measurement procedure involves human judges and these judges are aware of the experimental intervention. Such biased observers might confirm the presence of changed behavior when it really did not occur; it was merely a function of the observer's expectations.[10]

Threats to the external validity of the time-series design include both selection and treatment interaction and reactive situational effects.

## MULTIPLE TIME-SERIES DESIGN

The multiple time-series design is an extension of the time-series design that adds one or more naturally occurring comparison groups. By adding the comparison group, the evaluator gains increased confidence that any obtained differences between the treatment and the comparison groups are due to the experimental manipulation, not to alternative causes. This design actually allows the investigator to examine treatment effects in two ways: by comparing the pre-treatment measures with the post-treatment measures in the treatment group and by comparing the treatment values against the comparison group values.

This design has some distinct advantages: It adequately controls for all the threats to internal validity except the possible interaction between selection and history. It is always possible, for example, that the concurrent events impinging on the study participants may interact with the characteristics of the study participants to produce the observed effects.

The external validity of this design is threatened by a testing-treatment interaction, although this design is usually used in situations in which the testing is carried out as a matter of course or common practice with participants and is therefore not reactive. The design may also be threatened by a selection-treatment interaction. This is a caution one must always consider; effects may be due to the interaction between the uniqueness of the participants and their particular response to the intervention and would not generalize to other non-participants. Reactive arrangements may account for differences, but, again, these are unlikely given the circumstances under which most multiple time-series designs would be used.

The multiple time-series design provides a sound design choice when repeated measures are available anyway, and when a similar comparison group can be recruited. It is a design worthy of additional attention even though it is relatively absent from the literature.

## Non-Equivalent Control Group Design

The non-equivalent control group design is the same design as the pretest- post-test control group design considered under experimental designs except that it lacks randomization. In the non-equivalent control group design, the investigator takes advantage of two naturally occurring groups, one of which receives the experimental manipulation, one of which serves as the comparison group. (This design can be extended to include multiple comparison groups.) The absence of randomization means that the experimental and comparison groups do not have pre-experimental sampling equivalence; they are not technically the same at pretest. However, the careful selection of the two groups is focused on maximizing the similarity between the two occurring groups. Threats to internal validity are minimized the more similar the treatment group is to the comparison group based on both the selection process and the verification of equivalence using pretest scores. The more similar the experimental group is to the comparison group, the more confidence the evaluator can have in attributing any observed differences to the experimental treatment.

When pretest equivalence exists, this design controls for history, maturation, testing, and instrumentation. Both the treatment and the comparison groups would be equally affected by these potential threats to internal validity and the threats, therefore, could not account for any observed differences between the treatment and comparison groups. This design represents one of the most commonly used designs in evaluation studies.

This design does not control for possible interaction effects between selection and history, maturation, or testing. Although it has been argued that such interactions are unlikely, they are plausible under certain situations.[10] Let us consider, for example, a possible interaction effect between selection and maturation, even when the treatment and comparison groups are similar at pretest. Suppose that at pretest, eighth-grade children are similar in their attitudes toward sexual behavior. It is always possible, however, that the children in the experimental treatment group mature at a faster rate than do the children in the comparison group. These differences in maturation mean that observed changes in the experimental group could be inappropriately attributed to the effects of the program rather than to the maturation of the experimental participants. This selection-maturation interaction threatens the internal validity of the design.

The non-equivalent control group design also does not control for regression. If either the experimental treatment or comparison group were chosen because it represented extreme scores, then it is always possible that the difference between the two groups is related to the natural shift in scores – spontaneous regression toward the mean that would have occurred independent of the experimental manipulation. If the experimental group consisted of acutely grieving children of dead siblings, change in the experimental group could be attributable to a spontaneous change because they were an extreme group; this change could have occurred in the absence of an experimental manipulation anyway.

External validity is also threatened with a non-equivalent control group design by the interaction of the treatment manipulation with testing or selection, or by reactive arrangements. The threat to external validity due to interaction between testing and experimental manipulation is the same as with the experimental pretest- post-test control group design. The selection-treatment interaction is due to the possibility that the observed effects may be due to the uniqueness of the respondents selected to participate in the study; such results would not be expected to generalize to other potential participants. Reactive arrangements also prevent generalizability. However, threats due to reactivity are probably less with this design than they are in the true experimental control group design.[10] By using naturally occurring groups, the investigator may be less likely to create a reactive environment that produces the effects.

## Evaluations as Informing Policy and Practice

The selection of the evaluation design is guided ultimately by the evaluation question you want to examine. This means that there is no such thing as the perfect research design; rather, the design should fit the circumstances. Selected research designs were reviewed, including experimental and quasi-experimental designs and the related threats to internal and external validity. Throughout the chapter the advantages and disadvantages of each research design are considered.

Evaluation research, however, is not reducible to either sophisticated design questions nor methodologic wizardry. Rather, it should be viewed in the larger context of informing policy and advancing practice.[18]

No amount of statistical savvy nor psychometric circumlocution can replace the value of careful descriptive work, including detailed documentation of exactly what the program consisted of (versus what was planned); what behaviors the program elicited in the participants (versus what was predicted to be elicited); what the untoward effects or serendipitous impact of the program was; or what subgroups of the participants had unique or particular responses to the program. Documentation of these and related issues is what informs us of the program's effect, not just whether the outcomes reached statistical significance.

When evaluation is reduced to mere technical methodology issues it often isolates the practitioners. Audiences for evaluation findings are highly varied in terms of skills, needs, and background. Practitioners, for example, often have more interest in the programmatic component (what was it like; who responded well or poorly to it; where did it seem to fail or succeed; what refinements are needed in future applications of it) than in the technical aspects of the evaluation design. Increasingly there is the need to accommodate both research and program objectives.[19]

We are not deprecating "...quantification, comparison, controlled assignment, or objective measurement...but only that they be introduced as a result of reason and not reflex."[12] The issue is one of restoring balance between quantification and explanation. It also argues for bringing more players back into the evaluation field, including practitioners, not just formally trained evaluators.[3]

# REFERENCES

1. Gochman DS (ed): Health Behavior, Emerging Research Perspectives. New York, Plenum Press, 1988

2. Glanz K, Lewis FM, Rimer B (eds): Health Behavior and Health Education: Theory Research and Practice. San Francisco, Jossey-Bass, 1990

3. Green LW, Lewis FM: Evaluation and Measurement in Health Education and Health Promotion. Palo Alto, Mayfield Publishing, 1986

4. Perloff R, Perloff E, Sussna E: Program evaluation. Annu Rev Psychology 27, 569-594, 1976

5. Green LW, Lewis FM: Data analysis in evaluation of health education: Toward standardization of procedures and terminology. Health Educ Research 2(3), 215-221, 1987

6. Evans RI, Raines BE, Owen AE: Formative evaluation in school-based health promotion investigations. Prev Med 18, 229-234, 1989

7. Parcel G, Meyer MP: Development of an instrument to measure children's health locus of control. Health Educ Monogr 6(2), 149-159, 1987

8. Cook TD, Campbell DT: Quasi-experimentation Design and Analysis Issues for Field Settings. Chicago, Rand McNally, 1979

9. Pentz MA, MacKinnon DP, Dwyer JH et al: Longitudinal effects of the Midwestern Prevention Project on regular and experimental smoking in adolescents. Prev Med 18, 304-321, 1989

10. Campbell DT, Stanley JC: Experimental and Quasi-experimental Designs for Research. Chicago, Rand McNally, 1963

11. Lewis FM: Beyond technique and technology: Who and what is evaluation in health education to serve? Paper presented at 37th Annual Meeting, Society of Public Health Educators. Las Vegas, Nevada. September 26-28, 1986

12. Cronbach LJ, Ambron SR, Dornbusch SM et al: Toward Reform of Program Evaluation. San Francisco, Jossey-Bass, 1981

13. Cronbach LJ: Designing Evaluations of Educational and Social Programs. San Francisco, Jossey-Bass, 1983

14. Shortell SM, Richardson WC: Health Program Evaluation. St Louis, CV Mosby, 1978

15. Pentz MA, Johnson CA, Dwyer JH et al: A comprehensive community approach to adolescent drug abuse prevention: Effects on cardiovascular disease risk behaviors. Ann Med 21, 219-222, 1989

16. Windsor RA: The utility of time-series designs and analysis in evaluating health promotion and education programs, Advances in Health Education and Promotion. Greenwich, CT, JAI Press Inc., 1986

17. Windsor RA, Baranowski T, Clark N et al: Evaluation of Health Promotion and Education Programs. Palo Alto, Mayfield Publishing, 1984

18. Green LW, Lewis FM: Issues in relating evaluation to theory, policy and practice in health education. Mobius 1(2), 46-58, 1981

19. Pentz MA, Cormack C, Flay B et al: Balancing program and research integrity in community drug abuse prevention: Project STAR approach. J Sch Health 56(9), 389-393, 1986

# Index of Authors,
# All Three Volumes

# Index of Subjects,
## All Three Volumes

divorce as risk to child health, 8, 12
drop-out rates and drug use, 20, 148
**Drowning** as cause of death, 2, 18, 90, 97
childhood pool, prevention, 97
related to alcohol and drug use, 97
**Drug abuse/ use,** 146–151, 266, 405, 410-419, 602
and AIDS/ HIV, 146
and mental health, 532
and nutrition, 31, 44
and STDs, 633
and suicide, 536
costs of, 149
ethnic groups, 846
illicit, 21, 22, 147
in college athletes, 825
in college students, 613–619
patterns, 613–617
prevention, 617–619
model (CCCA), 618–619
in health science students, 810
intervention and treatment services, 619
nature and significance of the problem, 146
negative consequences of, 146
prenatal, and LBW, 266
prevalence, by category of drug, table 614
role in unsafe sexual behavior, 76
*see also* substance abuse
**Drug abuse prevention:**
implications for planning and policy, 151
prevention efforts, 149–151
communicable disease model, 149
public health model, 149
risk factor model, 149
model/ programs, 617, 618
social influences model, 412-415, 417-419
community, 418–419
Drug Abuse Warning Network (DAWN), 6
drug information network (RADAR), 620

EAP, *see* employee assistance programs
Early and Periodic Screening, Diagnosis, and Treatment (EPSDT), 6, 295

**Eating disorders,** 31, 44, 471, 706-713
and amenorrhea, 710
and mental health, 532
and nutritional counseling, 44
assessment, 709–711
diagnostic criteria, 706, table 707
epidemiology, 706–708
in the college population, 706–713
medical complications, table 711
prevalence, 707
prevention, 708–709
psychological features, 710
self-help group resources, 714
symptom assessment, 710
treatment, 712–713
*see also* anorexia; bulimia
Eating Disorders Consortium, Western College, 713
economic well-being of children, *see* well-being
Education for All Handicapped Children Act of 1975 (PL 94–142), 185, 189, 251, 352, 467
education, health, school, *see* health education, school
education, health, *see* health education
**Education:** minority, model for, 377–389
nutrition, 454
physical, *see* physical education
rape, 426, 732
sexuality, *see* sexuality education
special, *see* special education
educational plan, individualized (IEP), 189, 192
educator, health, *see* health educator
educators, peer health, *see* health educators, peer
educators, sexuality, 424
ELISA testing in HIV disease, 627
**Emergencies:**
college health services, 522–523
common, table, 338–340
diagnosing, 341
school health, 275, 337–342
treatment of, steps, 341
emergency information cards, 337, 346
employee assistance programs (EAP), 297

# APPENDIX A

## BIOGRAPHICAL SKETCHES OF
## CONTRIBUTING AUTHORS FOR VOLUME ONE

**Diana Abramo** is a doctoral candidate in Community Psychology at New York University, and is an AIDS consultant specializing in prevention education, outreach, and program development. Ms. Abramo was previously the Assistant Director of the Adolescent AIDS Program at Montefiore Medical Center, and has been a consultant for AIDS Family Service, AIDS Center of Queens County, and various AIDS prevention education projects. She is on the advisory committee of the National Pediatric AIDS Resource Center.

**Zili Amsel** is currently the Acting Director of the Division of Epidemiology and Prevention Research of the National Institute on Drug Abuse (NIDA). Dr. Amsel (ScD) was trained as a medical sociologist at New York University and as an epidemiologist at the Johns Hopkins University School of Hygiene and Public Health. She has written extensively in the areas of drug abuse, cancer prevention, and AIDS prevention. Additionally, Dr. Amsel has served as a consultant to several federal and international agencies.

**Suzanne Bianchi** is a demographer with the U.S. Bureau of the Census, Housing and Household Economic Statistics Division. Dr. Bianchi received her doctorate in sociology from the University of Michigan. Her research focuses on family compositional change and issues of race, gender, and economic inequality. She is co-author of American Women in Transition, a volume in the 1980 Census Monograph Series. Her publications on children include "Children's Contact with Absent Parents," Journal of Marriage and the Family, 1988; America's Children: Mixed Prospects, Population Reference Bureau, 1990; and a forthcoming Census Bureau report on "Family Disruption and Economic Hardship: The Short-Term Picture for Children."

**Anne Bourgeois** received a bachelor's degree in nutrition from Cornell University, and a masters degree in clinical nutrition from the Tuft's University School of Nutrition. Ms. Bourgeois then completed an internship program at the Frances Stern Nutrition Center/ New England Medical Center Hospital. She is a registered dietitian and a member of the American Dietetic Association.

**Willard Cates** received a masters degree in history from Cambridge University and a combined MD-MPH from Yale University School of Medicine. After clinical training in internal medicine, Dr. Cates joined the Abortion Surveillance Branch of CDC, and in 1982 became Director, Division of Sexually Transmitted Diseases. Under his leadership, the Division integrated HIV prevention activities into STD programs, changed its name to the Division of STD/HIV Prevention, and tripled in size. In 1991, he was chosen as Director of the Division of Training in CDC's Epidemiology Program Office to direct its scientific training functions. He has lectured and published widely on the subjects of epidemiology, contraception, and STDs; and is a past recipient of the American Public Health Association's Schultz Award for his research contributing to the health of American women.

**Carol D'Onofrio** is Associate Professor of Public Health at the University of California, Berkeley. Dr. D'Onofrio is active in the development, implementation, and evaluation of policy, research, and educational initiatives to promote the public's health. She has directed or co-directed several large-scale research projects involving children and youth in studies of tobacco-use prevention. As part of this work, Dr. D'Onofrio has collaborated with academic colleagues, teachers, adult volunteers, and youth in developing, field-testing, and disseminating the school-based Risk and Youth: Smoking (RAY:S) curriculum for students in grades seven through nine. She currently serves on the Board of Scientific Counselors for the National Cancer Institute's Division of Cancer Prevention and Control.

**Johanna Dwyer** received a BS in Food and Nutrition from Cornell, an MS in the same field from the University of Wisconsin, and MSc and DSc degrees in Public Health and Nutrition from the Harvard School of Public Health. Dr. Dwyer is Professor of Medicine in Community Health at Tufts University School of Medicine, and holds adjunct professor appointments at the Tufts University School of Nutrition and the Harvard School of Public Health.

**Nell Faucette** taught elementary physical education and was a public school administrator before receiving her EdD in physical education from the University of Georgia in 1984. Currently, Dr. Faucette is Associate Professor of Physical Education at the University of South Florida (Tampa) with primary responsibilities in the elementary physical education and teacher education programs. She is an investigator on a grant designed to increase children's physical activity through an elementary physical education and self-management intervention. Other primary foci for past research have been elementary physical education environments and the process of teacher change through in-service education.

**Karen Hein** is currently Professor of Pediatrics and Associate Professor of Epidemiology and Social Work at Albert Einstein College of Medicine in New York. Dr. Hein received her MD degree from Columbia University's College of Physicians and Surgeons, and completed her pediatric residency and an additional post-doctoral fellowship in Adolescent Medicine. She has written extensively, lectured, and made television appearances on the subject of adolescent health, focusing particularly on high-risk youth. In 1987, Dr. Hein founded and is the director of the Adolescent AIDS Program at Montefiore Medical Center in the Bronx. She has been awarded numerous grants related to HIV/AIDS in adolescents, and serves as a consultant to many federal and health organizations; she was the recipient of a 1989 U.S. DHHS Assistant Secretary of Health Award for leadership in HIV service. Additionally, Dr. Hein is a manuscript and abstract reviewer for many medical journals and has co-authored the book AIDS: Trading Fears for Facts, a guide for young people published by Consumer Reports Books in 1989.

**Alan Hinman** received a BA from Cornell University, MD from Western Reserve University, and MPH from Harvard University. Dr. Hinman's clinical training in internal medicine and infectious diseases took place at Cleveland Metropolitan General Hospital. Since 1965 he has been involved in public health and prevention programs at the state, national, and international level. In his current position as Director, National Center for Prevention Services, CDC, he provides coordination for national programs of immunization, tuberculosis prevention and control, sexually transmitted disease and human immunodeficiency virus prevention, dental disease prevention, and quarantine.

**Vince Hutchins** is a pediatrician who received his MD from the University of Iowa, and MPH from the University of California, Berkeley, 1968. Dr. Hutchins has held high administrative positions in the federal government, in the Maternal and Child Health field, for over 20 years, recently as Director of the Bureau of Maternal and Child Health. He is Consultant to the Carnegie Corporation in New York City. He has received awards from the American Academy of Pediatrics, the American Public Health Association, and the federal government for outstanding service in the field of Maternal and Child Health.

**Elaine Johnson** is currently the director of the Office for Substance Abuse Prevention (OSAP). Dr. Johnson received both masters and doctoral degrees from the University of Maryland. As director of OSAP, she oversees the administration of a variety of diverse and extensive alcohol and other drug prevention programs and activities for the nation. Additionally, Dr. Johnson is Associate Administrator for Prevention in the Alcohol, Drug Abuse, and Mental Health Administration (ADAMHA) of the U.S. Department of Health and Human Services. She provides consultation to major professional and national groups and organizations; and serves as consultant to the U.S. Department of State, the U.S. Information Agency, and the U.S. Department of Defense.

**Joel Kleinman** received both masters and doctoral degrees from Harvard University, where he was an assistant professor of biostatistics before joining the Public Health Service. Dr. Kleinman was director of analysis at the National Center for Health Statistics; he was recognized for his work with infant mortality and women's health as it related to the health of the fetus. As a biostatistician, he wrote and lectured extensively. Dr. Kleinman died at age 44 of complications of diabetes while this book was in publication.

**Richard Krugman** is an internationally regarded expert in child abuse and neglect, and is currently Director, C. Henry Kempe National Center for the Prevention and Treatment of Child Abuse and Neglect, as well as Professor of Pediatrics and Acting Dean of the University of Colorado School of Medicine. Dr. Krugman received his MD from the New York University School of Medicine; in addition, he was selected as a Robert Wood Johnson fellow in Health Policy, during which time he was Legislative Assistant (Health) in the U.S. Senate. He is Editor-in-Chief of Child Abuse and Neglect, The International Journal; and is an editor of the new edition of The Child Protection Team Handbook. Dr. Krugman provides expert clinical consultation as well as presentations and training at the national and international levels.

**Carl Leukefeld** is currently the director of the Drug and Alcohol Abuse Research Center at the University of Kentucky. Dr. Leukefeld received his masters degree from the University of Michigan and his doctorate in social work from the Catholic University of America. From 1967 to 1990 he was a commissioned officer in the U.S. Public Health Service; during much of that time Dr. Leukefeld was assigned to the National Institute on Drug Abuse in various clinical, management, and scientific capacities. His current research interests include the use of judicial sanctions, drug abuse treatment, and the impact of HIV on the drug abuser. Additionally, he is an editor or consulting editor for four professional journals and has served as a consultant to various organizations, including the World Health Organization, the National Institute of Justice, and the American Probation and Parole Association.

**Frances Marcus Lewis** is currently Professor, Department of Community Health Care Systems, University of Washington, Seattle; Evaluator, Cancer Information System, Fred Hutchinson Cancer Research Center, Seattle; and a member of the Emphasis Area Faculty in the Robert Wood Johnson Clinical Scholars Program. Dr. Lewis received her PhD from Stanford in the social sciences and did postdoctoral work in health education at The Johns Hopkins University. Her research interests focus on the psychosocial aspects of adaptation to life-threatening illness. She is co-author of Evaluation and Measurement in Health Education and Promotion; and is co-editor and co-author of Health Behavior and Health Education: Theory, Research, and Practice.

**Patrick O'Carroll** is Chief of the Intentional Injuries Section, Epidemiology Branch, Division of Injury Control, National Center for Environmental Health and Injury Control, CDC. Dr. O'Carroll received his MD from The Johns Hopkins University School of Medicine and his MPH from the School of Hygiene and Public Health at the same university. After completing a Preventive Medicine Residency at UCLA he was an EIS officer for the CDC. He has served on a variety of tasks forces involving injury control and suicide and has published extensively in the areas of homicide and suicide.

**Deborah Prothrow-Stith**, a graduate of Spelman College and Harvard Medical School, is currently the Assistant Dean for Government and Community Programs at the Harvard University School of Public Health and lecturer for the Health Policy and Management Department. Dr. Prothrow-Stith is a former commissioner of the Massachusetts Department of Public Health, appointed by Governor Michael Dukakis. Her professional initiatives have focused on adolescent health and have included strategies of community education, health education, media campaigns, research, and evaluation. Dr. Prothrow-Stith founded and directed a community-based violence prevention program that continued her pioneer work in health education for teenagers on anger and violence. She has been a consultant for several school systems and departments of public health, and has authored a book on adolescent violence entitled Deadly Consequences.

**Julius Richmond** is a pediatrician who is distinguished in the field of Child Health. He has held the positions of Professor of Pediatrics in the schools of medicine at the University of Illinois and at Syracuse University, and Professor of Social Policy at the Harvard University Medical School and at the School of Public Health. He was the first Director of the U.S. Head Start program. He has been Assistant Secretary of Health in the U.S. Department of Health and Human Services. He has received numerous awards for his outstanding contributions to the health of children and youth in the United States.

**Frederick Rivara** is currently Professor of Pediatrics and Adjunct Professor of Epidemiology at the University of Washington, and the Director of the Harborview Injury Prevention and Research Center. Dr. Rivara received his MD degree from the University of Pennsylvania and his MPH from the University of Washington in Seattle; additionally, he served as a Robert Wood Johnson Clinical Scholar, during which time his interest in injury control began. Dr. Rivara has been awarded the Ambulatory Pediatric Association Award for Excellence in Teaching and Research, and is recognized as one of the top scientists in the country in the field of injury control.

**Carolyn Rogers**, a demographer, is currently with the Economic Research Service (USDA). Ms. Rogers received her masters degree in sociology/demography from Brown University. Her research interests include family structure and change, children and child care, and the health status and living arrangements of the elderly. Formerly with the U.S. Bureau of the Census, she designed the June fertility supplement to the Current Population Survey, produced the annual Fertility of American Women report, and published articles on birth expectations and child care. Her publications on children include "Recent Trends in the Well-Being of Children in the United States and Their Implications for Public Policy," in The Changing American Family and Public Policy, and a 1991 USDA report on "The Economic Well-Being of Nonmetro Children."

**James Sallis** received his PhD in clinical psychology from Memphis State University in 1981 and then completed a fellowship in cardiovascular disease epidemiology and prevention at the Stanford University School of Medicine. Dr. Sallis is currently Associate Professor of Psychology at San Diego State University and Associate Adjunct Professor of Pediatrics at University of California, San Diego. He is currently principal investigator of a grant designed to promote physical activity in elementary school children through physical education and self-management. Dr. Sallis has also investigated the effects of a family-based diet and physical activity change program and completed several studies of measures of children's physical activity and fitness. He is involved in research to identify important determinants of physical activity in both children and adults.

**Linda Saltzman** is a Behavioral Scientist in the Intentional Injuries Section, Epidemiology Branch, Division of Injury Control, National Center for Environmental Health and Injury Control, CDC. Dr. Saltzman received her MS and PhD in Criminology from Florida State University, after which she was an associate professor at Mankato State (MN). Her professional interests and publications are in the area of family violence and suicide; she has been a participant on numerous committees, including the Council on Battered Women (Atlanta), and as the CDC representative to the U.S. Interagency Task Force on Child Abuse and Neglect.

Jack Smith is currently Chief, Statistics and Computer Resources Branch, Division of Reproductive Health, Center for Chronic Disease Prevention and Health Promotion, CDC. Mr. Smith received an MS in Biostatistics from Tulane University, and has spent 25 years in the Division of Reproductive Health at CDC.

Howard Spivak earned both AB and MD degrees from the University of Rochester, and followed pediatrics residency with a fellowship in ambulatory pediatrics. In 1988 he was honored by the American Medical Association Congress on Youth for the Boston Violence Prevention Project. Dr. Spivak is currently an associate professor in pediatrics at Tufts University School of Medicine, as well as an Associate in Pediatrics at the New England Medical Center Hospital in Boston. He has participated in numerous youth- and health-oriented committees and task forces in Boston, and expresses an interest in adolescent health (with a special focus on youth violence and violence prevention efforts); in public policy as it pertains to health (as Deputy Commissioner of the Massachusetts Department of Public Health); and in the relationship between health and social/environmental factors (especially the influences of poverty and racism on health).

Kenneth Troutman is currently Professor of Clinical Dentistry and Director, Pediatric Dentistry Post-doctoral Program of the Columbia University School of Dental and Oral Surgery. Dr. Troutman received his DDS degree from Temple University School of Dentistry, and an MPH degree in Maternal and Child Health from the University of California, Berkeley School of Public Health. He is a Fellow of the American Academy of Pediatric Dentistry, Fellow of the American College of Dentistry, Diplomate of the American Board of Pediatric Dentistry, past president of the American Academy of Pediatric Dentistry and coauthor of the textbook: Pediatric Dentistry - Scientific Foundations and Clinical Practice.

Deborah Klein Walker is currently the Assistant Commissioner for the Bureau of Parent, Child, and Adolescent Health in the Massachusetts Department of Health. Dr. Walker received her EdD from the Harvard Graduate School of Education in human development. Her current research interests focus on the social functioning of children with disabilities and chronically ill children in schools, and evaluation of secondary prevention programs for adolescent pregnant and parenting teens. Before assuming her current position, Dr. Walker was an associate professor of human development at the Harvard School of Public Health.

**Laurie Zabin** currently holds a joint appointment as Associate Professor in both the Department of Population Dynamics of The Johns Hopkins University School of Hygiene and Public Health, and the Department of Obstetrics and Gynecology of the JHU School of Medicine. Dr. Zabin received her PhD from the JHU School of Hygiene and Public Health, Department of Population Dynamics. She has worked for many years in the field of family planning, at the local, national, and international levels; and has served on the board of the Alan Guttmacher Institute since its inception. She is currently a member of the governing council of the American Public Health Association, and has served as chair of the section on population and family planning.

# APPENDIX B
## CONTENTS, VOLUME TWO

VOLUME TWO: **SCHOOL HEALTH**

**Section I.**  Nature and Organization of School Health

# Appendix C
## Contents, Volume Three

(See "Books Available," next page)

## Books Available From

## THIRD PARTY PUBLISHING COMPANY

| Code | Title and Authors | Calif. residents (inc. taxes) | Other USA states | Int'l cost (shipping) |
|------|-------------------|-------------------------------|------------------|------------------------|
| 0343 | **Principles and Practices of Student Health** (3 volume set) Wallace, Patrick, Parcel, and Igoe | $54.95 | $49.95 | $59.95 |
| 0289 | **Maternal and Child Health Practices**, 3rd Ed Wallace, Ryan, and Oglesby | 31.95 | 29.95 | 34.95 |
| 0319 | **Health Care of Women and Children in Developing Countries** - Wallace and Giri | 34.95 | 32.95 | 36.95 |
| A101 | **Handicapped Children and Youth** Wallace, Buehl, Taft, and Oglesby | 53.95 | 49.95 | 55.95 |
| A102 | **The National Adolescent Student Health Survey: A Report on the Health of America's Youth** ASHA/AAHE/SOPHE | 20.95 | 18.95 | 22.95 |
| 0149 | **The American Family: Life and Health** Patton | 24.95 | 22.95 | 26.95 |
| 0130 | **SOPHE Heritage of Health Education Monographs** (3 volumes, in Slip Case) | | | |
| | Classic (hard cover set) | 64.00 | 60.00 | 68.00 |
| | Library (paper cover set) | 48.00 | 44.00 | 50.00 |
| 0122 | **Expanding Health Care Horizons**, 2nd Ed Blum | 12.95 | 11.95 | 15.95 |
| 0076 | **Perspectives on Community Health Education** (Vol. 1 of series) Carlaw | 12.95 | 11.95 | 15.95 |
| 0254 | **Primary Health Care: The African Experience** (Vol 2 of series) Carlaw and Ward | 24.95 | 22.95 | 26.95 |

ORDER FROM

**THIRD PARTY PUBLISHING COMPANY**

P.O. Box 13306, Montclair Station
Oakland, California 94661-0306, U.S.A.

Telephone: 510/339-2323
Fax: 510/339-6729

**International orders, and orders from U.S.A. individuals, must be prepaid in U.S. dollars by check, money order, or VISA/MasterCard credit card.**